P9-CWE-727

Mentored by a Millionaire

Master Strategies of Super Achievers

STEVEN K. SCOTT

John Wiley & Sons, Inc.

Copyright © 2004 by Steven K. Scott. All rights reserved.

Published by John Wiley & Sons, Inc., Hoboken, New Jersey.
Published simultaneously in Canada.

No part of this publication may be reproduced, stored in a retrieval system, or transmitted in any form or by any means, electronic, mechanical, photocopying, recording, scanning, or otherwise, except as permitted under Section 107 or 108 of the 1976 United States Copyright Act, without either the prior written permission of the Publisher, or authorization through payment of the appropriate per-copy fee to the Copyright Clearance Center, Inc., 222 Rosewood Drive, Danvers, MA 01923, (978) 750-8400, fax (978) 646-8600, or on the web at www.copyright.com. Requests to the Publisher for permission should be addressed to the Permissions Department, John Wiley & Sons, Inc., 111 River Street, Hoboken, NJ 07030, (201) 748-6011, fax (201) 748-6008.

Limit of Liability/Disclaimer of Warranty: While the publisher and author have used their best efforts in preparing this book, they make no representations or warranties with respect to the accuracy or completeness of the contents of this book and specifically disclaim any implied warranties of merchantability or fitness for a particular purpose. No warranty may be created or extended by sales representatives or written sales materials. The advice and strategies contained herein may not be suitable for your situation. The publisher is not engaged in rendering professional services, and you should consult a professional where appropriate. Neither the publisher nor author shall be liable for any loss of profit or any other commercial damages, including but not limited to special, incidental, consequential, or other damages.

For general information on our other products and services please contact our Customer Care Department within the United States at (800) 762-2974, outside the United States at (317) 572-3993 or fax (317) 572-4002.

Wiley also publishes its books in a variety of electronic formats. Some content that appears in print may not be available in electronic books. For more information about Wiley products, visit our web site at *www.Wiley.com.*

Library of Congress Cataloging-in-Publication Data:
Scott, Steve, 1948–
Mentored by a millionaire / Steven K. Scott.
p. cm.
Includes index.
ISBN 0-471-46763-4
1. Success—Psychological aspects. I. Title.
BF637.S8S388 2004
158.1—dc22 2003018876

Printed in the United States of America

10 9 8 7

Dedication

To My Mentors:

In Life

My incredibly wise and loving wife, Shannon Smiley Scott.

My angelic mother, Minnie Joy Scott, and my courageous father, Gordon Scott.

Jim Shaughnessy, Dr. Gary Smalley, Pastor Jim Borror, and Herb and Helen Selby.

In Business

My mentor who changed everything, Bob Marsh.

To Those I Love Mentoring Most:

My wonderful children: Hallie Rose, Sean Kelly, Ryan, Devin, Zach, Mark, and Carol, and my sweet granddaughter, Madelyn.

My readers and listeners who come with hope and trust and leave with knowledge and skills.

CONTENTS

	PREFACE	**vii**
	Introduction	**1**
SESSION 1	A New Software Package for Your Brain	**17**
SESSION 2	Discovering Your Personality Type–You'll Like Your Style!	**31**
SESSION 3	No Time, No Talent, No Money–No Problem!	**47**
SESSION 4	Steven Spielberg's Masterful Strategy for Maximum Achievement in Minimum Time	**63**
SESSION 5	What You Say and How You Say It Changes Everything!	**83**
SESSION 6	Using Your Master Key to Open Any Door	**99**
SESSION 7	With This Technique You'll Superachieve; Without It You Won't!	**131**
SESSION 8	A Vision without a Map Is Worthless!	**144**
SESSION 9	The Secret Strategy of the World's Most Successful People	**160**
SESSION 10	The Billion-Dollar Difference . . . Better than Winning a Lottery!	**177**
SESSION 11	Removing the Single Greatest Roadblock to Achieving Your Dreams	**195**
SESSION 12	Bring On the Critics . . . and Beat Them!	**207**
SESSION 13	Taking Control and Keeping It	**221**
SESSION 14	It's Easy to Become Positively Amazing	**237**
SESSION 15	Discovering the High-Octane Fuel of the World's Most Successful People	**255**
	INDEX	**269**

Would You Rather Be Taught by a Teacher, or Mentored by a Millionaire?

The Strategies, Skills, and Techniques You Are About to Learn Have Empowered the World's Most Successful People to Achieve Their Impossible Dreams. As you use these strategies, skills, and techniques, you will begin to move toward a level of success greater than you have ever experienced. This will be true in any endeavor to which they are applied: your job, your career, even your marriage. Unfortunately these strategies, skills, and techniques are not taught in high school, college, or graduate school. You will not experience their power by simply reading self-help books or attending motivational seminars. They are known only to an elite few and are learned and mastered only through the mentoring process.

While a good teacher or motivator may increase your level of success by 25, 50, or even 100 percent, a good mentor can increase your level of success by 1,000, 5,000, or 10,000 percent! For example, my business mentor increased my personal income by more than 56,000 percent. My relationships mentor aided me in the critical skills I needed to win back the heart and hand of my ex-wife and build the happiest and most fulfilling relationship either of us has ever experienced.

How many self-help books have you read? How many motivational speakers have you heard? After reading a good self-help book or hearing a great motivational speaker, chances are you felt like a new person. But how long did the feeling last? Within a few weeks you were right back into the same old feelings you had experienced before. The changes you expected

Cheerleaders may supply a burst of emotional enthusiasm, but they don't throw the pass, score the touchdown, or win the game. Military generals plan great strategies, but they don't shoot the rifles, drive the tanks, or fly the planes. To win a game, a battle, or a war, you need more than cheerleaders and strategists. You need men and women who are (1) effectively trained and (2) adequately equipped to accomplish their objectives.

never materialized. You felt frustrated and perhaps even like a failure. Even though you may have blamed yourself for failing, it probably wasn't your fault. Many motivational speakers make a living speaking or writing, but have not achieved extraordinary success in starting, building, or managing a business. They often play the role of cheerleaders and can truly psych you up for a week or two. These talented and inspiring speakers and writers may have given you wonderful principles, exciting concepts, entertaining stories, and brilliant strategies. They may have truly inspired you to desire more success at work and at home. But, when they failed to equip you with the specific techniques and skills needed to apply their strategies to your daily endeavors, failure was unavoidable. You had no more chance of achieving extraordinary success than a soldier who is given a battle plan by a general, but sent into the battlefield without a weapon or any combat skills. So don't blame yourself for not achieving extraordinary success after attending a motivational seminar or reading a self-help book. Simply stated, you were not adequately trained and equipped.

Four Reasons Why This Book Is Going to Make a Phenomenal Difference in Your Professional and Personal Life

1. **You'll learn the 15 master strategies of the world's most successful people.** These strategies have catapulted hundreds of ordinary people to unimaginable heights of success and wealth. They are not taught in colleges or business schools, but were discovered through personal experience or learned from mentors.
2. **You'll learn and master specific techniques to instantly apply each strategy to your daily life at work and at home.** These techniques

are simple and easily learned, and yet incredibly effective, resulting in the mastery of lifetime skills.

3. **In 15 one-on-one mentoring sessions, you'll be led step by step through each technique and strategy with interactive exercises that enable you to begin using each technique literally overnight.**
4. **You're not being lectured by an educator or a motivational speaker. You're being mentored** by a man who lost 9 jobs in six years, yet became a multimillionaire on job number 10 because he too was mentored by a millionaire. Starting more than a dozen companies from scratch, my partners and I generated over $2 billion in sales, creating over $200 million in personal income.

How Do I Know These Techniques Will Work for You?

As you'll learn in Session 1, during my first six years after college I was a hopeless and habitual failure. Then, as I began to use these strategies and techniques that I learned from my mentors, they empowered me to achieve levels of success I had never dreamed possible. As I became acquainted with others who had achieved phenomenal levels of success, I discovered they too had used these same techniques. As I read the biographies of many of the world's most successful people, I realized that they had also used these same strategies and techniques. To my amazement, none of these life-changing dream-achieving skills are taught in high school, college, or graduate school. Every superachiever I have met or read about either learned these skills from a mentor or discovered them through personal experience.

As my success grew, I began meeting people who had wonderful dreams but had never succeeded in achieving those dreams no matter how hard they tried. As I helped these people to apply the 15 master strategies, they began to see their dreams come true, literally within weeks. In a number of cases, their incomes grew as well, rising from thousands of dollars per year to millions. To show how universally powerful these strategies and techniques are, I'll share a few examples.

An Assistant Minister in Waco, Texas

Gary Smalley had a dream of writing a book to teach couples how to have a better marriage. For 10 years he prayed for the chance to see this dream fulfilled. Gary and I got together in 1978 and created a strategy to fulfill this simple dream. Gary has since written 15 consecutive bestsellers, helping millions of couples to achieve happier relationships. His organization, Today's Family, has also impacted millions of marriages. His videotapes alone have sold over 6 million copies, making them the best-selling self-help tapes in history.

A Professor at Arizona State University

Professor Claude Olney created a seminar to help his struggling students at Arizona State University raise their grade point averages. He dreamed of offering a set of cassette tapes to college students at other universities. We created a plan that resulted in the creation of audio- and videotaped seminars for grade school, high school, and college students. The result was the best-selling educational tape series in history. These tapes changed the lives of millions of students and made the professor a multimillionaire within one year.

A Makeup Artist in Los Angeles

Victoria Jackson was a talented but struggling makeup artist in Los Angeles. She had created a cream makeup base that was unique, and she had tried to market it for eight years with little success. Although she had hundreds of jars of product in her garage, she had all but given up. Using the strategies from this book, we created a plan that resulted in the development of an entire makeup line with over 160 products. Within five years, Victoria Jackson Cosmetics had realized sales of over $300 million, and Victoria had become a multimillionaire.

Two Fitness Equipment Inventors in San Diego

Tom Campanero and Larry Westfall had created a wonderful but very big and heavy piece of fitness equipment. For nearly 20 years they demonstrated their machine at hundreds of conventions. Unfortunately, their sales reached only 5,000 units per year. In 1996 we created a plan using the strategies and techniques in which you are going to be mentored. Today, seven years later, the redesigned Total Gym has sold over 2.5 million units, generating nearly $1 billion in sales. In addition to becoming the single most popular piece of home fitness equipment in history, the Total Gym is currently used by over 7,000 athletic and sports medicine facilities to rehabilitate and train over 7 million people per year.

So Will These Strategies and Techniques Really Work for You?

The people in these examples were no different than you and me. They were ordinary people who had tried hard to succeed for years. And yet they had only achieved moderate success at best. You see, even though they had truly tried their hardest, they had not yet discovered the keys that could open the doors between them and extraordinary success. Once they were equipped with those simple keys, the doors were easily opened. These are the same keys that will be placed in your hands during our 15 mentoring sessions.

Now if you still don't believe that these strategies and techniques can make that big a difference in your life, maybe you'll believe what a few well-known Americans have written about these strategies and their awesome power to effect change in anyone's life.

> *"Steve Scott's uncanny insights and strategies are so specific and easily applied, I believe they can empower any reader, whether a college student, small business owner or the CEO of a Fortune 500 company to achieve levels of success they haven't yet dreamed of."*
>
> Donald Trump

> *"Steve Scott not only proves you can achieve your 'impossible dreams,' he takes you by the hand and gives you the knowledge, the steps, the confidence and the power to achieve every one!"*
>
> Chuck Norris

> *"Steve Scott gives us the specific strategies and techniques that we need to learn and use to achieve our most valued dreams. He not only shows us how to make our most impossible dreams possible, he shows us how to make them* probable!*"*
>
> Christie Brinkley

> *"He gives you a clear and concise roadmap to achieving more success than you would ever think possible. If you follow it, you're* sure *to get there."*
>
> Dick Clark

> *"If you follow his steps, you're sure to achieve your impossible dreams."*
>
> Joe Montana

So will these strategies work for you? Absolutely! All you need to do is learn them and then diligently apply them to your daily life. A house key left on your car seat won't open the door to your home as long as it remains on the seat. And yet, when picked up and placed into the door's lock and turned, it will easily open the door every time. The same is true here. Read about these keys and leave them on the pages of this book, and they will do nothing for you. Lift them off the pages and use them, and they'll open doors that you have never even dared to approach, much less attempted to open.

As you begin each of the 15 mentoring sessions, realize that these are not simply chapters in a book. There is no deadline to complete a session or finish this book. This book is not about me; it's about you. At the end of each session there is a section entitled "Actions for Traction," in which you'll find a set of interactive exercises that will enable you to apply and master the strategies and techniques you learned in that session. Complete each session and set of exercises in your own time. As you do, you will immediately see changes begin to take place. Your level of creativity and productivity will skyrocket. Your relationships at work, as well as at home, will begin to improve, gradually at first and then very dynamically. Your enthusiasm, passion, and fulfillment will reach levels that you only thought were possible for other people.

Because it's important that you only seek out mentors who are truly qualified in the area in which you are being mentored, this is the only section in this book that is about me, while the 15 mentoring sessions are all about you. So let's begin!

INTRODUCTION

From Habitual Failure to MultiMillionaire—All It Took Was a Mentor. Now It's Your Turn!

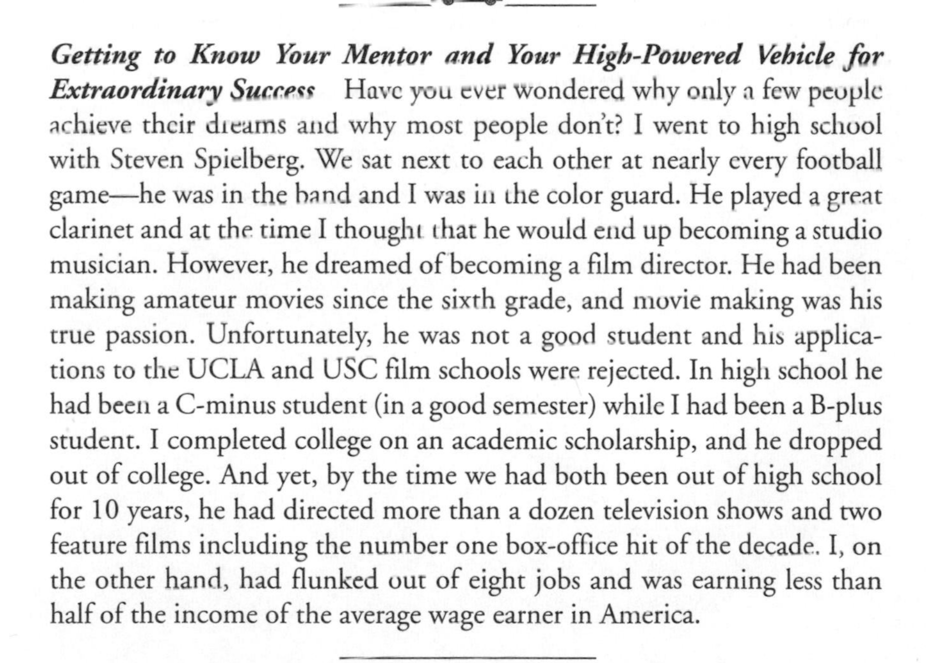

Getting to Know Your Mentor and Your High-Powered Vehicle for Extraordinary Success Have you ever wondered why only a few people achieve their dreams and why most people don't? I went to high school with Steven Spielberg. We sat next to each other at nearly every football game—he was in the band and I was in the color guard. He played a great clarinet and at the time I thought that he would end up becoming a studio musician. However, he dreamed of becoming a film director. He had been making amateur movies since the sixth grade, and movie making was his true passion. Unfortunately, he was not a good student and his applications to the UCLA and USC film schools were rejected. In high school he had been a C-minus student (in a good semester) while I had been a B-plus student. I completed college on an academic scholarship, and he dropped out of college. And yet, by the time we had both been out of high school for 10 years, he had directed more than a dozen television shows and two feature films including the number one box-office hit of the decade. I, on the other hand, had flunked out of eight jobs and was earning less than half of the income of the average wage earner in America.

So why was Steven achieving most of his dreams while I was failing to achieve most of mine? The answer was simple: He was doing the things that those elite few who achieve their impossible dreams do, while I was doing the things that the vast majority of adults do who don't achieve their dreams. Interestingly, those things that were driving Steven's success are not taught in high school, college, or graduate school, while I was doing all of the things we are taught to do in high school and college. Now if that doesn't pique your curiosity, maybe this will. *As soon as I began doing the same things that Steven had been doing, I too began achieving my impossible dreams.* My first eight jobs had lasted an average of eight months each and my annual salary had only reached $13,000 per year. I began using these strategies on my ninth job and doubled that company's sales from $30 million to $60 million within three months. Within a year I had found a mentor and formed a new company with him, and my income skyrocketed from $13,000 to $150,000. This job has now lasted over 26 years and has generated a personal income of over $200 million for my partners and me.

When Steven Spielberg and I ran into each other 20 years after we had graduated from high school, we discovered that we had done the exact same things, only in two different fields. He had applied these strategies to making films and I had applied them to marketing products. But Steven and I aren't the only ones who have used these strategies to achieve our most desired dreams. As I began to study the biographies of many of the world's most successful men and women, I discovered that they too had used these exact same strategies to achieve their extraordinary dreams. From Washington and Jefferson to Edison and Ford; from Helen Keller to Oprah Winfrey; from John D. Rockefeller to Bill Gates—it didn't matter how destitute their beginnings, or in which century they lived. Even their educational attainments seemed quite irrelevant. It didn't even matter to what kind of dreams they applied these strategies—whether creating a nation, building a new company, or merely breaking through to a better

The First Law of Extraordinary Success

People who achieve ordinary outcomes do so by using conventional approaches and methods taught in schools and used by the masses. People who achieve extraordinary to near impossible outcomes do so by using a different set of master strategies that are universally and consistently used by superachievers and are virtually unknown to the masses.

The Second Law of Extraordinary Success

Superachievers learn these master strategies from mentors (the fast way), or through the agonizing process of trial and error (the slow way).

way of life. They simply applied these strategies to their pursuit of their most cherished dreams, transforming those dreams into reality.

Four Types of People—Which Type Are You?

When it comes to levels of achievement, I've observed that there are four types of people: drifters, pursuers, achievers, and superachievers.

Drifters are those who move through life like a raft on a river, going with the flow wherever it takes them. They only exert as much effort and creativity as is necessary to stay afloat, no more and no less. This is the bottom level of achievers, which I believe represents about 50 percent of the adult population.

Pursuers are those who want to set their own course and pursue dreams, and though they achieve some of their dreams, they fail to achieve most. They lack the knowledge, resources, effective strategies, and critical skills necessary to achieve significant or extraordinary outcomes. I believe that this next level of achievers represents about 25 percent of the adult population.

Achievers are those who also set their own course and power their way to various destinations regardless of the flow of the river. They set significant goals in either their personal or professional lives and consistently achieve those goals. However, they rarely achieve extraordinary outcomes because their strategies are based on conventional wisdom and they rarely perform outside the box. They do not utilize the strategies, skills, and techniques that are critical for achieving extraordinary outcomes, or *superachieving*. This is the third level of achieving and represents the top 24.99 percent of the adult population. (If you are counting, this level brings the total of all three levels to 99.99 percent.)

Superachievers are those who get out of the river altogether. They use a set of strategies and skills that empower them to pursue and achieve extraordinary outcomes and impossible dreams consistently in their professional or personal lifestyle. Rather than being limited by the river, they know no limits. They consistently and habitually achieve extraordinary outcomes in any area to which they apply their master strategies for superachieving. Because they have learned the skills and techniques that are necessary to implement these strategies, doing so ultimately becomes second nature to them. The good news is that all of these master strategies, skills, and techniques are learnable. This level represents the top one-tenth of one percent of the adult population. Moving from the level of a drifter, pursuer, or achiever to the level of a superachiever is as easy as learning these strategies and skills and beginning to utilize them on a daily basis in every important area of your life. I know, because the first six years of my

Side-by-Side Comparison

Drifters	Pursuers	Achievers	Superachievers
Go with the flow.	Pursue but rarely achieve preset goals.	Achieve significant outcomes, but rarely extraordinary ones.	Consistently achieve extraordinary outcomes by using master strategies for superachievement.

postcollege life were spent drifting, and in a single year I moved to the level of a superachiever.

Comparison Charts

In each mentoring session I am going to give you side-by-side comparison charts such as the one above, where I graphically compare the differences between the strategies and actions of drifters, pursuers, achievers, and superachievers. You will likely see where you currently fall in any given comparison, and then you'll see what you need to do to move from where you are into the superachiever strategies, skills, attitudes, or behavior. Remember, the only difference between my first 10 years after high school and Steven Spielberg's first 10 years was the fact that I did what the masses did and he did what the superachievers did. As soon as I began doing what superachievers do, I too began to experience the kind of extraordinary outcomes that were a daily occurrence in Steven's life.

You've Just Been Given a Brand-New Porsche Turbo Carrera

Our dreams are like cities and towns on a map of America. Some are only a few miles away, while others are on the other side of the continent. Imagine that your dreams are represented by destinations scattered all over America. If your only method of transportation were walking, what would your chances be of ever achieving your dreams? While you might achieve those nearest to you or within a 50-mile walk, you probably wouldn't even start a journey that would require you to walk across the Rocky Mountains or swim across the Mississippi River. Unfortunately, our greatest and most desirable dreams are usually the most distant destinations. Once we become adults and realize how distant they really are, we don't even begin the journey, much less complete it.

Side-by-Side Comparison

How People Pursue Their Dreams

Drifters	Pursuers	Achievers	Superachievers
Walk through life in dress shoes.	Sprint in running shoes.	Run marathons in running shoes.	Drive toward their dreams in a 415-horsepower Porsche Turbo Carrera.

Now, imagine that, unlike everyone else who can only pursue their dreams by walking, you have just been given a brand new Porsche Turbo Carrera. It has a top speed of 180 miles per hour and the most advanced computerized navigational system in the world. What would your chances be of achieving your dreams now? Imagine being able to drive to any dream you have, no matter how far away or how rugged the terrain. While everyone else is giving up on their most treasured dreams and simply taking whatever they can get in a single day's walk, you can cruise to your most important dreams at 180 miles per hour. That's the incredible power of the 15 master strategies that make up your new "Porsche." In our mentoring sessions I will put this Porsche into your garage. I'm also going to give you the keys to start it, instructions on all of its incredible accessories, and all of the high-octane fuel you'll need to make your journeys to your most cherished and distant dreams. You'll not only be able to make the trip, you'll achieve your dreams in record time! However, before we begin our sessions I'd like to take a few minutes to tell you a little about my personal journey. Why? Because when you compare where you are now with where I was before I was mentored in these strategies, you will see that you are starting off a lot better than I did. I think you'll become convinced that "If Steve Scott with his dismal track record could succeed, then anyone can succeed using these strategies."

I Gave Up on Most of My Dreams within Two Years of Graduating!

I chose Marketing as my college major because I dreamed of a career in the advertising or marketing department of a major corporation. After receiving my degree in 1970, I quickly discovered there were no marketing jobs available for people without experience. I couldn't land a single interview with any marketing department of any corporation in my hometown of Phoenix. My dream had vaporized within 60 days of graduation. Consequently, I accepted a job as a management trainee for a life insurance agency. Unfortunately, the initial focus of that job was learning how to sell life insurance. While the other management trainees seemed to be selling one to two policies a week by the end of our first month, I wasn't selling a thing. In fact, in the five months that followed I only sold two policies—one to my best friend and one to myself. Even more frustrating to my boss, I quit the day before he planned to fire me. My first job had lasted only seven months.

I'll Bet My Resume Was a Lot Worse than Yours!

I didn't do much better with my second job. I was recruited to help start a new business. It was my first chance to make millions, but instead it left me broke. That job only lasted six months. Then came job number three. I actually got an entry-level job in the marketing department of a giant corporation 3,000 miles away from home. It looked like I was finally going to start a meaningful career path. Two days into the job, my wife had our first child, a gorgeous baby girl. This of course made me want to succeed more than ever. Even though I was only earning $12,000 a year, I gave this job my all. After my first nine months I thought things were going pretty well. I had just come back from lunch when my boss (the senior vice president of marketing) walked over to my desk and asked me to come into his office. I could feel my heart starting to race. I was sure he was calling me in to give me a raise. After all, when he hired me he told me that I would be qualified for a raise after a six-month probationary period. "Have a seat," he said as we walked into his spacious office. He walked over, sat on the corner of his desk, smiled, and said three simple sentences that I will never forget: "Steve, you are the single greatest disappointment in my entire career! You will never succeed in marketing! You have 20 minutes to clean out your desk."

I was shocked! I was 23, married with a child, and 3,000 miles from home. As I walked over to my desk I noticed the other employees in our department purposely looking the other way, and sneaking peaks at me as I tearfully began to clean out my desk. (While I was at lunch they had been told that I was going to be fired as soon as I returned.) I dumped the contents of each drawer into a paper bag, and the last personal item remaining on my desk was a picture of my newborn daughter. As I looked into her eyes, I felt sick. Daddy was a total failure. I had been out of college for less than two years and had already lost three jobs. It was obvious she was going to grow up playing in the courtyards of low-rent apartment buildings. Little did I know that I was going to lose six more jobs in the next three years. As I began each new job I acquired new dreams of how I would succeed. But my only means of pursuing those dreams were my walking shoes, and each dream was simply too distant with too many insurmountable obstacles to allow any hope of achieving them.

On my fourth job, I actually worked for two different subsidiaries of the same corporation. Even though my resume showed one job lasting nine months, it was really two that lasted a little over four months each. When my immediate supervisor warned me that I was going to be fired in two days, I beat my boss to the punch and quit. After five months on job number five, a real estate developer offered to back me in my own business. Thinking I couldn't do much worse than I had in a corporate environment, I took him up on his offer. Unfortunately he went broke eight months later, and so did I.

I was hired by a small catalog company on job number seven, and had real hopes of succeeding. My salary was only $1,000 a month, but the owner promised to give me a 50 percent raise in four months if I could double the customer response to his catalog. I completely revamped the catalog and doubled its response in three months. When my raise wasn't in my pay envelope the following month, I confronted my boss. Instead of giving me a raise, he gave me the boot. He was having an affair with the company bookkeeper and felt she needed a raise more than I did. So much for job number seven. Jobs number eight and nine lasted four months each. I was 27, a father of two, and had been out of college for less than six years when I left my ninth job. The only thing worse than my failure to hold any job for more than nine months was that my income had not grown to even half of the average

My Resume—May, 1976
Graduated from College, B.S. in Marketing, 1970

Year	Monthly Salary	Duration	Outcome
1971 1st job	$600	4 months	Quit
1971 2nd job	Started business	8 months	Failed
1972 3rd job	$1,000	9 months	Fired
1973 4th job	$1,000	9 months	Quit (about to be fired)
1974 5th job	$1,100	5 months	Quit
1974 6th job	Started business	9 months	Failed
1975 7th job	$1,000	4 months	Fired
1975 8th job	$1,100	4 months	Quit
1976 9th job	$1,500	4 months	Quit

income for wage earners in the United States. Not a very impressive resume, is it? How about you? How many jobs have you been fired from? How many have you quit? How many companies have you started that failed in less than a year? I'll bet your resume is a lot better now than mine was in May of 1976. The table on the previous page shows what it looked like.

Once a Failure, Always a Failure . . . Right? Wrong!

If you had been a personnel manager looking at my resume in 1976, chances are pretty good that you would not have considered hiring me. Of the nine jobs I had held since college, not one lasted more than nine months, and I had never received a pay raise in a single job. You would have likely reasoned, "This guy's a real loser!" Although you would have been justified in your reasoning, you would have been dead wrong. If you have ever heard the adage, "Once a failure, always a failure," I am now telling you that nothing could be further from the truth. I started job number 10 on May 10, 1976, and have now held that job for more than 27 years. More important, I have loved nearly every minute of it and have achieved countless "impossible dreams" that were an entire continent (even oceans) away. My partners and I have created more than a dozen multi-million-dollar businesses from scratch, selling over $2 billion in goods and services. And all of this was started with only $5,000 in cash and a dream.

So What the Heck Happened? How Could a Habitual Failure Become a Multimillionaire?

How could a total corporate failure see such an unimaginable turnaround? Did my IQ jump 100 points between job number 8 and job number 10? Did I go through a major personality change? Did I attend a success seminar or buy a set of get-rich-quick tapes? Nope, none of the above. Only two things changed—the same two things that are going to change in your life, beginning today. First, I found a mentor who had achieved many of his impossible dreams. Second, he put a Porsche Turbo Carrera in my garage, handed me the keys, and taught me everything I needed to know to drive it to each of my dreams, no matter how far away they were. It was the same Porsche I'm giving you, made up of the same master strategies, skills, and techniques. Best of all, these strategies, skills, and techniques are not complicated or difficult. They are easily learned and

American Telecast's Original Partners

Partner	Age	Background	Educational Attainment
R.M.	57	Entrepreneurial success/failure	High school graduate
S.S.	27	9-time corporate failure	College graduate
J.M.	27	Dog trainer	High school graduate
D.M.	25	Oil field worker	High school graduate
H.H.	25	Printing estimator	High school graduate
E.S.	19	Convenience store clerk	High school graduate

utilized regardless of your lack of talent, resources, educational attainment, or previous experience.

Now as hard as it may be to believe that these techniques could enable someone with little relevant skill or education to achieve extraordinary success, the fact is they will do just that. Look at the ages and backgrounds of my partners and me in 1976 when we started our business. My mentor (who was nearly broke at the time) mentored all of us into multimillionaires.

Notice that not one of us had any experience in direct response television marketing; writing, directing, and producing television commercials; business administration; media management; telemarketing operations; fulfillment operations; or manufacturing. And yet all of these functions were required for us to succeed. Each one of us is an irrefutable proof of the life-changing power of the strategies and techniques you are going to master in our mentoring sessions.

Critical Distinctions

Teacher: Someone who imparts information but relies on the learner to determine the importance, validity, and correct way to use that information.

Mentor: Someone who coaches the learner into a correct understanding of important information that is critical to achieving a specific goal, and coaches that person through the process of effectively applying that information.

Ideal mentor: A mentor who has achieved extraordinary success in an applicable or similar endeavor by using the information and processes in which he or she is coaching the learner.

Everyone Needs a Mentor

Every person I've ever known or read about who has achieved his or her dreams in any area of life has had at least one mentor in that particular area. Henry Ford credited one of his mentors—his former boss, Thomas Edison—for his success. Francis Ford Coppola mentored George Lucas; Sid Shineberg mentored Steven Spielberg; and Bob Marsh, Gary Smalley and Jim Shaughnessy have been my greatest mentors, professionally and personally.

In Which Areas of Your Life Do You Need a Mentor?

The fact is that you need a mentor in any area of your life in which you want to achieve significant success. Mentors will not only enable you to achieve extraordinary success, they will help you achieve it far more quickly than you would ever be able to without their help. I have been blessed to have had incredible mentors in every important area of my life. I've had business mentors, creative mentors, and a mentor for my marriage and parenting relationships.

How to Find the Right Mentors

Although you can't drive to your nearest shopping center and find a store called Mentor Mart, finding the right mentor for any given dream or project need not be as hard as you might think. It does take a little effort and little time. It can be as simple as finding a book written by an expert who has already achieved success in the area in which you are seeking help, or it can be as involved as identifying and recruiting someone you can interact with on a consistent, regular basis. You may choose to start your search in your own company or among people you currently know, but you don't have to limit your search to them.

For example, if you sell real estate for Century 21, your search for a mentor might begin by looking for the most successful salesman currently working for Century 21. However, you should also consider seeking out the most successful Century 21 salesmen who have retired. Or, you can choose someone who's been incredibly successful selling something other than real estate. And then there are sales experts who now write and teach seminars for a living. You can study their books or attend their seminars. Even though I haven't talked with Zig Ziglar for years, I consider him a great mentor. His books and tapes have significantly changed the way I look at life and relate to others.

Unfortunately, it's just as easy to recruit a wrong mentor as it is to recruit a right one. A few years after my company began marketing Gary Smalley's video series on relationships, the airwaves became full of so-called relationship experts touting their books and videos on relationships. And yet, two of these "experts" received their degrees from a non-accredited diploma mill from which you could buy a Ph.D. for a few thousand dollars. One of these experts was currently in her fifth marriage. One of her many failed marriages had been with one of the other experts who was selling his books and tapes. In fact, his book on relationships has become an all-time best seller. I don't know about you, but the last person I want to mentor me in my relational skills is someone who hasn't been able to succeed in his or her own relationships. These people tend to teach what they think will work rather than what they have personally experienced and proven to work.

Four Questions You Should Answer Before You Commit to a Potential Mentor

1. **What degree of success has he or she personally achieved in his or her area of expertise?** I would never recruit a mentor for my marriage who had failed in a marriage, and I would never recruit a mentor in business who has never succeeded in business.

2. **How legitimate are his or her credentials?** Today people can buy degrees in just about any field they want. I would rather be mentored by a person with no credentials than one with bogus credentials. My mentor in business didn't have an MBA. In fact, he never attended college at all. But he was a marketing and entrepreneurial genius.

3. **Is he or she a man or woman of integrity?** This may be a little harder to check out, but it's worth it when you can. Discover all you can about potential mentors' reputation. Do they practice what they preach?

4. **Does his or her personal experience reflect the degree of success you are dreaming of achieving?** Only recruit mentors who are living examples of what you want to achieve. Millions of couples seek marriage counseling from counselors who are not happily married themselves or have even failed in their own marriages. The wife of one of my best friends sought advice from a female counselor who was totally unqualified by virtue of her

credentials and personal experience. The counsel she received was terrible and resulted in a devastating divorce. When it comes to your marriage and family, please check out your counselors' credentials and personal experience in depth. Good counselors are great mentors for couples wanting a better marriage. Bad counselors are more destructive than dynamite.

Strategies and Tips for Identifying and Recruiting Mentors

1. **Determine the specific dream or area of your life for which you want a mentor.** Do you need a mentor to help you in relationships; to help you in your profession in general; or to help you in a particular area of your job, career, or profession, such as managerial or marketing skills? I've had two important mentors in the area of relationships and one key mentor in business.

2. **Create a list of potential mentors for each dream or area you've decided on.** Using your prioritized list of dreams, and starting with your most important dream, make a list of the people you respect most who might be able to give you insight, wisdom, and advice for each dream. List the names in order of preference. In other words, the person at the top of each list should be the person you would choose if you could pick anyone in the whole world. Even if you don't think there's a prayer of this person giving you a minute of his or her time, he or she should be at the top of your list.

3. **Starting with the mentors at the top of your list and working down, write down the status of your current relationship with each one.** (Boss, friend, acquaintance, friend of a friend, total stranger, and so forth.)

4. **Write down everything you know about that person through either your personal experience with them or second- or third-hand knowledge.**

5. **Research everything you can about your potential mentors.** What are their likes, their dislikes, their passions? How do they spend their time on and off the job? What motivates them?

6. **If your potential mentors are mere acquaintances or strangers to you, do you know anyone they know?** If you do, begin to find out all you can from that person, and consider using that person as a reference when you make your initial contact with a potential mentor.

7. Prepare to contact a potential mentor on the phone or in writing with a brief proposal or request. Whether you plan to make your contact in person, on the phone, or in a letter, you need to prepare your proposal or request well before you make the contact. If you are contacting someone who knows your reference but doesn't know you, your reference should be stated in your opening sentence. Your next sentence should touch on the quality or qualities that you so admire about this person. You should then briefly explain why those qualities are so important to you and how you want to gain this person's insight and wisdom in making those qualities a part of your life. Finally, ask if the person could spare a brief amount of time each week or month (a lunch, breakfast, coffee break, or round of golf) in which you could ask questions that might help you grow in this particular area.

8. Make the contact. Nothing beats a personal appointment. Depending on your potential mentor, that strategy may or may not be practical. If you can't make an appointment to see him or her, the next best thing is a phone call. Only use a letter when you have failed to get a meeting or make the contact by phone. Regardless of how you make your contact, make it brief and to the point. Any mentor worth his or her salt (unless retired) already has a very busy schedule, and if he or she thinks future contacts with you are going to take too much time, he or she will either turn your proposal down outright or simply avoid you like the plague.

9. Follow up. After you've made your first contact, follow up with a brief note of appreciation, commenting on something specific that the potential mentor said or did.

10. Go to the next person on the list. If your first choice for a mentor turns you down, be sure to find out why. Then go through this same procedure with the next person on your list.

What Qualifies Me to Be One of Your Mentors?

You can see that I believe that you should never recruit advisors, counselors, or mentors in any area of your life until you know they are truly qualified by their own experience to serve in any of these critical roles. So the first question you should ask is, "What qualifies Steve Scott to be one of my mentors?" I am not qualified to be your mentor by a genius IQ, a Ph.D. in business, or my skills as a writer or speaker. Nor am I qualified simply because I have made millions of dollars. What does qualify me to be your mentor is a single fact: I have learned and effectively used a specific set of strategies, skills, and techniques that have enabled me to achieve my impossible dreams in my business pursuits, my financial goals, and my relationships with my wife, my children, and my friends. My partners and I have enjoyed a successful batting average and have set sales records that have never been equaled in our industry of direct response television. Financially, with less than 80 employees, we have generated billions of dollars in sales and achieved all of our financial goals, making tens of millions of dollars in personal income. But I also know the power of these strategies because they have not only worked for me, they have worked miraculously for many others whom I have known personally. If you allow me to mentor you in these strategies and skills, and apply them to the pursuit of your professional, financial, and personal dreams, they will work for you as well.

"But Nothing's Ever Really Worked for Me Before. Why Will This Be Any Different?"

If this is your question, it's a great one. If pursuing your most cherished dreams requires you to metaphorically cross the continent or traverse overwhelming obstacles such as the Rocky Mountains or the mighty Mississippi River, will changing brands of walking shoes make any significant difference in your chances of successfully "walking" to your dreams? Absolutely not! If I were simply handing you a different pair of shoes, I would say that the chances of our sessions making any difference in your life would be zero. It really doesn't matter to me how many things you've tried in the past or how many times you've tried them. They are like changing shoes. In this book I am not handing you one more pair of shoes. Unless you have been personally mentored by someone who has achieved extraordinary success—even the near impossible—you have not ever received what I am going to give you in this book. I am going to put you in the seat of a Porsche Turbo Carrera, teach you how to drive it, fill the tank with the highest-octane fuel, and give you a credit card to keep it filled, just like my mentor did with me. That is why our sessions together are going to change your life, regardless of how many times you have failed in the past.

In our first session you are going to discover something about yourself that no one has ever told you—not your high school teachers, your college professors, your corporate bosses, your minister, or even your mother. Simply stated, you are going to discover the incalculable computing power of your Porsche's onboard computer and how it can be used to accomplish goals you never imagined possible.

Actions for Traction

WHERE THE RUBBER MEETS THE ROAD

You'll Need Two Tools for Our Mentoring Sessions

If you are simply reading this book for entertainment or to acquire a little knowledge, you will need nothing besides this book to do just that. However, if you want to be mentored and master the strategies of the world's most successful people, then you will need two tools: (1) A loose-leaf notebook in which you can perform the exercises that I give in the "Actions for Traction" section at the end of each session and (2) a second loose-leaf notebook that will become the road atlas to each of your dreams. Your only assignment for this session is to get the two notebooks, along with a dozen tabbed dividers and paper that you will need for each of the mentoring sessions that will follow.

Note: If you would like to save a lot of time, you can purchase preprinted copies of each notebook by calling my assistant at (800) 246-1771 or visiting my Web site at www.stevenkscott.com. The first is entitled *Mentoring Session Notebook,* and the second is entitled *Vision Mapping Journal.* Both are provided for your convenience. You can make your own, but I've found that most people I have mentored have preferred the convenience and ease of the preprinted notebook and journal.

SESSION 1

A New Software Package for Your Brain

Reprogramming Your Onboard Computer for Extraordinary Success

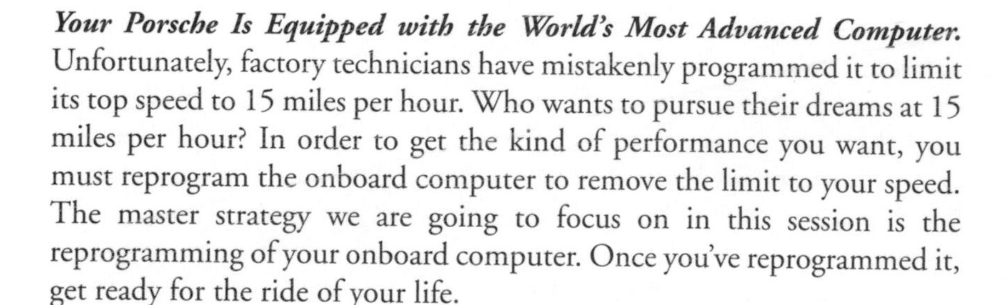

Your Porsche Is Equipped with the World's Most Advanced Computer. Unfortunately, factory technicians have mistakenly programmed it to limit its top speed to 15 miles per hour. Who wants to pursue their dreams at 15 miles per hour? In order to get the kind of performance you want, you must reprogram the onboard computer to remove the limit to your speed. The master strategy we are going to focus on in this session is the reprogramming of your onboard computer. Once you've reprogrammed it, get ready for the ride of your life.

For years, Michael L.'s mother had told him he would never amount to anything. By the time he graduated from high school, he was convinced she was right. He graduated number 299 out of a class of 301.

Bill L. didn't make it as far as Michael. He dropped out of school in the sixth grade.

Tom E.'s mom believed in him, but his schoolteachers didn't. He only made it through his first three months of first grade. The school headmaster thought he was mentally retarded.

George R.'s mom and dad dropped him off at an orphanage at the age of seven and never had anything to do with him again.

Tom M. was only four when his father died. His mother handed him and his brother over to an orphanage.

Knowing their beginnings, the oddsmakers in Vegas would have gladly bet against any of these boys ever achieving anything significant with their lives. And yet, even though all five had rough starts in life, their names or their achievements have become known to all of us.

Master Strategy 1–Reprogram Your Mind and Attitude to Achieve Extraordinary Outcomes

Michael L.

After graduating from high school at the bottom of his class, Michael L. did even worse in college. However, because he could throw a javelin farther than any other high school student in America, he landed a track scholarship to the University of Southern California. Unfortunately he flunked out his freshman year and ended up sleeping on park benches in Santa Monica. Even though Mike failed to achieve any success whatsoever in high school or college, he went on to become the most successful television actor, writer, and director in Hollywood history. Every single television series that he wrote, directed, or starred in became a huge prime time hit. No other actor, writer, or director has ever batted a thousand in television. How could someone who had failed so miserably become so extraordinarily successful? And yet, that is exactly what Michael Landon did.

During the 1980s, Mike became one of my best friends in Hollywood. As we got to know each other, I discovered that the same strategies that had been responsible for Steven Spielberg's success and mine had also worked miracles in Mike's life. Although each of us had plenty of evidence to justify our early beliefs that we would never succeed, all three of us made an awesome discovery—one that changed the course of our futures from unrelenting failure to unimaginable success. Interestingly, none of us made this discovery on our own. Instead, it was revealed to each of us by our mentors. They were the first to see it in us, the first to point it out to us, and the first to make us true believers. As one of your mentors, it is now my privilege to lead you into this same discovery. Before I do, let me tell you the rest of the stories about the other would-be losers. Like Steven Spielberg, Michael Landon, and myself, these boys seemed destined to failure by their early beginnings. And yet their destinies began to change as they discovered and became believers in this same truth.

Bill L.

Had Bill Lear not dropped out of school in the sixth grade, he would have read in the high school physics books of his day that it was impossible to make a radio small enough to fit into an automobile. Fortunately, he never read those books and went on to invent the first car radio. You could say that this was a fluke had he not also invented the autopilot, which radically changed the course of aviation. And later in his life, when the world's leading aviation companies said that there was no corporate market for small jets, and that building a prototype of such a jet would cost more than $100 million, Bill created his prototype business jet for under $10 million and provided corporate aviation with affordable, practical, and reliable Lear Jets years before the aviation giants followed his lead.

Tom E.

And who would have given Tom E. even a prayer for success? After being pulled out of the first grade by his mother and being judged mentally retarded by the school's headmaster, Tom's business life didn't seem any more promising. Working for the railroad at the age of 12, he was fired after only a few months on the job. And yet, this grade-school dropout not only invented the process of recording sound and making motion pictures, he gave us the first electric light bulb and over 1,000 other patented inventions. Even though he created more breakthrough inventions than any man in history, Thomas Edison would be the first to tell you that he was not a genius. Instead, he made the same discovery that you are about to make, and built his future on the exact same strategies that you are going to learn and begin to implement in our remaining sessions.

The Orphans

And then there are the orphans. George Ruth became known as the greatest baseball player of all time (and gained the nickname of "The Babe"), while Tom Monoghan and his brother started a pizza store that Tom turned into a chain with dominoes as its logo.

While each of these men achieved their impossible dreams by implementing these life-changing strategies, the foundation for doing so was securely laid when they discovered one truth that is just as true of you as it was of them. Although you may believe it about them, you may find it hard to believe about yourself, but I will give you all the proof you will need. First, let me clue you in on a secret. In our last session I told you that I was putting a brand-new Porsche Turbo Carrera in your garage. Guess what? You're not only the driver, you are the Porsche! Each strategy we will be discussing is part of your new design and is just waiting to be utilized.

The first component of your Porsche that we're going to look at is your onboard computer. It's not only the most advanced computer ever put into an automobile, it's the most advanced computer ever created! And since you are the Porsche, this awesome computer is already in you! Now before you dismiss this truth as hogwash and tell me there's no way you've got such a powerful onboard computer, let me tell you that in our early years, Steven Spielberg, Mike Landon, Bill Lear, Thomas Edison, Babe Ruth, Tom Monoghan, and I would have told you we didn't have it either. (And our teachers would have agreed.) But we did have it, right from the very beginning. We came straight from the factory with it built in! We just didn't know we had it. It took our mentors to reveal its true power to us and make us believers.

One Simple Life-Changing Truth

The most powerful computer ever created isn't a mainframe, it's a micro and it's housed within the few cubic inches of your head.

In 1976 my mentor invited me to quit job number nine and form a marketing company with him. He had acquired the marketing rights to a product that had never been marketed. He told me that he wanted me to negotiate a contract with a famous celebrity and then write and produce a two-minute commercial to sell this product on television. How could he ask me to do any of these things? I had never negotiated a contract; I had never written, directed, or produced a television commercial. And yet, he not only asked me to do all of this, he was going to bet his last $5,000 on my successfully accomplishing all of this. Although he really believed in me and believed that I could do it, I had no confidence whatsoever. And here's where his brilliant mentoring came in. He gave me two simple strategies and a few techniques, and like software downloaded them into my "onboard computer." The result? I negotiated the contract with one of the most famous celebrities in America; I wrote and produced the commercial, and it yielded sales of more than $1 million per week for 20 weeks. I had discovered that what my mentor had believed was indeed true: I possessed the world's most advanced computer. All it needed was to be reprogrammed with the right software to achieve extraordinary outcomes. (A $5,000 investment producing $20 million in sales is a pretty extraordinary outcome.)

"Just because Steve Scott, Steven Spielberg, Michael Landon, Thomas Edison, Babe Ruth, and Thomas Monoghan have the world's most advanced computer doesn't mean *I* have it. My brain may be a lot less powerful . . . right?"

If this is your first reaction, welcome to my club, because it was mine as well. But the fact is, your brain is just as powerful as mine—it just hasn't been programmed with the same software. But you and I are going to change all of that.

Back in the mid-1970s a friend of mine was one of the engineers who built the world's most advanced scientific computer. His eyes lit up with pride as he told me it could receive over 1 billion bits of information per second. And yet, he looked somewhat puzzled when I asked how many of those bits it could process simultaneously. He answered, "Just one." Even though the computer could process 1 billion bits per second, it could only process them one at a time. I then asked him how many computers would he need to process 4 million bits simultaneously. He replied, "Four million." I then asked him how much space would be needed to house that many computers. "Hundreds of acres," he replied, "but why are you asking such ridiculous questions?" "What would you say if I said that such a computer already exists?" I asked. "I'd say you're nuts!" he replied. He was even more incredulous when I told him that this supercomputer could be contained in a few cubic inches of space. Finally the light went on with my engineering friend. Of course I was talking about the human brain.

Unlike man-made computers, your brain doesn't just process one bit of information at a time. For example, right now as you read this sentence your brain is processing 4 million bits of information simultaneously just from your two eyes! Amazingly, it converts the 4 million photoelectric binary signals it receives from your eyes instantly into a vision of your surroundings, perceiving that picture in three dimensions with color, depth, and motion. And all of this is done in one tiny little portion of your brain. At the same time, your brain is receiving and processing hundreds of millions of other bits of information from your other senses, organs, and living tissues and sending out millions of commands! It's doing all of this without any conscious thought or effort on your part. And as if that's not enough, there are all of the other aspects of this supercomputer—the reasoning, communication, and emotional functions it performs. If you're still not in awe, realize that it does nearly all of this 24 hours a day, seven days a week for 70, 80, even 100 years, without any mechanical breakdown or outside maintenance. Can you think of any machine ever made that has worked around the clock for decades with no mechanical maintenance, replacement parts, or breakdowns?

So why am I telling you all of this? Because I want to show you that you were given this unbelievably awesome computer for a reason. It didn't just happen, and it wasn't placed inside your cranial cavity simply to support a mundane, mediocre, or unfulfilling life. To the contrary, *you were equipped with the world's most advanced computer in order that you might achieve extraordinary outcomes from your efforts, both for your benefit and the benefit of others.* If you are having a hard time believing that this is really true, let me ask you a question. Do you think any team of brilliant engineers would create the world's most advanced computer just to perform simple single-digit addition and subtraction? Of course not; that would be lunacy. The same is true about your Creator. He did not give you the world's most advanced computer so you could simply exist in mediocrity from day to day. That would be like giving your kids a million-dollar super-computer so they could play tic-tac-toe.

So here's the first revelation that changed my destiny and is foundational to changing yours. Because you've been equipped with the world's most advanced computer, you have everything it takes to achieve extraordinary success at work and at home. However, if your personal and professional life doesn't reflect this truth, don't panic. It does not mean that you were given an inferior computer. It simply means that you have not yet reprogrammed your computer for extraordinary achievement.

Like most people's, your computer was programmed for mediocrity by the time you graduated from high school. Going back to our analogy of your Porsche, even though it came from the factory equipped with the world's most advanced computer, that computer was preprogrammed to allow the car to be driven at a top speed of only 15 miles per hour. Until it's reprogrammed, the car will never perform anywhere near its intended capability. Once it's been reprogrammed and its speed cap has been eliminated, you'll be able to drive to any of your dreams at 180 miles per hour. However, if you don't take the time and make the effort to reprogram it, it will always be governed by its original program, and mediocrity and failure are likely to characterize both your personal and professional existence for the rest of your life. The good news is, reprogramming it for extraordinary success is easy—and I'm going to lead you through this process step by step.

The Third Law of Extraordinary Success

Regardless of past programming for mediocrity, anyone can reprogram their brain for extraordinary outcomes. All they need is the right software and the commitment to use it.

Side-by-Side Comparison

Drifters	Pursuers	Achievers	Superachievers
Have an onboard supercomputer but never replace past programming for mediocrity.	Have an onboard supercomputer but never replace past programming for mediocrity.	Have an onboard supercomputer and replace past programming with achievement efforts.	Have an onboard supercomputer and replace past programming with master strategies for superachievement.

How We Were Erroneously Programmed for Mediocrity

Before we start this reprogramming process, you need to understand how you were originally programmed for mediocrity. For most of us, our programming for mediocrity was complete by the time we graduated from high school. Why? Because we were programmed to judge ourselves based on a set of false standards—namely those of academic success, popularity, or athletic achievement. If you didn't get straight A's, weren't elected homecoming king or queen, or didn't quarterback the football team, you probably thought of yourself as average or a little above or below average. Chances are that your judgment was reinforced by your teachers, peers, and maybe even your parents. The result of this kind of programming is usually a life of average accomplishment (or a little better or a little worse than average) on your job, in your marriage, and with your family.

Before You Reprogram, You Have to Trash Your Old Programming

Before you can begin to reprogram your brain for extraordinary achievement, you have to trash your old programming for mediocrity. This is done by deciding to judge yourself by real standards rather than false standards. As adults, a few of the false standards by which we judge ourselves are job titles, paychecks, material possessions, and a forever young and thin appearance. None of these standards accurately reflect our true worth or value. The true standards against which we should judge ourselves are what we accomplish with our time, talents, and efforts and the amount of happiness, fulfillment, and benefit those accomplishments bring into our lives and the lives of others. When a person's time, talent, and efforts bring a tremendous amount of fulfillment and benefit to his or her life and the lives of others, he or she is then extraordinarily successful, regardless of job title, paycheck, or material possessions. So from this point on, we are not going to measure your success by false standards, but rather by true standards with real value.

"Wait!" you say. "I thought this was a book about making millions!" It is and it isn't. The strategies contained in this book have made me and countless others millions of dollars, and if applied to your career and business pursuits could do the same for you. However, what is the good of having millions of dollars if you, your wife, or your children are unhappy and unfulfilled and bring little benefit to the lives of others? My goal is to equip you for extraordinary success. If you apply these strategies and techniques to your professional life, you will achieve extraordinary success on the job. Apply them to a field that rewards success with money and you will have a great chance of making millions. However, if you apply them to a field that doesn't reward success with money, you won't make millions, but you won't be any less happy. My son Mark recently graduated with his degree in secondary education and in English. As he applies these strategies to teaching high school students he will likely become one of the most effective high school teachers in America, but he won't get rich. Mark is also a rock musician and composer who is extremely talented on the drums, guitar, bass, and synthesizer. If he applies these strategies to making and selling music, he could make millions of dollars more than his father has made. But to apply these strategies to either his teaching or his music, he must first do the same thing you must do now—namely, reprogram his computer for extraordinary achievement.

The Three-Step Process of Reprogramming Your Brain and Attitude

Step 1: Realization

The first step in reprogramming your computer is to realize the following facts:

- Your future success is not going to be based on or limited by your own know-how or resources (your time, talent, or money).
- Your future success is not going to be limited by your lack of achievement in the past or by your past failures.
- Your future success at home and on the job *is* going to be based on the fact that your computer is programmed for extraordinary success

with a specific set of strategies, skills, and techniques that you are going to learn in our sessions and utilize in your daily life.

Said another way, this awakening is realizing that you have everything it takes to achieve extraordinary success right now—except the strategies, skills, and techniques, and you will soon have those. In computer terms, you have the hardware and all we have to do is install the software and then start to use it. By the time you complete our final session, you will have installed all of the software and will have learned the skills necessary to use it.

Step 2: Personal Commitment

After the realization comes the second step: a critically important commitment. If I told you that I deposited $20 million into your bank account and you didn't believe me, you wouldn't write a single check on it, even if the money really were in your account. And if you didn't write checks on it, you wouldn't gain a single benefit from having that $20 million in your account. You would go right on living your life like you always have. On the other hand, if you did believe that I put $20 million into your checking account, you would probably start writing checks on it instantly. Everything in your life and the lives of those you love would begin to change. Educations and retirement would be secured. Mortgages, car loans, and credit cards would be paid off. Financial stress would be relieved, and hopefully you could bless the lives of countless others in need. All because you believed me and made a commitment to begin to utilize the funds that I had placed in your account.

You have been equipped with the world's most advanced computer; you can either believe it and make a commitment to act on it, or you can choose not to commit and continue to achieve whatever level of success you are accustomed to achieving. I am going to teach you strategies, skills, and techniques that have propelled the world's most successful people to their impossible dreams. You can believe in them and begin to use them, or you can choose not to believe or use them. Anytime you are asked to believe and commit to something new, you have to make the same choice: Do you believe it and act on it, or do you choose not to believe it and continue in your current path? If you wish to reprogram your computer for extraordinary success, this is the commitment you must make: You must choose to believe that these strategies will make the difference that I claim and act accordingly by beginning to use them on a daily basis.

Step 3: Strategy

The final step in reprogramming your onboard computer for extraordinary success and cruising toward your dreams at 180 miles per hour is to utilize a specific master strategy. That strategy in itself is the single most powerful way to reprogram your computer for extraordinary success. It is so powerful that it always works, 100 percent of the time. I call it the vision mapping process, and it will be the focus of our sixth, seventh, and eighth sessions. Earlier I mentioned that your dreams are like destinations on a map—some nearby, some more distant, and others clear across the continent. The vision mapping process will enable you to see clearly where each of those dreams resides and will provide you with a detailed road map that will enable you to achieve each of those dreams far more quickly than you would ever imagine possible.

Actions for Traction

WHERE THE RUBBER MEETS THE ROAD

1. Whose brain is bigger—Thomas Edison's, Bill Gates's, Oprah Winfrey's, or yours?
2. Whose brain performs more functions—Thomas Edison's, Bill Gates's, Oprah Winfrey's, or yours?
3. Who has experienced the most failures in business and personal life—Thomas Edison, Bill Gates, Oprah Winfrey, or you?
4. What will be the greatest determining factor in your future success—your past education, your current knowledge, your talents, your resources, or your mastery and utilization of the strategies and techniques you are going to learn in our future sessions?
5. What will be your most important activity in reprogramming your brain for extraordinary success personally and professionally?

Answers: 1. They are all the same size. 2. They all perform the same number of functions. 3. Thomas Edison 4. Your mastery of the strategies and techniques you are going to learn in future sessions. 5. The vision mapping process.

– Bonus Section –
Activating Your Photographic Memory

I once worked with man who had a photographic memory. He could memorize a *Time* magazine from cover to cover as fast as he could read it (about 30 minutes). He even memorized the entire Bible in a matter of weeks.

How about you? Do you have a photographic memory? If I were to give you a list of 15 unrelated words and you weren't allowed to write them down, could you remember them in order, even if you didn't try to memorize them? Could you memorize them in order in less than three minutes and then recite them back to me now, six weeks from now, and even six months from now?

Now we're going to run through a quick exercise. I don't want you to even try to memorize these words. I just want you to envision in your mind the events I'm going to describe. Do not attempt this exercise when you are in an environment with possible disruptions (kids, telephones etc.). If you are not already in a room all by yourself, go to such a room before you start this exercise.

I'm going to give you a series of little paragraphs. Do not move from one paragraph to the next until you have envisioned the statement or paragraph you've just read.

Right now, look across the room at the wall that's directly in front of you. Pretend you hear a banging on the other side of that wall. *(Look at the wall and pretend you hear the banging before you read the next statement.)*

All of a sudden a giant **yellow fish** comes right through the wall, floating through the air around the room above you. *(Stop reading and look up and picture the yellow fish coming through the wall.)*

The fish now opens its mouth, and a giant **bubble** comes out, floating through the air, and guess who is inside the bubble? **Bill Clinton** is inside the bubble, looking down at you, smiling and waving. *(Look up and watch the bubble come out of the fish's mouth. See Bill in the bubble and wave back at him and say out loud, "Hi, Bill.")*

Bill reaches into his pocket, pulls out a handful of bright red **marbles,** and drops them onto the floor. They magically move into the shape of a **star.** *(Look up and see Bill pull the red marbles out of his pocket and drop them onto the floor. Then look down at how they've formed the shape of a star.)*

Inside the star is a **Wal-Mart store.** You think, "Great, I need to do some shopping anyway." So you go inside the Wal-Mart and look down the aisles. Amazing . . . every aisle is filled with bags of **Fritos.** Fritos bags are everywhere . . . nothing but Fritos in every aisle. *(Look at all of the bags of Fritos.)*

You think to yourself, "I'm kind of hungry," so you grab a bag of Fritos. You open up the bag and it's full of **broccoli.** Yuck . . . but you're so hungry you pull a piece of broccoli out of the bag and take a bite of it. To your amazement, **chocolate** comes oozing out of the broccoli and gets all over your **blue sports coat.** *(See yourself pulling a piece of broccoli out of the Fritos bag, biting into it, and chocolate oozing out and getting on your blue sport coat.)*

Now let's review the first 10 words. What comes through the wall? _________

What comes out of its mouth? _________

Who is in the bubble? _________

What does he pull out of his pocket and drop on the floor? _________

They magically go into what shape? _________

What store is inside that shape? _________

What's on every aisle? _________

What's inside the bag that you take a bite of? _________

What oozes out when you bite down? _________

What article of clothing does it ooze onto? _________

Now let's cover the next five words. Since you've got chocolate all over your blue sports coat, you quickly grab a ***National Enquirer*** off the rack at the checkout stand and try to rub the chocolate off of your sport coat. It doesn't work, so you grab a bottle of **Coca-Cola** and pour the Coke onto your coat and once again try to rub the chocolate out. As you rub, your blue sport coat magically turns into a bright **red shirt.** *(Picture yourself grabbing a* National Enquirer *off the rack, rubbing the chocolate off your coat, and then pouring a bottle of Coca-Cola onto the blue sport coat and rubbing the chocolate. As you rub it, picture your blue sports coat turning into a red shirt.)*

Oh no! You look down the aisle and there's an angry **bull** pointing his horns right at your red shirt, starting to huff and puff. Your heart starts to race. All of a sudden, the bull stands up on tiptoe and grabs a plastic **toy guitar** off the rack and starts to play it. *(Look down the aisle, see the bull* *looking at you, then see him stand on his toes, grab the toy guitar, and start playing it.)*

What did you first grab to try to rub the chocolate off of your coat? ______________

When that didn't work, what did you grab next to rub on your coat? ______________

As you rubbed that onto your coat, it magically turned into what? ______________

When you looked down the aisle, what did you see, staring back at you? ______________

What did he grab off the rack and start playing? ______________

Now, without looking back at what you just read, answer these questions. If you get stuck on an answer, go back to the story you just visualized.

You hear a banging against the wall. What comes through the wall and floats through the air? A giant yellow ______________. What comes out of its mouth? A ______________. Who is inside, looking down at you and waving? ______________. What does he pull out of his pocket? ______________. He drops them on the floor, and they magically form what shape? A ______________. What's in the middle of that shape? A ______________ store. You go inside, and what fills every aisle? Bags of ______________. You open up a bag and what's inside? ______________. You take a bite and what oozes out? ______________ It gets all over your ______________. You grab a ______________ off the rack and start to rub your ______________. The spot doesn't come out, so you pour ______________ on the ______________ and rub some more. It magically turns your ______________ into a ______________. You look down the aisle and see a ______________. He points his horns at you and huffs and puffs. Then he stands on his tiptoes and pulls a ______________ off the rack and begins to play.

Congratulations! You've just memorized 15 unrelated words in order, and you didn't even write them down.

What does this exercise show? A few minutes ago, when I asked you if you could memorize 15 words in order in under three minutes without writing them down, you could have passed a lie detector test with your answer of no. If I asked you the same question now, you could pass a lie detector test answering yes. What happened in those few minutes? Did your IQ go up 100 points? No. Did your mental ability instantly improve? No. All that happened was that you learned a very simple yet effective memory technique that forced you to memorize with the right side of your brain (the visual and feeling side) instead of the left side of your brain (the analytical side). Normally, when we try to remember something, we simply do it by rote, which uses the left side of the brain and is a much more difficult and much less effective way to memorize.

I took you through this exercise for two reasons: (1) to demonstrate that you and your incredible onboard computer are capable of achieving things you never imagined possible and (2) to show you that achieving impossible dreams is not a matter of a higher IQ or more education, but rather learning and using very simple yet highly effective strategies and techniques. This memory technique is not one of the master strategies or necessary skills or techniques that you will be learning. However, the next time you need to remember any kind of a list, you now know to make up a very visual story weaving the items on the list into the story. By practicing and using this one simple technique, your ability to memorize has just been improved more than 10-fold. And that's what our future sessions are going to do over and over again—teach you remarkably simple strategies and techniques that are so effective that they can radically change your life and raise the level of your personal and career achievement higher than you've ever imagined possible. I'm handing you a set of keys, and you will begin to see that even the heaviest and most formidable door can be easily unlocked and opened by a tiny key.

SESSION 2

Discovering Your Personality Type—You'll Like Your Style!

The Springboard for Playing to Your Strengths, Strengthening your Weaknesses, and Selecting Your Partners

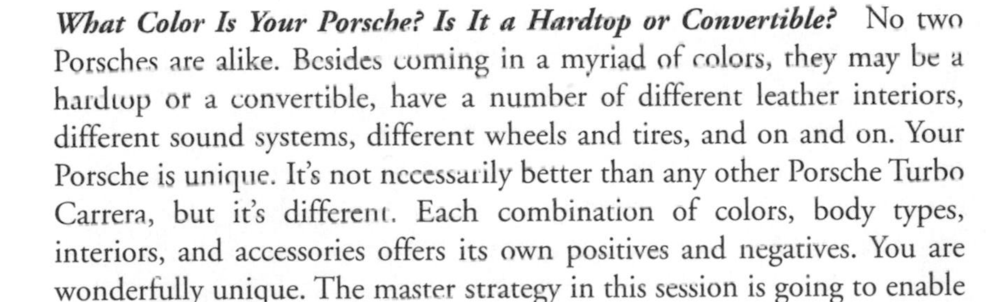

What Color Is Your Porsche? Is It a Hardtop or Convertible? No two Porsches are alike. Besides coming in a myriad of colors, they may be a hardtop or a convertible, have a number of different leather interiors, different sound systems, different wheels and tires, and on and on. Your Porsche is unique. It's not necessarily better than any other Porsche Turbo Carrera, but it's different. Each combination of colors, body types, interiors, and accessories offers its own positives and negatives. You are wonderfully unique. The master strategy in this session is going to enable you to play to your strengths, strengthen your weaknesses, and prepare yourself for effective partnering.

Why do some people seem to be natural born talkers, while others find talking harder and listening easier? Why do some people always take charge in any situation, while others find it much easier to follow? Why are some people so optimistic and others so naturally pessimistic? Why are some more concerned about projects than people and others more naturally sensitive to the needs of people and less concerned about projects? All these questions and hundreds more about you and the people you relate to are quickly answered when you understand that it's all a matter of personality. No wonder what's easy for others is hard for you, and what's easy for you is hard for others.

We are all born with a personality type and exhibit its natural inclinations, strengths and weaknesses, and drives and motivations within months of our birth. As the years pass, we balance those natural drives with learned behaviors. And yet, despite all of our education and efforts, when it comes right down to it, our personality type is usually the greatest determining factor in our behavior, our motivation, and our fulfillment in life. Understanding your personality type and the personality types of those with whom you live and work is critical to your success. This is true both on the job and in your most valued relationships.

You Are a Brand-new Porsche Turbo Carrera, Not a 1957 VW Beetle!

I'll never forget the first time I drove a Volkswagen Beetle. My best friend in high school had purchased a used 1957 black Bug and invited me to take it for a spin. As I stepped on the accelerator, it seemed like we were barely moving. Concerned that I might stall out in the middle of the intersection, I tromped the gas pedal all the way to the floor. To my amazement, we still barely moved. My buddy smiled and said, "But it gets great gas mileage." Twenty-five years later I drove another friend's car for the first time. This one was a brand-new 1991 Porsche Turbo Carrera. He handed me the keys in the parking lot of Gladstone's Restaurant in Malibu, on the corner of Sunset and the Pacific Coast Highway. I pulled out of the parking lot and rolled up to the stoplight. When the light turned green, I tromped the pedal to the metal. Wow! It seemed like we hit 60 before the car in the other lane had even crossed the intersection. The acceleration reminded me of my first ride in a jet fighter. It riveted me to the seat like igniting the afterburner of a jet engine.

So what was the difference between the '57 Beetle and the '91 Carrera? In addition to its acceleration, speed, and power, the Porsche was far more maneuverable and had a more beautiful body style and color, plush leather seats, a great sound system, and a convertible top. Both the Beetle and the Carrera were automobiles. Both would get you from point A to point B. However, their very essence was radically different owing to the nature of their design. One was designed and built to provide basic transportation, the other to provide the ultimate in speed, power, and beauty.

Like that Porsche, you too have been designed and crafted with extraordinary built-in features that will last a lifetime—features that were designed for maximum achievement, happiness, and fulfillment. However, until you know and understand your personality type, there's a good chance you will drive around thinking of yourself as a '57 Beetle and perform with minimal expectations. How tragic to be a Porsche Turbo and live, act, and perform like a '57 Beetle.

While you and I are both Porsches, we may be radically different in our personality types. You may be a bright red convertible; I may be a cobalt-blue hardtop. The good news is that no one type is better than another; they are only different. Each type has tremendous strengths and natural weaknesses.

Master Strategy 2—Play to Your Strengths, Strengthen Your Weaknesses, and Prepare to Partner

Why Is an Understanding of Your Personality Type and the Personality Types of Others So Important?

Even though you can be happy and successful without an understanding of your personality type and the personality types of others, the chances of significantly increasing your success and happiness are greatly enhanced when you gain this understanding. There are five extraordinary lifetime advantages that you will acquire as you learn your personality type and the types of those around you.

1. **The most obvious advantage is that you will be able to play to your strengths.** Your personality type brings with it tremendous natural strengths, and when they are revealed you can draw on them even more effectively. You will also learn how to control and balance those strengths and natural drives that are inherent in your personality type. What others consider to be our flaws are often our strengths out of balance. Even though your Porsche may have a $2000 set of tires, if they are out of balance you won't be able to drive it more than 70 miles per hour without terrible vibrations and a higher risk of an accident. When our strengths aren't balanced by learned behavior, they too can create stress and other difficulties in our work and our relationships.

2. **Understanding your personality type will reveal and clarify your inherent weaknesses.** This is not a negative! To the contrary, it is extremely beneficial. Once you are aware of your natural weaknesses, you can strengthen them or use your strengths to compensate for them. Equally important, understanding those weaknesses will become a major

factor in helping you identify the right kinds of mentors and partners you need to recruit to effectively complete a project or achieve a dream. For example, my personality type is great at gaining a vision for a project but terrible at completing the myriad of details necessary to achieve that vision. Consequently, I recruited a partner in my television productions whose personality type is extremely detail oriented. Without him, hundreds of details would fall between the cracks on every production. With him, I never even worry about a single detail being overlooked. The natural strengths of his personality type are the perfect complement to my natural weaknesses. As a result, my productions are infinitely better with him than they would be without him.

3. **As you learn the personality types of your spouse, children, coworkers, employees, and supervisors, you will have a much greater understanding and appreciation of their strengths.** You will also gain a lot more tolerance for their weaknesses. You will realize that many of the things they do that bother you, they do because it's inherent in their personality type rather than because of a lack of love or respect for you. This knowledge will also be extremely beneficial when it comes to completing projects, because you will be able to make project assignments based on people's personality types, playing to their individual strengths and natural drives.

4. **Understanding the personality types of those with whom you relate will enable you to be far more effective in your communication with them and in motivating and encouraging them.** Each personality type gives and receives communication differently and is motivated and encouraged by factors entirely different than those that motivate and encourage the other personality types.

5. **Knowing your personality type and the personality types of others can make your daily life a lot less stressful, a lot more enjoyable, and infinitely more productive.**

Discovering Your Personality Type with All of Its Incredible Strengths and Surmountable Weaknesses . . . In Five Minutes

In the next few minutes you are going to take a test you cannot flunk. In fact, you're guaranteed an A plus. No matter how you answer this test, you are going to receive a great score because that score will enable you to determine your personality type. There are four basic personality types. None of us are totally one type, but rather we are each a unique combination of all four personality types, with one or two usually being stronger than the others. The strongest is called our dominant personality type and the second-strongest is our subdominant type. After you take the test, we will score it and then take a detailed look at what it all means.

The Five-Minute Personality Test

Following is a chart of horizontal lines with four words on each line, one in each column. On each line, put the number 4 next to the word that best describes you in that line. Then put a 3 next to the word that describes you next best, a 2 by the third-best word, and a 1 by the word that least describes you. On each horizontal line of words you will then have one 4, one 3, one 2, and one 1. Do not put more than one of any number on any horizontal line of words.

For example, my choice for the first line of words would be as follows:

Likes Having Authority 3 Enthusiastic 4 Sensitive Feelings 2 Likes Instructions 1

L		O		G		B	
Likes having authority	2	Enthusiastic	3	Sensitive feelings	4	Likes instructions	1
Takes charge	4	Takes risks	2	Loyal	3	Accurate	1
Determined	4	Visionary	3	Calm, even keel	2	Consistent	1
Enterprising	3	Likes talking	4	Enjoys routine	2	Predictable	1
Competitive	4	Promoter	3	Dislikes change	2	Practical	1
Problem solver	2	Enjoys popularity	4	Gives in to others	3	Factual	1
Productive	2	Fun-loving	1	Avoids confrontation	4	Conscientious	3
Bold	4	Likes variety	1	Sympathetic	3	Perfectionistic	2
Decision maker	3	Spontaneous	4	Nurturing	2	Detail-oriented	1
Persistent	4	Inspirational	2	Peacemaker	3	Analytical	1
Total L	32	**Total O**	27	**Total G**	28	**Total B**	13

Scoring the Test

When you've completed the test, add the numbers for each vertical column. If the column adds up to more than 40 or less than 10, you've added wrong. Now add the total scores for all four columns together. That total should equal 100. If it doesn't, then make sure there is only one 4, one 3, one 2, and one 1 on each line and add the columns again. The most you can score in any given column is 40, and the total for the entire test will equal 100. For example, my scores for each column were L 36, O 30, G 14, and B 20. Adding these scores together equals 100.

Here's What It All Means

Each lettered column represents a specific personality type. The column with the highest score is your dominant personality type, while the column with the second-highest score is your subdominant type. While you are a combination of all four personality types, the two with the highest scores reveal the most accurate picture of your personality type with its inherent natural inclinations, strengths and weaknesses, drives and motivations, and communication and relational behavioral styles. The higher your score in any column, the more dominant the strengths and weaknesses inherent in that personality type. Dr. Gary Smalley likens the four personality types to animals because it makes them easier to visualize and remember than the numbers, letters, colors, or technical terms that are usually used to label personality types. I agree with Gary, so I will use his animal analogies.

Which column did you score highest in? If you scored highest in the L column, then your dominant personality type is that of the lion. If you scored highest in the O column, then you are an otter. If you scored highest in the G column, then you are a golden retriever, and if you scored highest in the B column, then you are a beaver. Next, look at the column with your second-highest score. That is your subdominant personality type. Remember, the higher you score in your dominant type, the stronger its characteristics will be and the more you will identify with those characteristics. If your score is 30 or higher in any of the four types, you can expect those characteristics to be very strong in your life. I am a lion/otter combination, and my wife is an otter/golden retriever. Because we both score above 30 in both our dominant and subdominant types, we see the characteristics of both the dominant and subdominant very clearly in our natural inclinations and drives.

Approximately 10 percent of you will score in the mid-twenties in all four personality types and not receive a high score (upper twenties and above) in any type. Don't panic. This situation means you are very well balanced and can draw on the strengths of all four types equally. It also means that there is no single group of strengths that are driving you and no single group of weaknesses that are devastatingly powerful in your life. When Larry King took this test he scored 26, 24, 24, and 26. No wonder he is such a great interviewer. He can truly become all things to all people. It means he can make friend and foe alike feel comfortable in his presence.

Now let's look at the individual characteristics for each personality type. I suggest that before you read the descriptions of all four, you should first read your dominant type and then your subdominant type. Place a check mark by the characteristics that you identify with in each. Once you clearly understand your own dominant/subdominant combination, then read the others. Being familiar with all four types will help you identify the personality types of your family and others. For each personality type, I will first give you a list of its characteristics and then a few brief comments about that type.

L = Lions

Natural Strengths

- Decisive
- Goal-oriented
- Achievement-driven
- Gets results
- Independent
- Risk taker
- Takes charge
- Takes initiative
- Self-starter
- Persistent
- Efficient
- Driven to complete projects quickly and effectively
- Competitive
- Enjoys challenges, variety, and change

Natural Weaknesses

- Impatient
- Blunt
- Poor listener
- Impulsive
- Demanding
- May view projects as more important than people
- Can be insensitive to the feelings of others
- May run over others who are slower to act or speak
- Fears inactivity, relaxation
- Quickly bored by routine or mechanics

Basic disposition: Fast-paced, task-oriented.

Motivated by: Results; challenge, action, power, and credit for achievement.

Time management: Focus on now instead of the distant future. They get a lot more done in a lot less time than their peers. They hate wasting time and like to get right to the point.

Communication style: Great at initiating communication; not good at listening (one-way communicator). Like to cut through the fluff and get right to the point.

Decision making: Impulsive; make quick decisions with goal or end result in mind. Results-focused; need very few facts to make a decision.

In pressure or tense situations: Take command and can even become dictatorial in tense situations.

Greatest needs: Results. Want to experience variety and face new challenges. Need to solve problems and want direct answers.

What the lion desires: Freedom; authority; variety of challenging assignments; opportunity for advancement.

Lions are the "take charge and get it done" personality type. They are usually the bosses at home or at work . . . or at least they act like they are! They are decisive, bottom-line folks who are observers, not watchers or listeners. They love to solve problems and solve them *now.* They are usually individualists who love to seek new adventures and opportunities. Lions are very confident and self-reliant. In a group setting, if no one else quickly takes charge, the lion will. When they gain a vision for a project, they want to accomplish it as quickly as possible and move on to their next vision. They need very little input to make decisions and often seek little or no advice from others before making a decision. They may feel challenged or threatened when questioned. They work great under pressure. Completing a project quickly or on time is more important to a lion than taking more time to do everything perfectly. Unfortunately, if lions don't learn how to tone down their aggressiveness, their natural dominating traits can cause major problems with others. Most true entrepreneurs are strong lions, or at least have a lot of lion in them.

If you are a lion, here are a few areas for improvement that you should begin to focus on. You need to learn how to relax. It's not a crime to take a vacation and just rest and have fun; it's a way that you can add health and years to your life. It's also a way that you can meet tremendous needs of your wife and children. You need to force yourself to listen to others, and to give encouragement rather than instantly giving solutions to their problems. At home and at work, you need to be more patient with others and help them to complete projects at their pace rather than jumping in and taking over or simply running over them. You need to partner with beavers, who are great at focusing on the details of a project that you will easily overlook. You need to give others a chance to talk at their own pace without rushing them to get to the point. You need to realize that if you don't learn to balance your natural drives with patience, kindness, and concern for the needs of others, you will dishonor them and ultimately be regarded as rude, uncaring, and arrogant. You have tremendous strength and power in your character that you need to balance with love and gentleness. If you want to see how this is done, watch the golden retrievers in your life. All of these qualities are as easy and natural to them as your strengths are to you.

O = Otters

Natural Strengths

- Enthusiastic
- Optimistic
- Good communicator
- Emotional and passionate
- Motivational and inspirational
- Outgoing
- Personal
- Dramatic
- Fun-loving

Natural Weaknesses

- Unrealistic
- Not detail-oriented
- Disorganized
- Impulsive
- Listen to feelings above logic
- Reactive
- Can be too talkative
- Excitable
- Avoid drudge work

Basic disposition: Fast-paced, people-oriented.

Motivated by: Recognition, approval of others.

Time management: Focus on the future and have a tendency to rush to the next exciting thing.

Communication style: Enthusiastic and stimulating; often one-way (talking rather than listening), but can inspire and motivate others.

Decision making: Intuitive and fast. Make lots of right calls—and lots of wrong ones.

In pressure or tense situations: Attack. Can be more concerned about popularity than about achieving tangible results.

Greatest needs: Social activities and recognition; activities that are fun, and freedom from details.

What the otter desires: Prestige, friendly relationships, opportunity to help and motivate others; opportunities to verbally share their ideas.

Otters are excitable, fun-seeking cheerleader types who love to talk! They are a party waiting to happen. They are great at motivating, encouraging, and even inspiring others. They need to be in an environment where they can talk and have a vote on major decisions. Otters' outgoing nature makes them great networkers. They usually know a lot of people who know a lot of people. Otters are the life of any party and most people really enjoy being around them. They have a strong desire to be liked and enjoy being the center of attention. Popularity and the applause of the crowd is often more important than tasks and deadlines. They are often very attentive to style, clothes, and flash. Although otters are quick to gain a vision for the big picture, they are quickly bored by the drudgery of a project and tend to avoid routine work. They are also not naturally inclined to focus on the specific details or minutiae of a project and therefore should not be depended on to manage the details. Otters often neglect the present and focus on the future, whether it's tonight's dinner, the party this weekend, or the vacation next summer. Otters hate confrontation and try to avoid it at all costs. Because of their need to be popular, otters can be very vulnerable to peer pressure. However, under pressure or when backed into a corner, they will attack. They tend to use their strong verbal skills as their primary weapon when they attack.

If you are an otter, here are a few areas for improvement that you should begin to focus on. There is more to life than just having fun, and you need to learn how to become more attentive to the needs of others and how to get serious about meeting those needs. You need to learn how to focus on follow-through and completing existing commitments before you take on new projects and commitments. You are great at talking, but you need to learn listening skills and learn to honor others by listening to them with your mind as well as your ears. You also need to balance your natural impulsiveness by taking time to seek the advice and counsel of others before you make important decisions. You need to set realistic deadlines (Session 10 on persistence and 14 on managing your time and priorities will make you more able to quickly and effectively complete projects than you've ever imagined possible). As far as partnering at work or in business, you definitely need to partner with beavers and lions. Beavers will help you make sure important details don't fall between the cracks, and lions will help you to achieve your important projects and dreams in a reasonable amount of time.

G = Golden Retrievers

Natural Strengths

- Patient
- Easygoing
- Team player
- Stable
- Empathetic
- Compassionate
- Sensitive to feelings of others
- Tremendously loyal
- Puts people above projects
- Dependable
- Reliable
- Supportive
- Agreeable

Natural Weaknesses

- Indecisive
- Overaccommodating
- May sacrifice results for the sake of harmony
- Slow to initiate
- Avoids confrontation even when needed
- Tends to hold grudges
- Fears change
- Ignores or sacrifices own needs

Basic disposition: Slow-paced, people-oriented.

Motivated by: Desire for good relationships and appreciation of others.

Time management: Focus on the present and devote lots of time to helping others and building relationships.

Communication style: Two-way communicators; great listeners and provide empathetic response.

Decision making: Make decisions more slowly, want input of others, and often yield to that input.

In pressure or tense situations: Give in to the opinions, ideas, and wishes of others. Often overly tolerant.

Greatest needs: Security; gradual change and time to adjust to it; environment free of conflict.

What the golden retriever desires: Quality relationships, security, and a consistent known environment; their own area or specialty; a relaxed and friendly environment and freedom to work at their own pace.

Golden retrievers are first and foremost loyal and people pleasers. They're so loyal that they more than any other personality type can absorb the most emotional pain and punishment in a relationship and still stay committed. They are great listeners, incredibly empathetic, and compassionate and warm encouragers. Golden retrievers are quick to defend and slow to attack. They put people above projects and can react very negatively to the way lions tend to put projects over people. They are the best friends you could ever have. They'll always find time to listen, comfort, and encourage, even if you don't deserve the time of day. People who marry golden retrievers are often the luckiest people on earth. My first son is a golden retriever and is without a doubt one of the most compassionate and loving people I have ever known. Interestingly, his personality type was as obvious as a neon sign right from the time he was a toddler. He was always quick to share, and the first to comfort any child (or adult) in distress. Today he is a 27-year-old and married to another golden retriever.

My wife's subdominant personality type is that of a golden retriever. However, with a score of 36, she exhibits all of the strengths and weaknesses of a golden retriever. On the weakness side, golden retrievers tend to be such people pleasers that they can have great difficulty being assertive in a situation or relationship even when it's needed. It is really hard for golden retrievers to seriously discipline their children, even when discipline is desperately needed. If they have a child who is a lion, they are dead meat.

Golden retrievers also have a hard time standing up for themselves and asserting their own personal needs to their spouses, friends, bosses or coworkers. They hate confrontation. They have a very strong need for close relationships and often bury their hurts and needs for the sake of maintaining harmony in their relationships. However, their unwillingness to express their needs or hurts doesn't mean their needs and hurts aren't important to them; they simply store them up. This can have devastating consequences for them and their relationships. Dr. Smalley points out that golden retrievers can store needs and hurts for five to seven years. But while they are storing them, they are being eaten alive on the inside. Finally, they explode and the relationship can come to a devastating end. It becomes very hard for the golden retriever to then forgive, and holding a grudge becomes automatic. Like the dog they are named after, they can become very stubborn at holding on to what they feel is right. If you've ever played tug of war with a real golden retriever holding onto its favorite toy, you will have a good mental picture of just how stubborn this personality type can be.

If you are a golden retriever, you are truly awesome; however, there are areas in which you can improve with a little learned behavior. First, you need to learn that there's nothing wrong with making your opinions, needs, and hurts known to those with whom you relate. You need to become more assertive when necessary. Making your opinions, needs, and hurts known will ultimately strengthen your relationships, and not doing so will not only hurt you, but will ultimately weaken your most valued relationships. *No* is not a dirty word, and you need to learn how to say it more often. You need to learn to politely say no more often to the requests and demands of others, whether your spouse, your children, or even those you serve at work or in church. If you don't, you will ultimately become drained emotionally and physically. You need to establish boundaries with others and honor your own needs. None of this comes naturally or easily to you, but you need to choose to do so for your sake and for the sake of those you love. You also need to learn how to replace grudges with forgiveness. Not to forgive makes you a prisoner of the very person you're displeased with. They win, you lose. When you forgive, you both win. While forgiveness is much easier said than done, when we get into Session 14, you'll learn a process I call *treasure hunting* that will make forgiving people easier than ever. In Session 6 you will learn two communication techniques (emotional word pictures and drive-through talking) that will make expressing your needs to others easier than ever.

B = Beavers

Natural Strengths

- Accurate
- Analytical
- Detail-oriented
- Thorough
- Industrious
- Orderly
- Methodical and exhaustive
- High standards
- Intuitive
- Controlled

Natural Weaknesses

- Too hard on self
- Too critical of others
- Perfectionistic
- Overly cautious
- Won't make decisions without all the facts
- Too picky
- Overly sensitive

Basic disposition: Slow-paced, task-oriented.

Motivated by: The desire to be right and maintain quality.

Time management: Tend to work slowly to make sure they are accurate and make the best decisions. They are pressured by deadlines, and would rather be right and miss a deadline than be wrong and make one.

Communication style: Good listeners; communicate details; usually diplomatic.

Decision making: Avoid making decisions; need lots of information before they will make a decision.

In pressure or tense situations: Try to avoid pressure or tense situations. They will ignore deadlines when they interfere with making the best decision or doing a project the right way.

Greatest needs: To be correct. They feel an inner pressure to be right and accurate.

What the beaver desires: Clearly defined tasks; stability; security; low risk; tasks that require precision and planning.

Thank God for beavers! Without them, our skyscrapers and bridges would be falling down, our medical surgeries would be a lot riskier, and business bankruptcies would be more the rule than the exception. You see, beavers are those wonderful people who do things right, no matter what the cost or how long it takes. Beavers have a strong need to do things by the book and as perfectly as possible. In fact, they are the only personality type who actually read instruction manuals. And unlike others who only consult the instruction books when they are in trouble, beavers read the instructions before they begin a project. They are great at providing quality control in an office, factory, or any situation or field that demands accuracy. They are often found in occupations such as accounting, engineering, architecture, medicine, and others that demand accuracy. Because rules, consistency, and high standards are so important to beavers, they are often frustrated with others who do not share these same concerns. Their strong need for maintaining high (and sometimes unrealistic) standards can short-circuit their ability to express warmth in a relationship. In fact, they can become so focused on doing something right that they become totally insensitive to the needs and concerns of those around them.

The higher you score in the beaver column, the more perfectionistic you are likely to be. Your need to do everything as near perfectly as possible can become a major stress factor in your life and a devastating factor in your relationships with others. The wife of one of my friends is so high in beaver traits that she grounds her children for two weeks if they leave a single thing out of place when they are finished using it. She no longer lets them make their own beds because they don't do it as well as she does. Needless to say, her relationships with her children are highly stressed, to say the least.

As a beaver, your wonderful strengths are your attention to detail, your focus on quality, your analytical nature, and your thoroughness. Unfortunately, you also may have a tendency to start a lot of projects and only finish a few. You can be extremely hard on yourself. You can also be hard on others who are not as attentive to details, quality, and correctness as you are. You are a partner who is desperately needed by the other personality types, and you can increase your value in any partnership with just a few adjustments. First, you need to remind yourself that perfection is not always necessary. Even though there may only be one perfect way, in most situations there are many good ways. You need to be more accepting of others doing things their own way, even if your way is better. Begin to lighten up with others and try to become more flexible. Practice saying the sentence, "It's okay to make mistakes."

Of all the personality types, beavers are the most prone to depression. When you make mistakes, you get angry with yourself and keep that anger bottled up inside. Anger turned inward is a primary cause of frustration and depression. For the sake of your emotional and physical health, it's critical that you learn to be more forgiving of yourself and your mistakes. You also need to become more forgiving of others and tolerant of their mistakes. You'll learn secrets for doing this in our future sessions, especially Sessions 11 and 12. Doing things right comes naturally to you . . . being happy with yourself and others does not. But, as you will learn in these future sessions, this is easily fixed!

Side-by-Side Comparison

How People Deal with Their Strengths and Weaknesses

Drifters	Pursuers	Achievers	Superachievers
Do whatever comes naturally. Think everyone should act the way they do.	Play to their strengths to pursue their projects, goals, and dreams.	Play to their strengths. Strengthen their weaknesses. Balance strengths and weaknesses with learned behavior.	Play to their strengths. Strengthen their weaknesses. Balance strengths and weaknesses with learned behavior. Partner with people who have strengths that complement their weaknesses.

Great News about Your Personality Type

As you focus on your dominant and subdominant personality type, it is critical that you understand that these traits are only your natural inclinations. The weaknesses and negative inclinations in your personality type can be strengthened, balanced, compensated for, or even eliminated by choosing to do what is right and best in a situation rather than simply letting your personality's natural inclination dictate your behavior. As you'll discover in Session 4, it's impossible to achieve our most cherished dreams all by ourselves. We need to recruit the ideas, talents, energy, and resources of others. Knowing your natural weaknesses will also become your greatest ally in helping you determine the kinds of partners you need to recruit to achieve any of your most important projects or dreams. Understanding the personality types of those in your family will equip you to draw on their natural strengths and enable you to become more understanding and tolerant of their weaknesses. As you study the characteristics of each of the four personality types, you will learn the best ways to communicate with and motivate each one. Because I know the personality types of my wife and each of my seven children, life is a lot less stressful and a lot more enjoyable for all of us.

Foundational Lists from Your Personality Profile

1. List what you believe are your greatest strengths from your dominant and subdominant personality types.
2. List what you believe are your greatest weaknesses from your dominant and subdominant personality types.
3. Write down what you believe will be some of the best ways you can strengthen or compensate for your greatest natural weaknesses.
4. List what you believe are the personality types for your spouse, each of your children, your boss, and those with whom you work most closely.
5. In light of their personality types, review and write down what you believe will be the best ways to motivate, encourage, and communicate with each member of your family and with the people you relate to at work.

No Time, No Talent, No Money—No Problem!

Your Lack of Know-How and Limited Resources Will Never Limit You Again!

The Two Roadblocks that Have Always Stood between You and Your Dreams Are No Match for Your Turbo Carrera. Anyone trying to cross America on foot would be greatly disheartened by the sight of the Rocky Mountains. There's no easy way to cross this continental divide. While this massive mountain range is nearly impassible to those seeking their dreams on foot, it's not even a worry to you and your 415-horsepower Turbo Carrera. The two master strategies in this session will empower you to overcome the two most formidable roadblocks that have always stood between you and your dreams.

"I would love to do that, but I don't know how." "I would love to do that, but I don't have the time, talent or money to do it." How many times have thoughts like these kept you from pursing an opportunity or dream?

Ray Kroc was a 52-year-old salesman of milkshake machines. He knew nothing about running a restaurant, starting a franchise, or running a major corporation. He did not have the money, time, or talents that were needed to start a new restaurant franchise business, and yet, he created the most successful restaurant franchise system in history—McDonald's.

Frank Phillips's only training was that of a barber and a bank teller. He had absolutely no knowledge of geology or the oil business. He did not have the time, talent, know-how, or money to look for oil, find oil, or start an oil business. And yet he looked for it, found it, and created one of the greatest oil companies of all time—Phillips Petroleum.

Master Strategy 3—Power-Pass Your Lack of Know-How

"What You Don't Know . . . Can Make You!"

We've all heard the adage, "What you don't know can kill you." That is certainly true. Had I been left alone in the cockpit of a sailplane before I learned to fly, I would have never survived my first flight. For the vast majority of adults, the lack of knowledge or the lack of know-how appears to be such an insurmountable obstacle that when it stands between them and a dream, it might as well be Mount Everest. They usually give up on that dream immediately. Occasionally they may start the hike, but as soon as they hit the first storm they quickly retreat and choose a much more attainable dream, one that lies within their know-how or comfort zone of knowledge. However, one of the greatest secrets for extraordinary achievement known by the world's most successful people is that the opposite of this famous adage is also true; namely, "What you don't know can make you!" In fact, what you don't know can be a springboard to levels of success you haven't even imagined.

How can this be? How can the obstacle that instantly defeats most adults be a launching pad for superachievers? When superachievers are confronted with their lack of know-how, instead of seeing it as an insurmountable roadblock they simply see it as signal, a green light that tells them that this is a situation in which outside help must be recruited. When Steven Spielberg decided to make a movie about dinosaurs, he didn't panic because of his lack of know-how in the area of visual effects and model making. Equally important, he didn't enroll in courses on model making or digital visual effects. Instead of panicking or trying to increase his own knowledge, he simply recruited the best model maker in Hollywood, Stan Winston, and the best digital effects company in the entertainment industry, Industrial Light and Magic. As a result, *Jurassic Park* was the most realistic (and terrifying) dinosaur movie ever made.

The Fourth Law of Extraordinary Success

Lack of know-how only appears to be an insurmountable obstacle. For superachievers, it serves as a springboard to extraordinary achievement.

I know what you're thinking! "Steven Spielberg can afford to recruit any outside resource he wants . . . I can't!" The good news is, recruiting the outside resources you need when pursuing your personal and professional dreams doesn't necessarily require money. When I was in high school, I wanted to learn how to fly, but I didn't have any knowledge of flying or any money for flight lessons. And yet without spending a dime I received my private pilot's license for gliders by the time I was 17. When I was in college, I wanted to form a contemporary music group. Unfortunately, I knew nothing about music. And yet, in less than a week I had recruited 17 singers and 18 instrumentalists, nearly all of them music majors at Arizona State University. Then, without a penny in our piggy banks, and without borrowing a dime, we acquired the thousands of dollars worth of sound equipment we needed. Finally, we recruited one of the top choral arrangers and directors in America to be our arranger and director. Within a month we were performing on college campuses throughout the state and other large venues. The group remained together for years. The critical key in both attaining my pilot's license for free and creating a successful music group was utilizing the strategies we'll look at in our next session—those of effective partnering.

When my mentor and I started my current business, national advertisers were spending more than $100,000 on the average 30-second commercial. We only had $3,600 to produce our two-minute commercial. Having never written or produced a television commercial, I had neither the know-how nor the talent to do so. And with a budget of $3,600, no ad agency in America would have given us a snowball's chance of succeeding. And yet, we were able to do it (although I went $600 over our tiny budget). As I mentioned earlier, that commercial created $20 million in sales and launched what became a multi-billion-dollar business.

Illustrations like this are not limited to my personal experience. I could give you hundreds of examples of men and women throughout history whose lack of know-how did not keep them from achieving their impossible dreams. For example, although Charles Lindbergh was one of the greatest aviators in history, he had no medical training or know-how whatsoever regarding medical devices. Yet he created two medical devices that became cornerstone advancements in modern medicine: the blood centrifuge to separate plasma from blood cells, and the artificial heart and lung machine to keep organs alive outside of the body. Without these inventions and their successors, today there would be no heart surgery of any kind, nor would there be an effective treatment for many diseases of the blood, including leukemia.

Five Facts You Need to Know about Your Lack of Know-How

There is only one kind of person who is permanently locked out of moving up into the category of superachievers, and that is a know-it-all. Know-it-alls don't really know it all, they just think, talk, and act like they do. Unfortunately, their belief that they know more than those around them and that they can single-handedly accomplish anything they set their mind to actually prevents them from seeing the critical need to recruit outside resources to achieve extraordinary outcomes. And if there is one fact in life, it is that no one can achieve extraordinary success in any area without recruiting outside resources. If you have a know-it-all attitude in your personal or professional pursuits, you will be limited to a lifetime of disappointments and mediocrity at best. Your only hope for extraordinary achievement and fulfillment is to come down to reality and acknowledge that you are in the same boat as the rest of us. Even though you do have the world's most advanced computer, a critical part of its reprogramming for extraordinary success is installing reality software regarding your lack of know-how. Here are five facts we all must accept and believe as the first step to overcome our lack of know-how.

1. We don't have to be geniuses to achieve extraordinary outcomes and impossible dreams. Of the dozens of superachievers I have met, I have only known one whose IQ was over 140. However, I have met a number of geniuses that have worked for superachievers but weren't superachievers themselves. Thomas Edison, one of my favorite superachievers of all time, not only denied being a genius, he redefined the term when he said, "True genius is 1 percent inspiration and 99 percent perspiration." If I use his definition rather than an IQ measurement, then every superachiever I have ever known is a genius. And the good news is, by Edison's definition, anyone can become a genius.

2. We all know a little, and don't know a lot. There are only a few things I know how to do really well and millions of things I don't know how to do at all. When it comes to producing a television show, there are hundreds of details that must be efficiently and effectively accomplished, and I don't have the knowledge, training, or skills to do any of them. I know how to write a script and direct a cast and crew, and that's it. I can't even operate a camera or read a light meter. And yet, my productions have been good enough to attract and enlist Academy Award–winning actors such as Charlton Heston, Jane Fonda, and Cher, as well as dozens of television stars and recording artists. The secret? I have produced award-winning productions because I have partnered with a great producer who recruits crews that include many of the most talented and highly skilled craftspeople in Hollywood. All of this is to say that you only need to know a little because whatever you don't know is known by others who often are easily recruited.

3. **We all have a few skills, and don't have most skills.** Here again, the entertainment industry gives us a perfect example of this truth. While Steven Spielberg is arguably the greatest film director and producer of our generation, the next time you watch one of his films, notice how many credits follow the movie's end. While Steven is a master storyteller and director, nearly every one of those 300 to 600 credits identifies someone who performed a skill that Steven does not have. And yet, had that skill not been superbly performed, his film would have not turned out as well. If Steven Spielberg doesn't have most of the skills required to achieve any of his dreams, what would make you or me think that we have all of the skills we need to achieve our dreams? We don't. The great news is, every skill we would ever need to achieve any of our dreams is possessed by someone else, and therefore can become available to us.

4. **We don't even have to know how to do those things that are critical to the success of a project or the fulfillment of a dream.** What does barbering or banking have to do with finding oil and building an oil empire? Frank Phillips had none of the skills critical for doing either, and yet he did both. Helen Keller could neither see nor hear, and yet she became one of the most inspirational writers and speakers of the twentieth century. Nearly everyone I have ever known has mistakenly thought that if they want to achieve something they must at least know how to do those things that are critical to the success of the project or endeavor. Nothing could be further from the truth. I know absolutely nothing about retailing fitness equipment, and yet I started a fitness company with my partners that has sold nearly $1 billion worth of equipment. Never turn your back on a project, opportunity, or dream simply because you do not know how to perform the elements necessary to succeed in the project, seize the opportunity, or achieve the dream.

5. **We have a few natural talents and abilities, and don't have most.** This is one area where I really come up short. I'm not athletic, artistic, musical, or mechanically inclined. However, I do have a natural ability to see things in a logical order and a talent for being able to simplify complex concepts and make them easily understood. I do have a natural ability for speaking and encouraging people. Other than these four natural talents or abilities, every other talent or ability that I have acquired has been learned with a great

deal of effort. But for each of the natural talents and abilities that I have, there are thousands or even millions that I don't have. Yet that has never stopped me from achieving my impossible dreams. I'm not athletic, but I've built a number of successful fitness companies. I'm not musical, but I've created two successful musical groups and directed a nationally renowned symphony. I'm not artistic, but many of my television shows have included scenes that were true works of cinematographic art. Your lack of talent and abilities need never prevent you from achieving your impossible dreams.

I share these five facts with all of their don't-haves to reinforce the absolute truth that everyone has a tremendous lack of know-how, including every superachiever who has ever lived. Coming face to face with your own lack of know-how is nothing to fear, nothing to be worried about, and most of all nothing to be ashamed of. Seeing and acknowledging your lack of know-how in any given situation is critical to achieving extraordinary success in that situation. Anything less will keep you from reaching outside of yourself and recruiting the outside resources that are critical to achieving extraordinary success.

Even though your lack of know-how looms in front of you like a giant mountain standing between you and your dreams, in reality it is more like rain on your Porsche's windshield. Even though it may impair your vision for a moment, it's easily dealt with by simply flipping a switch to activate your windshield wipers. Turning your lack of know-how from an insurmountable obstacle into a springboard to extraordinary achievement is also simply a matter of flipping a switch. You simply turn your gaze away from yourself and toward the outside resources you will need to recruit.

Side-by-Side Comparison

How People Deal With Their Lack of Know-How and Lack of Resources in Relation to Their Pursuit of an Opportunity, Project, or Dream

Drifters	Pursuers	Achievers	Superachievers
View obstacles as insurmountable and give up on opportunities, projects, and dreams when these obstacles appear.	Try to figure out a solution or an alternative approach, but usually give up when a solution isn't quickly or easily achieved.	Try to increase their know-how and find alternative solutions, and occasionally succeed when pursuing moderate achievement.	Use their lack of know-how and lack of resources as a signal to look outside of themselves and recruit the know-how and resources of others to achieve extraordinary outcomes far greater than they could have ever achieved on their own.

Flipping the Switch

Turning your lack of know-how into a springboard or launching pad to extraordinary achievement is a process that involves two specific strategies. First, you must gain an accurate assessment of your own strengths and weaknesses in general, and then in particular as those strengths and weaknesses relate to your pursuit of a specific project, opportunity, or dream. Gaining an accurate and thorough assessment of your strengths and weaknesses will provide you with a personal profile that will serve as the foundation on which the elements critical to your success and happiness will be built. Although foundations are neither attractive nor appealing, they provide the essential base on which every significant structure is built. In the "Actions for Traction" section at the end of this session I'm going to ask you to create a number of lists that will provide you with all of the information you need to properly lay this foundation.

The second strategy that is required to turn your lack of know-how into a springboard to extraordinary success is the strategy of effective partnering. You must identify, recruit, and effectively utilize the right partners whose strengths will more than compensate for your weaknesses. Effective partnering is the single most powerful strategy you will learn in our mentoring sessions. Without this strategy, no impossible dream would have ever been realized and no extraordinary outcomes would have ever been achieved . . . by anyone! This one strategy has been used by every superachiever who has ever lived and will be the focus of our next session. Before you throw up your hands and say, "Who would ever partner with me?" or "I can't afford to recruit partners," let me assure you that my definition of partners and partnering is radically different from your definition, and by my definition, you will be able to effectively partner, regardless of your circumstances or resources. All you need to do is learn and utilize the strategies and skills that you're going to learn in that session. But before we move on to that session, there's one more area we need to cover in this one—namely, your limited resources.

"But I Don't Have the Time or Money." So What!

When I talk to individuals about achieving their most desired dreams, there's one roadblock that they cite more quickly and more often than their lack of know-how, and that is their lack of resources. They say they don't have the time or the money needed to achieve their dreams. How about you? How many times have you walked away from a dream, a deep desire, an opportunity, or a project because you didn't have enough money or time? Guess what. You are not alone! No one has enough time or money to achieve his or her most cherished dreams. We all come up short. Even billionaires have dreams they don't have the money to buy. Fortunately there are two ways to expand and multiply our limited resources. Let's start with the most precious and limited resource of all, time.

Master Strategy 4—Remove the Limits of Your Limited Resources

Without a doubt, the single most limited, irreplaceable, and precious resource we have is our time. It is the only resource we have that is irreplaceable. When a day passes, it can never be reclaimed or replaced. Money lost can be replaced, and talents lost can be replaced with substitute talents, but there is no substitute for time. When people get into financial trouble or lose a job, they can cut their expenses dozens of ways and slow the rate at which they burn through their cash, savings, and credit. But unlike money, there is no way to slow down the "burn rate" of time. The average adult in America only lives for 3,950 weeks. If you are 30 years old, you've already used 1,560 of those weeks. If you are 40, you've used up 2,080, and if you are 51 you may only have 1,300 weeks left. And that's if you make it to the average. You could have a few more years than that, and you may have a lot less. But regardless, every seven days you are going to lose another week, and you will never get it back. A former acquaintance of mine was the president of NBC television. When he turned 40 he had no idea that he only had about 110 weeks left. When I filmed Michael Landon's last project, he thought he was in the best physical shape of his life. He looked great and felt great. He had no idea that he only had 18 weeks left.

Now, as bad as all of this may sound, there's something even worse. Time is not only our most limited resource, it is also the least appreciated and most easily wasted of all our resources. Most people waste it as freely as they flush water down the toilet.

That's the Bad News. The Good News Is . . .

Don't get too depressed. I'm not telling you all of this to bring you down, but rather to bring you into reality. Time is truly the most precious commodity we have and it needs to be treated more wisely than you would treat a bank account or a treasure chest of priceless jewels. The good news is that in this session and the sessions that follow, you are going to learn how to become far more productive with your time than ever before, and

The Fifth Law of Extraordinary Success

Superachievers remove the limits of limited resources by accurately assessing their resources, wisely allocating them, and expanding them by recruiting outside resources.

how to greatly expand it and use it to achieve your most important dreams more quickly than you would ever think possible.

There are three steps that you must take to implement this fourth master strategy of removing the limits of your limited resources of time and money.

1. They must be accurately assessed and correctly valued.
2. Their use must be wisely allocated.
3. They must be expanded.

The good news is that all three of these steps can be implemented with each limited resource. Although implementing these steps goes against our human nature, as you implement them you will begin to receive their immeasurable benefits, and eventually they will become second nature to you.

Making the Most of Your Time, 30 Hours a Day, 10 Days a Week

The first step in removing the limits of your limited and diminishing resource of time is to gain an accurate assessment of how you currently spend it, and then choose to begin to value your time more highly as the priceless commodity that it is. Because most people place such a low value on their time, they waste vast amounts of it without even thinking about it. For example, most adults could pass a lie detector test swearing that they watch less than 15 hours of television per week. And yet, the fact is that American adults watch between 35 and 56 hours per week. In Session 13, I will lead you through a simple exercise that will give you a very accurate assessment of your time. Most of us don't waste our time doing terrible things; rather, we waste it doing good and acceptable things. Unfortunately, doing that which is merely good and acceptable can rob us of the opportunity to use our time to do what is best. And the ramifications and consequences of this can be enormous.

Side-by-Side Comparison

How People Use or Misuse Their Limited Resources of Time and Money

Drifters	Pursuers	Achievers	Superachievers
Fail to accurately assess the value of their limited resources and squander those resources by simply doing what comes naturally. Their resources are consumed by the demands of the moment and by their focus on instant gratification rather than the wise allocation of limited resources.	Accurately assess and value their limited resources but fail to effectively and strategically expand those resources.	Accurately assess and value their limited resources and try their hardest to expand those resources. However, they try to expand their resources from within through better investing, spending, and saving, rather than by strategically recruiting outside resources.	Accurately assess and value their limited resources. Seek outside counsel in how they allocate their resources. Most important, they are very quick to effectively and strategically recruit outside resources. They realize that this is the fastest and most effective way of expanding their limited resources. They also seek lots of outside counsel to make sure they make the best use of their limited resources rather than simply accepting a good use of those resources.

Imagine that you own one piece of property in New York City, and your only income for the rest of your life is going to be derived from leasing that property to a business. A convenience store chain offers to pay you $50,000 per year for 50 years. That sounds like a good deal, so you sign the lease and receive a check for your first year's rent. The next day there's a knock on your door. It's Donald Trump, and he tells you that he wants to lease that same piece of property for a 90-story office tower and will pay you $1 million per year for 50 years. Unfortunately, you've already leased the property. Your good use of that property robbed you of its best use and all of its incredible benefit. This same principle is especially true of time. Every block of time you manage is like that single piece of property; you only get to use it one time and in one way. Once it has been committed to be used for one purpose, it can't be used for another. Since time is our most limited resource, using it for good, acceptable, and mediocre uses can rob us of its best uses and of all of the benefits that accompany the best use. In Session 13 you will learn a simple technique that will assist you in making the best use of your time in relation to achieving your most important goals. It will also enable you to accomplish more each day than you would have ever thought possible.

The second step in removing the limits of this limited resource is learning how to more effectively allocate your time to accomplish those things that you value and desire most. Much of our time is consumed by responding to the demands and priorities of other people or the demands of momentary circumstances. One of the techniques you will learn in Session 13 will enable you to take control of your time, your life, and your future like never before through the optimum allocation of your time.

The third and final step of removing the limits of your limited resource of time is to expand your time. There are 168 hours in a week, and most people are awake for at least 112 of those hours. However, there is a way that we can expand the number of hours in our days and weeks through the process of delegating a portion of our workload to others. Even though I only work about eight hours a day, I expand my effective hours through the delegating process and consequently I accomplish at least 20 hours of work per day. I do this by doing only those things that I alone can do. The other things that I need to accomplish on my job that can be done by others are delegated to my assistant and a project manager. Now just because you may not be able to afford an assistant doesn't mean you can't delegate. In Session 13 you'll learn how to delegate work both on the job and at home in ways that will expand your time significantly.

Removing the Limits of Your Limited Resource of Money

The same three steps of assessment, allocation, and expansion that remove the limits of the limited resource of time work just as effectively with your limited resource of money. Believe it or not, nearly every person, every company, and every nation in the world does not have the money they need to do everything they want to do. Yet, superachievers do not let their lack of money prevent them from achieving their impossible dreams.

Ray Kroc did not have the money he needed to start a restaurant franchise. Bill Gates and Paul Allen didn't have the money they needed to start a software company. Thomas Edison didn't have the money he needed to fund his research for an electric light bulb. In fact, if you were to look at the 1,000 greatest success stories of all time, you would discover that not one of them had the money they needed to pursue and achieve their rags-to-riches success. Perhaps the greatest impossible dream ever conceived by a handful of men was that of an independent democratic nation. Unfortunately, even though Washington, Jefferson, and our other founding fathers desperately wanted an independent nation, they did not have the money to fund a war with the greatest military power in the world. They not only had no money, they had no credit. And yet, by implementing the strategies in this session and the next session, they were able to acquire the money and credit they needed to wage their war and win their independence. So when people tell me they have a great idea but can't pursue it because they don't have enough money, I usually say, "So what!" I then go on to say that a truly good idea can nearly always find funding when the funds are correctly pursued.

As was the case with time, the first step in removing the limits of your limited resource of money is to gain an accurate assessment of what you have, your current flow of income, and how you currently spend it, and then to choose to begin to value your money more highly, viewing it as a limited resource that at some point may be very hard to replace. As basic as this may sound, most people don't follow this step. They are shocked when they go into a divorce settlement and make an accounting of how much income they've taken in and how much was spent in each category of expenditures. By the way, when I say *choose to value your money,* I don't mean chose to love it, adore it, or hoard it in a miserly fashion. What I mean is to begin to value its rarity. You literally trade lots of hours of your life for each paycheck you receive, and to spend it foolishly or make it captive to large balances on your credit card is to devalue the worth of your time and labor. While this step of accurately assessing and valuing won't remove the limits of your limited resource in itself, it will provide a foundation for the next two steps that will remove those limits.

Once you have an accurate assessment of how much money you have, what comes in, and how it is spent, the second step is to begin to allocate the use of your money, income, and assets wisely. Here again, as with time, a good use of our money can rob us of a better or best use. In 1948, a thriving and growing company hired my friend's father. By the end of the year he had enough in savings to buy his first brand-new automobile. He had been driving a clunker all through college and at last he could afford to spend $3,000 on a new car. However, the day before he bought the car he was told he could buy company stock for only $5 a share, and the company would match his stock purchase one to one. My friend's father wisely reasoned that while every new car depreciates as soon as it is driven off the lot, the stock, on the other hand, might appreciate. His company had been a public company since 1919 and had a good history of appreciation. As good as a new car would have been for his young family, he decided that the stock purchase would be a better use of his money. When he cashed out his stock many years later, it was worth millions of dollars. Had he chosen to make good use of his money and buy his family a brand-new car, he would have robbed himself of making the best use of his money by buying his company's stock. While buying company stock is not always the best use of one's money (Enron employees would have been better off buying new cars), in my friend's case it was definitely the best use.

The question for most people is, "How can I determine the best use versus good or bad uses of my money?" Because everybody is in a different boat on this one, I hesitate to give general advice. This is one area where outside counsel is needed by nearly everyone. There are lots of books on saving, spending, and investing. I highly recommend anything Clark Howard writes, such as *Get Clark Smart* (Hyperion, 2001). Also, there are financial counseling companies and financial planners that can help you with steps 1 and 2.

The third and most important step in removing the limits of your limited resource of money is that of expanding your financial resources. You expand your financial resources in three ways: good investing, good saving, and recruiting the financial resources of others. Recruiting the financial resources of others has long been the most preferred path of superachievers. Our founding fathers turned to Robert Morris, who not only provided $2 million of his own money but also cosigned loans from France. France refused to loan Washington the money he desperately needed unless Morris would personally guarantee the loans. Without the funds and financial guarantees of Robert Morris, the Revolutionary War would have never been waged, much less won. What was true for Washington and our founding fathers has been true with every superachiever I have ever known or studied. Not one achieved his or her impossible dreams without first recruiting the financial resources of someone else.

Do you realize what great news this is? It means that your level of achievement never need be dictated by or limited by the level of your personal financial resources. This has been true of everything I have achieved throughout my life. My dream to get my pilot's license in high school was paid for by the United States Air Force, no strings attached. My music group's need for sound equipment was fulfilled by a donation from a kind benefactor. My company's ability to roll out our first product in a national television advertising campaign was financed by credit extended to us by the nation's television stations. So the question now facing us is, How does a person recruit the financial resources of others that are needed to fund an idea, a project, or a business? Simply stated, there are six general steps that must be taken.

1. **Your idea, project, or business must be a truly worthy idea, project, or business.** For every legitimate, good, and worthwhile idea, there are thousands of bad ones. Inventors present nearly 1000 new products to my company each year with the hope that we will take their products to market. The vast majority of these products are mediocre at best and worthless at worst. Before you seek the financial resources of others, do your homework and get lots of outside opinions on the validity and true worth of your ideas. The goal isn't just to validate the worth of your idea or project, but to use wise counsel to sharpen your ideas and make them even better.

2. **You must create an accurate assessment of your resources and demonstrate your ability to wisely allocate those resources.** Nobody in his or her right mind would commit financial resources to someone whose own resources are misused, poorly managed, or lightly accounted for. A financial resource wants to make sure that you wisely and tightly control your own funds and that your tracking of your own resources is thorough and accurate. You may have a great idea or project, but if you can't prove that you are a capable manager of your own resources, no one will take the risk of letting you manage his or her resources. If you are terrible at this discipline, don't panic—I am too. This is when you reach outside of your own know-how and recruit a partner who is great at this discipline. You'll learn how to do this in our next session.

3. **You should use the strategies and techniques that you will learn in our next session to identify, recruit, utilize, and motivate the right financial partners.** You may have a great idea or project, and you may run a tight ship financially, but potential financial partners could still turn you down. It's not enough to just hit the streets looking for financial resources. To successfully recruit outside resources of any kind requires using a successful strategy for identifying, recruiting, utilizing, and motivating the right partners. This involves a set of strategies and skills that I'm going to mentor you in in our next session.

4. **You should use the vision mapping process that you'll learn in Session 7 to create a well-defined and powerful vision of your idea, project, or business.** I never cease to be amazed at how many people present ideas, products, and projects that are only partially conceived. I'll ask,

"Well, how are you going to do this?", and instead of a clear and detailed answer, I only hear a vague idea. Regardless of how good a project may be, if you haven't created a precise and detailed plan for every aspect of that project, the chances of acquiring outside resources are near zero. In Session 7 you'll learn a skill that I call the vision mapping process, which will give you all of the detail and clarity you need to present any idea you may want to communicate.

5. **You should use the skills for effective and persuasive communication that you will learn in Session 5 to communicate your vision to your would-be financial partners.** Most good and even great ideas never get out of the starting gate because the person presenting the idea communicates his or her vision ineffectively. Once you learn the communication and presentation techniques in our fifth session, you will never have to worry about this problem again.

6. **You should always keep foremost in your mind and presentation that your would-be financial partners (whether your boss, an investor, a company, or a bank) are only interested in what your opportunity will do for them, not what their participation will do for you.** You wouldn't believe the stories I have heard from people who have wanted my company to back their projects. At least 60 percent of the time their focus is on what we can do for them, rather than on what their idea or project can do for us. The only reason a would-be financial partner would ever provide his or her resources to help you fulfill your vision is because your vision presents a wonderful opportunity to further fulfill his or her vision for his or her resources—namely a great return on his investment and the highest and best use of those assets.

Don't let this list scare you, but rather let it guide you. There are trillions of dollars of unused financial resources in America. Getting a piece of that pie is a lot easier than anyone may think when you go about it the right way. As we close this session, let me remind you that the single greatest strategy for overcoming your lack of know-how and removing the limits of your limited resources is the strategy of effective partnering. It is the one strategy that has been used by every superachiever in history to achieve extraordinary levels of success and impossible dreams. That is why effective partnering is the focus of our next session.

Actions for Traction

WHERE THE RUBBER MEETS THE ROAD

Creating Your Personal Profile for Extraordinary Achievement: Gaining an Accurate Assessment

1. List your personal strengths. Start with the personality strengths you listed from your personality type and add to them any additional strengths, talents, or abilities that you have.
2. List your business strengths (such as sales, administrative abilities, managerial abilities, marketing abilities, and so on).
3. List what you consider to be your personal weaknesses—for example, your lack of education, lack of success, or lack of patience. Are you too quiet or too talkative? Are you too tolerant or not tolerant enough? And so on. Here again, start with your natural weaknesses revealed in your personality test and add to the list.
4. List what you consider to be your business or professional weaknesses. For example, maybe you are a terrible salesman. Maybe you're a bad communicator. Maybe you're not detail oriented or are too focused on detail. Other potential weaknesses are lack of managerial, marketing, and communication skills. If you have a hard time developing a lengthy and accurate list of weaknesses and faults, ask your spouse or people at work. They often see these more clearly than we do.
5. List the things you love to do (your passions, hobbies, work projects, etc.).
6. List what you do really well, both personally and on the business side.

SESSION 4

Steven Spielberg's Masterful Strategy for Maximum Achievement in Minimum Time

Techniques for Accelerating Your Success through Effective Partnering

Your Porsche's Five-Gear Transmission Will Enable You to Reach Your Most Distant Dreams in Record Time. As powerful as your turbocharged engine is, what good would it be if your transmission only had first gear? How frustrating to have a car that could cruise at 180 miles per hour, but can only be driven down the highway at 5 to 10 miles per hour in first gear! Fortunately, your Porsche has a five-speed transmission that can efficiently transfer all of the horsepower of your turbocharged engine to the drive train that turns your wheels. The master strategy we're going to discuss in this session is that five-speed transmission. Without it, you'll never achieve your impossible dreams—but with it, you'll achieve them in record time.

Who were Maurice Clark and Henry Flagler? Who was Harry Sonneborn? Who was Ubbe Iwerks? You probably don't recognize any of these names. But you do know the names of their partners who achieved their impossible dreams. None of the famous partners would have achieved their fame or their impossible dreams had they not teamed up with these unknown partners.

As you discovered in the last chapter, without Robert Morris, George Washington and Thomas Jefferson would have never realized their impossible dream to defeat the British. There would have been no Revolutionary War, and there would be no United States of America. Without Maurice

> ***The Sixth Law of Extraordinary Success***
>
> It is impossible to achieve extraordinary success in any arena without effectively partnering. Every extraordinary or impossible dream ever achieved has been achieved through partnering.

Clark and Henry Flagler, John D. Rockefeller would have never created Standard Oil, which made him the richest man in the world. Without Harry Sonneborn, Ray Kroc's dream of McDonald's restaurants on thousands of street corners would have died a terrible, profitless death after only 200 franchises had been sold. Kroc's McDonald's Corporation was barely making ends meet until Sonneborn gave Ray the idea that turned McDonald's into a multi-billion-dollar empire almost overnight. Walt Disney arrived in Hollywood with $40 in his pocket and a suitcase of clothes. If it weren't for Ubbe Iwerks and Walt's other partner, his brother Roy, there would have never been a Mickey Mouse—and without Mickey, the movie and theme park empire that followed would never have materialized. Yet, because Walt Disney, George Washington, John D. Rockefeller, and Ray Kroc all discovered the unlimited power of strategic partnering, their impossible dreams became unimaginable success stories.

These examples are not the exception, but rather the rule. Every person in history who has achieved his or her impossible dream has done so by effectively using this same strategy. If that doesn't tell you something, maybe this will: No one in history has ever achieved his or her impossible dream without employing this strategy. So, if the greatest superachievers of all time could not achieve their impossible dreams without effective partnering, what makes you or I think that we can? The fact is, we can't! How about you? How many partners have you recruited in your pursuit of your most important dreams? Show me your past, present, and future partners (or lack of them), and I will show you the level of your past achievement and the level of your future success.

Master Strategy 5—Identify, Recruit, and Effectively Utilize Partners

What Is Effective Partnering?

There are two terms that must be understood in order for you to utilize this fifth master strategy in the pursuit of your important goals,

Side-by-Side Comparison

How People View and Utilize Partners

Drifters	Pursuers	Achievers	Superachievers
Do everything they can on their own. They only partner as a last resort when there is no other way to get what they want. Because they usually go with the flow, they see no need to partner.	Are hard workers and mistakenly believe that getting what they want is simply a matter of trying harder and working harder, so they pursue their dreams alone or with minimal or ineffective partnering.	Set moderate goals that are often achievable without the need for extensive and effective partnering. Occasionally partner when they see the need to do so, but they view partnering as a weakness rather than a strength.	Set extraordinary goals that they know are impossible to achieve without the recruitment of strategic partners. They view partnering as a critical part of their strategy from the very outset of their plan. Effective partnering is the single most powerful strategy they utilize. It becomes part of their nature.

projects, and dreams. First you must understand what I mean by the term *partner.* When I speak of a partner, I am not referring exclusively to a legal relationship that exists between two people or companies. Rather, I am referring to any individual or company that can be recruited by someone to perform tasks that are necessary for the optimal achievement of any important project, goal, or dream. This can include counselors, consultants, advisors, experts, authors, friends, key employees, financiers, investors, lenders, mentors, and literal or legal partners. Most of our attention in this session is going to be focused on the last two groups—mentors and literal or legal partners.

The second term that must be clearly understood is *effective partnering.* Effective partnering involves four sequential components: (1) identifying the right type of partner needed for a given situation; (2) identifying the right person within that type; (3) recruiting the right person with the right kind of offer; and (4) effectively utilizing the partner for optimal results. When any of these components are absent, partnering becomes far less effective and potentially disastrous.

The Seventh Law of Extraordinary Success

Effective partnering raises the level of success exponentially, accelerates success meteorically, and reduces risk enormously.

In 1899, the founders of the newly formed Detroit Automobile Company recruited Henry Ford away from the Edison Illuminating Company to be a senior officer and part-owner of their new company. The founders had achieved three of the four components of effective partnering: They had identified the right type of partner they needed and the right person within that type, and they recruited him with the right kind of offer. And yet, once they had recruited Ford, they did not effectively utilize him. Instead, they neutralized him with directives that prevented him from following his instincts. As a result, they failed to produce a single car in their first two years, and Henry Ford was summarily fired. Within two years the Detroit Automobile Company was defunct, while Henry had found the right partners who fulfilled all four components. The result was the creation of the Ford Motor Company. Within a few years, even though the new car market was divided between 250 different automobile manufacturers, one out of every two cars in the world was a Ford!

The Incalculable and Unparalleled Benefits of Effective Partnering

The two facts that no one in history has ever achieved extraordinary success in any arena without effective partnering, and that 100 percent of all extraordinary achievements have been accomplished through effective partnering should provide ample incentive to utilize this strategy in every important endeavor we ever pursue. However, if these two general facts do not motivate you to do so, perhaps this list of specific benefits of effective partnering will.

The 11 Incomparable Benefits of Effective Partnering

1. It's the fastest and most beneficial way to overcome your lack of know-how. I had no idea how to write, direct, and produce television commercials. Partnering with a mentor and skilled craftsmen has enabled me to write, produce, and direct over 800 national television commercials that have now produced over $2 billion in sales for our companies and $200 million in personal income for my partners and me. Unlike the process of learning, which can take years for any single discipline, partnering can utilize hundreds of disciplines and accomplish far better results in a matter of hours or days.

2. It's the fastest and most beneficial way to remove the limits of your limited resources. No person or business has ever achieved extraordinary success without recruiting the time, talent, or money of other individuals or companies. The more successful the person or company is, the more outside resources they have recruited. The fastest and most effective way of removing the limits of limited resources is through resource expansion. Time is expanded by delegating; talents are expanded by recruiting the talents of others; and money is expanded by recruiting the money of others from lenders, investors, or credit extended by suppliers.

3. It raises your chances of success geometrically. In my industry, the average success rate of our competitors is less than 5 percent. Our company's success rate runs between 50 percent and 72 percent. Our competitors typically would rather own 100 percent of their projects than give up a percentage to form strategic partnerships. For 27 years, a critical key to our success rates has been the strength of our internal partnership and our ongoing efforts to quickly form strong strategic alliances with inventors, celebrities, and vendors. Before joining forces with my mentor and partners in 1976, my personal success rate for new business start-ups was 0 percent. My success rate for my corporate jobs was 11 percent (I had failed eight out of nine times). My personal success rate since teaming up with my partners has ranged from 50 percent to 90 percent, depending on the year, and my 27-year average has been approximately 70 percent. Remember that I have had the same IQ and educational background before and after 1976. So what moved me from 0 percent in successful start-ups to 70 percent? Two words . . . effective partnering!

4. It raises your level of success exponentially. Some strategies can increase your success arithmetically and some can increase it geometrically. But effective partnering is the only strategy I know of that can increase your level of success exponentially.

How dramatic is that kind of increase? Suppose you start with $10.

An arithmetic increase is demonstrated by $10 + $9 = $19.

A geometric increase is demonstrated by $10 × 9 = $90.

An exponential increase is demonstrated by $\$10^9 = \$1$ billion.

That is the kind of incredible difference effective partnering can make in the level of success you achieve in a given endeavor. Sound too good to be true? With an ineffective partnership Henry Ford produced no cars and made no sales or profits, and the company dissolved. With the right set of partners Henry Ford produced more cars in a day than most of his competitors produced in a year and, by 1928, half of all the cars in the world were Fords. That is an exponential increase. In my case, I started two businesses on my own. One was a sole proprietorship and the other was an ineffective partnership. Both businesses failed. In one, I grossed $25,000 in sales and experienced a loss of $2,000. The second business grossed $20,000 in sales and lost $10,000. My current business utilizes effective partnering. We have grossed over $2 billion in sales and made profits of $200 million. Sales of $25,000 without effective partnering versus $2 billion with effective partnering; a $2,000 loss versus a $200 million profit. That is the exponential power of effective partnering.

5. It *accelerates* your achievement of success meteorically. At the time Thomas Edison decided to pursue the concept of a practical electric light bulb, renowned scientists had already been trying to invent one for more than 50 years. Edison had neither the degrees nor the depth of knowledge that any of these scientists had. And yet the power of his strategic partnerships with a handful of staff and a patient group of investors enabled him to do in 3 years what far more qualified scientists had not been able to achieve in 50. After six years of hard work, my income was in the bottom 25 percent of American wage earners, and my net worth was about minus $15,000. Within six months of forming our partnership in 1976, our company was generating $1 million per week in sales, my net worth had soared into the millions, and my income was in the top 1 percent of American wage earners.

6. It increases your knowledge and broadens your expertise. Walt Disney returned to the United States after World War I to go to work as an illustrator for an ad agency in Chicago. He knew absolutely nothing about animation. His first partnership was with an animator from the agency. This not only put him on the fast track of building an animation business, it enabled him to learn the art and skill of animation from a brilliant animator at the same time. In my case, prior to partnering with directors and producers, I knew absolutely nothing about producing and directing television commercials. Yet within a matter of months of partnering, I had gleaned the necessary skills to produce and direct on my own.

7. It increases your offensive power against competitive forces and reduces your vulnerability to their attacks. Since 1976, my company has partnered with more than 70 celebrities who have appeared in my commercials and infomercials as spokespersons for our products. These celebrities have included Academy Award–winning movie stars, Emmy Award–winning television stars, and Grammy award–winning recording artists. Their sincerity, commitment, and credibility has made nearly all of our products impervious to competitors and to copycat products. While many business experts questioned our wisdom for paying out more than $100 million in royalties to our celebrity partners, I can tell you that these partnerships have been absolutely critical to our success. Without our celebrity partners, our company would have failed on nearly every project because no consumer would have preferred our products over the more established brand-name products. Our partnerships have enabled us to grab market share away from our competitors as well as defend our market share from aggressive competitive efforts to take it away. Nothing beats a good offense better than a good offense *and* defense, and that is exactly what effective partnering achieves!

8. It reduces your risk of failure. The wisest man who ever lived (also the richest) wrote in the biblical book of Proverbs, "Without counsel, people fall; but in the multitude of counselors there is safety" (Proverbs 11:14). Effective partnering radically reduces the risk of failing in any given endeavor or situation. The reasons are simple. When you have an effective partnership, each partner's weaknesses are compensated for by another's strengths. When one partner no longer has the ability, energy, or will to persist, another does. When one partner's vision is clouded or blinded on an issue, another partner will see clearly from a different point of view. And last but not least, when the partnership is under attack from competition or adversity and one partner's defenses are down, the other's are up. When I produced our first infomercial on the Total Gym with Chuck Norris and Christie Brinkley, I thought we had a surefire home run. It was the best show I had ever produced. But when we tested it on the air it only produced mediocre results at best. With the number of orders generated from the test, we knew we could not roll the product out in a national television campaign. I had done the absolute best I could, and it wasn't enough. Chuck and Christie had performed their best, and it wasn't enough. Then one of my partners had ideas for two seemingly insignificant changes. We made those changes, and the Total Gym became the most successful product and program in our company's history. Our Total Gym sales are approaching $1 billion, making it the most successful single piece of fitness equipment in the history of the industry. Had I been a sole proprietor, the product would have died in the test phase and Total

Gym sales would not have even hit the $10,000 mark. Gaining my partner's input and point of view turned a strikeout into the greatest grand slam our company has ever hit.

9. It reduces the quantity and the degree of failures you will experience. Nothing, including effective partnering, ever eliminates failure completely. However, effective partnering will radically reduce the percentage of failures you will experience and the severity of each failure as well. When I produce a project, I become emotionally tied to the project, the inventors, and the celebrities who partner with us. About 25 to 30 percent of the projects we test fail to get enough response to merit a national rollout of the campaign. As these failures begin to develop, my natural drive is to make a string of revisions, hoping that we can turn a loser into a winner. Sometimes my partners will conceive of great ideas that will turn a project around, as in the case of the Total Gym. Thus they reduce the number of failures we experience. At the same time, they are great at recognizing when it's time to stop throwing good money after bad and give up on a project. In this way they limit the depth of the loss we experience. When it comes to failing, I'd take a $1 million failure over a $2 million dollar failure any day.

10. It reduces your personal workload. During the first 12 years of our business, I ran myself ragged. I wrote our commercials, worked with artists to create the props, worked with set designers for our sets, shopped for clothes with our wardrobe stylists, and held long casting sessions for principal performers and extras. Then I would direct our shoots and complete the commercials through all phases of the editing process. I had almost no personal life because my life was totally consumed by my projects. Then, beginning in 1986, I partnered with another producer. Gradually he took on 90 percent of my workload. This not only allowed me to make a better living (our productions were greatly improved), but, even more important, enabled me to enjoy a lot more personal and family time. Today, all I do is write the shows, show up at the shoots and direct, and then show up for the edits. Hundreds of other details that used to control nearly every waking minute are now performed by my producer.

11. It reduces your level of personal stress. No worthwhile business endeavor is a cakewalk. Every project has its ups and downs, and producing more ups than downs takes a lot of effort and creates a lot of stress. The fact that effective partnering allows you to share the workload and responsibilities with someone else radically reduces the amount of stress you will experience. Stress produces very destructive hormones that leave our cellular structure more vulnerable to illnesses and life-threatening conditions such as heart disease, stroke, and even cancer. If we want a longer, healthier, and happier life, offloading stress is critical, and effective partnering gives us a great way to do that.

While any one of these 11 benefits of effective partnering should provide ample incentive for you to pursue partners in any important project you take on, when combined they demonstrate conclusively the incalculable value of effective partnering. Now that you see how critical effective partnering is to your achievement of extraordinary success, let's review two important definitions and then focus on the all-important how-to's.

Important Definitions

- ***Partners:*** **Counselors, consultants, advisors, experts, authors, friends, key employees, financiers, investors, lenders, mentors, and literal or legal partners who are recruited to fulfill tasks that are necessary to the optimal achievement of a goal, project, or dream.**
- ***Effective partnering:*** **Partnering that involves four essential components:**
  1. **Identifying the right type of partner needed for a given situation.**
  2. **Identifying the right person within that type.**
  3. **Recruiting the right person with the right kind of offer.**
  4. **Effectively utilizing the partner for optimal results.**

Ineffective Partnering Prevents Extraordinary Success, Raises Risk, and Accelerates Failure

Just as effective partnering can ensure and accelerate success, ineffective partnering can ensure and accelerate failure. Unfortunately it is a lot easier to partner ineffectively than it is to partner effectively. In fact, if you don't follow the steps we're about to look at, there is a much greater chance that you will partner ineffectively than there is that you'll "get lucky" and partner effectively. In Henry Ford's first venture into the automobile business, he picked the wrong partner and wasted two years of his life and ended up with nothing to show for it. His partner, the Detroit Automobile Company, picked the perfect partner in Henry Ford, but they blew the fourth step of effective partnering and failed to effectively utilize and motivate him. They could have become the greatest automobile company of the twentieth century, but instead they vaporized in a little over two years.

Walt Disney picked the wrong distribution partners—Charles Mintz and a movie studio—for his first series of theatrical cartoons centered around a character called Oswald the Lucky Rabbit. Disney had unknowingly signed a contract that gave the ownership of Oswald to the studio. When they saw the success of this cartoon series, rather than renew Disney's contract for a second year, Mintz and the studio dumped him, hired away all of his animators except one, and decided that they knew how to keep the character entertaining better than Disney did. Disney ended up with nothing. Mintz and the studio thought they could make Oswald a hit without Disney's input, so instead of effectively partnering with the greatest entertainment visionary in history, they simply put the screws to him and threw him away. While you may have never heard of Charles Mintz and Oswald the Lucky Rabbit, you have heard of Disney's next cartoon character and the entertainment empire that Disney built around him. The difference between the short-lived success of Oswald and the never-ending success of Disney's second character (a mouse named Mickey) was Disney himself and the partnership that lasted a lifetime with his brother Roy and the animator that co-created Mickey, Ubbe Iwerks.

A close friend of mine founded a company in the early 1980s and built it into a thriving concern worth hundreds of millions of dollars. After he took his company public in 1997, his stock was trading at $27 per share. That year he decided to merge with another company that was making an attempt to compete with his core business. I knew enough about the owners of that company to urge my friend not to go through with the merger. The other company was run by Harvard MBAs who were great theorists and terrible businessmen. When he told me that they would be taking control of the marketing, sales, and training aspects of the business, I told him that this would be the death of his company. Unfortunately, he went through with the merger and the Harvard MBAs drove the company nearly into the dust. At the time I am writing this book, their stock is trading at $1.02 per share. If you had owned $10,000 of their stock in 1997, today your investment would be worth $377. That's the power of *ineffective* partnering!

As I mentioned a moment ago, it's much easier to partner ineffectively than it is to partner effectively. That's why the remainder of this session is so critical. If you follow the four steps for effective partnering and the strategies and tips for identifying and recruiting the right partners, you will experience the awesome benefits of effective partnering and avoid the terrible consequences of ineffective partnering.

Implementing the Four Steps of Effective Partnering

Step 1—Identify the Right Type of Partner(s) Needed for a Given Situation

Identifying the right type of partner you need for a given situation requires the completion of five tasks.

1. **You must gain a clear and precise vision** of what you want to achieve in that situation. You'll master the technique for doing this (the vision mapping process) in our fifth and sixth sessions.

2. **You must have an accurate assessment** of your own strengths and weaknesses and how they apply to your pursuit of the particular vision. This can be drawn from the lists you created at the end of our last two sessions. Determine what critical elements of the vision your strengths will enable you to accomplish and what critical elements will be difficult or impossible to accomplish because of your weaknesses, lack of know-how, and limited resources. Create a detailed profile of those critical elements for which a partner or partners are needed to compensate for your weaknesses, lack of know-how, and limited resources.

3. **You must determine the category of partner** (advisor, counselor, expert, financier, mentor, legal partner, etc.) that is needed to provide the necessary complement to the detailed profile that you have created in task 2.

4. **You must determine the role the partner** or partners will play in the fulfillment or accomplishment of each critical element; the type of commitment you need from them (time, expertise, money, instruction, etc.); and the commitment you are willing to make to them in return.

5. **You must create a profile or description of the ideal partner** or partners that you realize you need for each role (personality type, relevant experience, strengths, commitment, motivation, character, etc.).

Step 2—Identify the Right Person within That Type

Using the profile of the ideal partner or partners, make a list of the people you know who would fit that profile. Your list can include known experts; authors; people in your company; or even competitive companies, friends, or relatives. Prioritize your list, starting with your first choice. If you don't have any idea who could fit your profile for the ideal partner, do your homework. Tell your friends and associates what you are looking for and see if they know anyone who fits the bill. In this day and age you are no more than two or three people away from knowing just about anyone. If the kind of person you need would be a member of a professional association, go on the Internet or to an association meeting or trade show. There are hundreds of ways to build your list of potential partners. If individual names don't instantly come to mind, don't panic—start networking. Two projects that my company recently adopted came to us from parents of kids on my son's football team. If they had confined their search for a marketing partner to their known business associates, they would have missed a great opportunity. Instead they brought their ideas to "Ryan's dad."

It's also important to remember that in many cases partnering doesn't necessarily involve the full-time commitment of the would-be partner. For example, for a personal vision such as improving your marriage, finding a good marriage counselor, a friend who has a great marriage, or even a good book to give you the help and direction you need is a form of partnering.

Step 3–Recruit the Right Person with the Right Kind of Offer

Once you have identified your A-list of potential partners, you have to recruit them. This is the one step where people nearly always blow it. They approach their would-be partner (1) from the wrong point of view, (2) with an ineffective presentation, or (3) with a weak offer. For example, the wrong point of view for your approach would be to tell the prospective partner what he or she can do for you. Most people are far too busy and consumed with their own concerns to involve themselves in helping someone else achieve a goal or a dream just for the sake of that person. The right point of view for your approach is creating an effective presentation of what your goal, project, or vision can do for the partner. If they see enough personal benefit in taking on your project, prospective partners will at least be inclined to pay attention to your offer.

The second mistake people make when trying to recruit a partner is that they ineffectively communicate their vision. You may have the best opportunity that person will ever hear, but if you don't effectively and persuasively communicate that opportunity you are very likely to fail in your recruiting effort. I recently met with a professor from Harvard Medical School. He is a true genius and has created an enormous breakthrough in the early detection of diseases. Yet he has not been able to secure funding for this project—not because it isn't a great project, but because he has not created an effective and persuasive way to communicate it. In our next session I'm going to mentor you in four powerful communication techniques and the six steps of creating an effective and persuasive presentation. As you learn these techniques and utilize these steps, you will never again have to worry about failing due to ineffective communication. I have used these communication techniques to persuade more than 25 million people to get up off of their sofas, pick up their phones, and order my products. These techniques will work for you as well as they have worked for me.

The third mistake that nearly everyone makes in their efforts to recruit a needed partner is that they make a weak offer. I recently formed a partnership with a revolutionary Internet service provider that has created what I believe is the greatest business opportunity that has crossed my desk in 27 years. I believe that this project could grow from a net worth of zero to a net worth of $1 billion to $5 billion within three years. Two other companies had the chance to partner with this group, and in both cases made offers that were insultingly low. In my opinion they lost the greatest financial opportunity they will ever encounter, just because they lowballed their offer. When you find an ideal partner for a project, make the best offer you can afford to make in order to recruit that person in a way that elicits his or her total commitment. Such an optimum offer doesn't always have to be synonymous with money. Sometimes people will commit to a partnership based on a shared vision or on the role that they will play. Perhaps they need authority, recognition, or other perceived and real benefits.

In college, my music group was in dire need of a good arranger and director. I knew the name of the finest choral arranger and director in the state, and inarguably one of the finest in America. We had no money to offer him, so our only hope of recruiting him was to use something that he would value more than money. Fortunately for us, we were able to present our vision for the group, its mission, and his role in such a way that he decided he wanted to be a part of that vision and joined our group following a single rehearsal.

Throughout my life I have enjoyed the incredible benefit of having wonderful mentors. Not one of them ever cost me a penny, and yet each one brought value to my life that was beyond measure in dollars or any other way. On pages 12 to 13 you'll find 10 strategies and tips for recruiting mentors that should be used in the pursuit of your dreams and goals.

Step 4—Effectively Utilize the Partner for Optimal Results

The final step in effective partnering is one that people fail to achieve more often than not. We saw earlier how the Detroit Automobile Company had successfully recruited the greatest visionary in automotive history, and yet failed to produce and sell a single automobile during his two-year employment. We saw how Charles Mintz and a movie studio had recruited a relationship with Walt Disney, and yet the profit they extracted from that relationship never amounted to anything significant.

In my case, in 1972 I worked for a mail-order insurance company as an assistant product manager. Time after time I took my creative ideas for our advertising campaigns to my boss, and each time he told me that this was not a part of my job description and summarily dismissed my ideas. This was the same boss who said to me, "You are the single greatest disappointment in my entire career. You will never succeed in marketing; you have 20 minutes to clean out your desk." During my nine months with this company, I had performed the mechanics of my job but the company had never given me a chance on the creative and marketing side. Four years later, my current partner and I started our business of marketing products on television through the use of two-minute television commercials. After a year of extraordinary success, we decided to go to the insurance company with an idea to sell its life insurance policies direct to consumers through the use of a two-minute television campaign. Even though my ex-boss fought it, he was overruled by the company's founder and I created a campaign that became the single most profitable marketing campaign in that company's history. This campaign not only made millions of dollars for the insurance company, it made millions for our company as well. Had my ex-boss effectively utilized me, he could have had this campaign for the cost of my salary of $12,000 per year. Instead, because he was now paying my company as an outside vendor, it cost his company millions of dollars.

While this serves as a great example of how a company ineffectively utilizes someone, my mentor provides a perfect example of how to effectively utilize a partner. When he hired me in 1976, I would have gladly worked for him for a salary. However, because he knew the power of effective partnering, he offered me a percentage of the ownership of the marketing companies we would create. At that time his company was barely getting by financially. Although a percentage of ownership in companies that were yet to be formed was worthless at the time, I knew that my participation in ownership gave me a potential for extraordinary financial success if we could make any of those future companies successful. This prospect motivated me unlike anything had ever motivated me before.

Because my mentor effectively utilized me, and the other partners we eventually recruited, my campaigns have produced over $2 billion in sales. The percentage of ownership my mentor had given me had not only made me millions of dollars in income, it made him, his children, and his grandchildren millions as well. Always remember that in a business situation, sharing the financial rewards with key people will buy you far more than it will cost you. My mentor reduced his share of the company by 20 percent when he gave me a 20 percent ownership. He gave up 45 percent ownership to other partners he recruited in the next 10 years and ended up with 35 percent of the company. However, the profits of the company rose from $0 to over $200 million. None of this would have happened had he not shared ownership with his key people. Would you rather own 100 percent of $0 in profits or 35 percent of $200 million? Sharing the wealth is one of the single most important elements in effective partnering.

Four Essential Components to Effectively Utilize Partners

So what does it take to effectively utilize the partners you recruit for any given situation? I have found that there are four essential components that are critical to the effective long-term utilization of a partner. Remember that even if a key individual isn't a legal or literal partner, because he or she is key to your ultimate success, he or she should still be effectively utilized, which requires these four elements.

1. **Provide the opportunity and authority.** To effectively utilize partners, they must be provided with an opportunity to fully apply to your endeavor all of the knowledge, talent, and passion they can muster. Equally important, they must be given enough authority to accomplish their mission. While the Detroit Automobile Company provided Henry Ford with the opportunity to apply his know-how, talents, and passions to the production and sales of automobiles, they did not give him the authority to make decisions critical to the company's direction and commitments. They had partnered with a visionary but failed to give him the authority to fulfill that vision.

2. **Provide the right environment.** For people to produce to the max, they need to be provided with an environment that is conducive to their

optimum productivity. The most important environmental issue is not the physical environment, but rather the mental and emotional environment. This means an environment where people are free to express their thoughts, ideas, and opinions without the fear of being inappropriately criticized or ignored. It also means an environment where partnering is encouraged and partners work according to their personal styles, not a style dictated by job descriptions, traditions, or the work styles of others. Because I have attention deficit disorder (ADD), I like to work on multiple projects simultaneously. While this was very threatening to most of my past employers (they wanted me to finish one job before starting another), my mentor and current partners realize that this is how I work best. The result is that I finish my primary project in record time and am well into my secondary projects by the time I finish my primary project. Others would lose their sanity if forced to work on multiple projects simultaneously, and they should be allowed to follow their style of finishing one before starting another.

Providing this kind of environment may seem risky, but when used with achievers or superachievers, the outcomes are far greater than can be predicted. The reward is far greater than the risk. Providing the right physical environment is also important when possible. In 27 years of writing television commercials and infomercials, I have never been able to write even one in my office. When it's time to write, I get away to a secluded place that's very conducive to writing. During our first 10 years, I would rent a hotel room and stay there until my writing was finished. Then our company leased a beach house where I did all of my writing for the next seven years. Now I live near the mountains, so I escape to my mountain home. Had my partners insisted that my office should be all I need to write, I doubt that I would have ever written a single commercial, and we would all be working for other companies.

3. Provide the right incentives. Providing the appropriate reward is critical to effectively utilizing partners. By giving me a piece of the action, my partner provided incentive that was greater than I could have ever imagined. When approaching a project, I gave it everything I had in terms of time, effort, and creativity. If my projects succeeded, I would achieve financial security like I had never known. If they failed, I would be just as broke as my partner who was funding the projects. While incentives such as promotions, job titles, and added authority are moderately effective, nothing motivates like money; the greater the financial opportunity, the greater the motivation and commitment.

4. Use the greatest long-term motivating strategy. The two great motivating forces in anyone's life are fear of loss and desire for gain.

Correspondingly, there are two primary ways to impact another's behavior: using fear to manipulate behavior or using love to motivate behavior. I'm not talking here about romantic or emotional love. In a partnering context, I'm talking about providing partners with honor, value, kindness, and security. The most important word here is *value.* We value partners when we listen to their input and respond to it in an honoring way. The more people feel valued, the more they will contribute. Of course we show value with monetary reward, but equally important, we honor people's opinions and give them the authority they need to implement their ideas when possible. In a corporate environment, this one element is often abundantly absent.

The Xerox Corporation provides one of my favorite examples of the ineffective utilization of partners by not valuing their opinions or contributions. As companies began to install mainframe computer terminals at individual workstations, Xerox management became concerned that copying machines could one day become obsolete. Instead of sending paper copies of documents, a company could distribute information to employees via a corporate network of computer terminals. Consequently, Xerox created a research facility known as the Palo Alto Research Center (PARC) and staffed it with some of the world's brightest technological wizards. They provided these people with a great working environment that fostered creativity and productivity. The first technological breakthrough the PARC researchers developed was the world's first personal computer. Management's response was a total rejection of the product. Their reasoning went, "Why would any company buy personal computers when terminals connected to mainframes could easily be put on anyone's desk." They also reasoned that there would be no consumer market for personal computers, because who is qualified to use a computer at home? And even if they were qualified, what on earth would they use it for?

The next breakthrough created by this brilliant research team was the graphical user interface, or GUI. They explained to management that this would so simplify working with a computer that anyone at home or at work would be able to easily operate their own personal computer. Instead of using complicated command codes, a user could use a mouse and simply point and click. Management rejected this product as well. So when Steve Jobs (who had started a personal computer company called Apple) asked the PARC researchers if he could study their GUI and learn from it, they were happy to see that someone valued their ideas and gave him carte blanche in his examination of their breakthrough. Not only did it become the basis of Jobs's biggest breakthrough, the Macintosh, it became the basis for Bill Gates's graphical interface product, Windows.

As discouraged as they were, these brilliant researchers didn't stop with inventing the personal computer and the graphical interface. Their next breakthrough came in the way they were able to link different computers together. They called it Earthnet. Their vision was that every computer in the world could communicate with every other and users could share information. Once again, Xerox management rejected the breakthrough. "The world is full of competitors; why would anyone want to share information with anyone else? What a crazy idea!" Of course the Earthnet provided the technology that became the Internet.

Had Xerox management valued the ideas and breakthroughs of their researchers (who in effect were their partners), they would have owned patents on the personal computer, the graphical interface, and the Internet. In other words, they would have owned it all. There would be no other PCs or Macs, no Windows, and no AOL. In their place there would only be one company, Xerox. As you apply these four components to effectively utilize your partners, unlike Xerox, you will reap unfathomable rewards.

A Word about Manipulating with Fear

While the most effective way to motivate another's behavior for long-term success and a stronger relationship is with love (value and honor), the easiest and most often used way to motivate behavior is with fear. While using fear may accomplish your short-term goal of getting something done quickly, it never works for the long-term benefit of any project you undertake. Yes, it can get a particular job or project completed on time, but it can cause permanent damage to a relationship. So although it can manipulate a partner or anyone else to perform for the moment, it weakens their commitment, trust, and motivation to perform in the future.

American Telecast became the single most productive company in America (*Forbes* defines productivity as profit per employee) because all of our partners and employees were motivated by love by our founding partner. Our revenues and profits per employee have been more than double those of most productive public companies in America, including Microsoft. But our company is not alone. One of the most successful software companies in the world (SAS) is also run by a man at the top who motivates his employees with love rather than fear. The same is true of one of our nation's most successful airlines (Southwest) and two of the most successful restaurant franchise systems (Wendy's and Chick-fil-A). Manipulating behavior with fear is always faster and easier, but is never more productive or beneficial to you, your endeavors, or your partners.

In closing this session, it might be helpful to give you a list of strategies and tips for recruiting partners. After you've reviewed this list, take a break and then tackle the exercises in the "Actions for Traction" section. In our next session we're going to look at the key to your Porsche. As it turns out, this key will not only open your Porsche and start its engine, it will open any door in your world, from your boss's office to your banker's vault.

Strategies and Tips for Identifying and Recruiting the Right Partners

1. **Assess your own strengths and weaknesses.** What you don't need is a partner who is a carbon copy of yourself.

2. **Identify the talents, abilities, and strengths that you need in a partner to compensate for the areas of your weaknesses, inabilities, and lack of interest.**

3. **Look for a person who shares the same vision you have for your business venture or personal dream.** Your partner not only needs to see it, he or she needs to be overwhelmed by it. If such a person doesn't currently exist, then it is your responsibility to effectively and persuasively communicate your vision to any potential partner. (Our next two sessions will give you the most powerful communication and persuasion techniques I have ever found, and they will enable you to communicate your vision more effectively than ever before.)

4. **Look at the character and integrity of your would-be partner.** This is a lot harder to evaluate than his or her talents, but it's far more important. If a partner's ethics and morals aren't extremely high, sooner or later there's a pretty good chance he or she will betray you, someone else in your company, or your customer. I've really failed at this one. Because I've been so enamored by the charisma, talent, and salesmanship of three individuals, I did not check out their character and integrity. The result? I lost $7.5 million in three bad partnerships.

5. **Look for a partner who is willing to be totally committed to your vision to achieve its success.** If you are totally committed and he or she isn't, I can promise you that the partnership won't last long. Look at how the partner has performed in other situations where he or she has been committed. Are his or her commitments short-lived, or faithful until the end?

6. **Is your would-be partner a positive person or a negative person?** People who are generally negative tend to be very poor partners. A partner

doesn't have to be as positive or as optimistic as you, but if he or she is quick to tear down others or find the negative in situations, he or she is likely to jump ship when the going gets tough—or worse, steer the ship in the wrong direction.

7. **Look at your would-be partner's natural drive and gifts rather than his or her resume.** Is he or she a theorist or a doer? How do you know? It's simple: Look at what he or she has personally done, not what he or she has had other people do.

Effective partnering is the single most powerful strategy you will ever apply to your personal or professional life. In Session 9 we are going to talk about a strategy that I call *shooting for the moon.* Once you shoot for the moon, effective partnering is the only strategy that will provide you with the power to actually hit the moon.

Actions for Traction

WHERE THE RUBBER MEETS THE ROAD

1. Which of your personal or business areas, dreams, endeavors, projects, or goals do you think would benefit significantly by your recruitment of a partner or mentor? Prioritize your list, beginning with your most important areas first.
2. Identify the specific kinds of partners or mentors that you should try to recruit that would enable you to more quickly and effectively achieve your most important dreams or projects. In addition to your strengths and weaknesses, you should also take into account your personality type with its natural strengths, weaknesses, and drives.)
3. For each kind of partner or mentor that you have identified, make a list of specific individuals who fit your qualifications for each kind of partner or mentor you want to recruit.
4. In your notebook, using the methods outlined in this session, lay out your plan for recruiting the partners and mentors you need for your most important dreams.
5. How do you currently motivate your peers, your loved ones, and those under your authority? Do you usually motivate with fear or with love? In your notebook, write down some of the people you want to motivate, and any ideas on how you can begin to motivate those people with value, honor, kindness, and security.

SESSION 5

What You Say and How You Say It Changes Everything!

Laying the Foundation for Effective and Persuasive Communication

Your New Porsche Comes with the Most Incredible Master Key Ever Made. Without its key, your Porsche won't take you anywhere. Without that key, you will be like everyone else—relegated to pursuing your dreams on foot. And like everyone else, if your only means of pursuing your dreams is walking, then you will only achieve those mediocre dreams that are the nearest and most easily reached. Dreams that are extraordinary, whether personal or professional, will forever remain at an unreachable distance. Fortunately, I'm going to give you the key to your Porsche in this session.

And this key is the most amazing key that will ever be placed into your hand. This key will not only open the door of your Porsche and start your 415-horsepower engine; it will open any door that will ever stand between you and your most cherished dreams. It can open your banker's vault and your customer's checkbook. It can even open the door to your spouse's heart and the door to your child's mind. This incredible master key is the skill of effective and persuasive communication.

What a Difference This Key Can Make!

If you are a salesperson: This key can be the difference between making a sale on 75 percent of your calls instead of 5 percent; making the sale on your first appointment instead of your third; and making a sale in minutes rather than hours.

If you are trying to climb up the corporate ladder: This key can be the difference between your boss ignoring your ideas or implementing them; the difference between your words falling on deaf ears or being received with anticipation and enthusiasm; the difference between being looked down on for what you say or appreciated for what you say.

If you are a supervisor, manager, corporate executive, or business owner: This key can be the difference between your subordinates' eyes glazing over while you are speaking or scratching their heads while reading your memos, and catching your vision and running with it.

If you are in a relationship: This key can be the difference between your partner being blind to your deepest needs and desires, or understanding and fulfilling those needs and desires.

If you are a parent: This key can be the difference between your children not focusing on or responding to what you say, or gaining their undivided attention and motivating them to respond to your words the way you would like them to respond.

Your Communication Skills Will Either Accelerate Your Achievement or *Slam the Brakes on It!*

Even though 100 percent of the people I have met in my lifetime have been able to speak and write, fewer than 2 percent have been effective

Side-by-Side Comparison

How People Communicate in Important Matters

Drifters	Pursuers	Achievers	Superachievers
Communicate in important matters the same way they communicate in unimportant matters; they shoot from the hip, saying or writing whatever comes to mind just as it comes to mind.	In important matters, they think before they speak or write, and often compile a written list of the important points they want to make before they begin their written or verbal communication.	Prioritize their list of important points and often create an outline of what they want to say and how they want to say it. In the case of a verbal presentation, likely rehearse their talk before they give it.	Either utilize the critical skills of effective and persuasive communication or rely on partners who utilize those skills. They learn the frame of reference of their listeners, anticipate their objections and excuses, and formulate their communication accordingly.

The Eighth Law of Extraordinary Success

Achievement is accelerated by effective and persuasive communication skills and is retarded by the lack of those skills.

communicators, and fewer than 1 percent have been persuasive communicators. The tragedy is that most people will go through life communicating in an ineffective and nonpersuasive way even though becoming an effective and persuasive communicator is not a difficult task. To the contrary, effective and persuasive communication is a learnable skill that only requires mastering a handful of easily learned techniques. Regardless of how effective and persuasive you are right now, the techniques you are going to learn in this session have the power to turn you into one of the most effective and persuasive communicators you will ever meet. They may not necessarily turn you into an eloquent speaker or a Pulitzer Prize–winning writer, but they will give you effective and persuasive communication powers that will enable you to consistently motivate others to do what you believe is in their best interest.

Can just a handful of communication techniques really make that big of a difference in your professional and personal life? Absolutely! The skills you are going to learn in this session and the next have enabled me to achieve extraordinary outcomes beyond my wildest imagination.

Here are a few examples. These communication techniques have enabled me to:

- Persuade more than 80 famous celebrities, along with their agents, managers, and attorneys, to partner with my companies and endorse our products and services.
- Persuade more than 25 million consumers to get up from their sofas, go to their telephones, and order more than $2 billion in goods and services from my companies. Without these powerful communication techniques, I would not have made a single sale!
- Repair and win back the heart of my wife after we had gone through a devastating separation and divorce.
- Enrich my marriage to the point of its being the most fulfilling aspect of my life.
- Build wonderful relationships with each of my children.
- Build and strengthen lifetime friendships.

Master Strategy 6—Become an Effective and Persuasive Communicator

***A Few Words from* The Richest Man Who Ever Lived**

"The heart of the wise teaches his mouth, and adds persuasiveness to his lips." (Proverbs 16:23)

"The tongue of the wise makes knowledge acceptable" (Proverbs 15:2)

After graduating from college in 1970, my first job was with a life insurance company. Even though that job only lasted five months, I learned two things from my boss. The first was that on average, it takes a good life insurance salesman at least three one-hour appointments with a client to sell a life insurance policy. The second was a communication technique that was extremely powerful. My boss was the single most successful life insurance agent in the company's 100-year history, and he credited his success to the power of this one technique. Think about it; in 100 years of business, with thousands of insurance agents selling this company's life insurance policies, my boss had set a sales record that nobody else had ever come close to achieving. And he gave the credit for his success to one communication technique. Unfortunately, I wasn't very good at using that technique, and during the five months I worked for the company I only sold three policies. But that's not the end of the story. Six years later, on job number 10, I learned three communication techniques from my two mentors that were infinitely more effective and persuasive than the technique I had learned from my first boss. In fact, their relative power over the first technique would be like comparing the supersonic Concorde airliner to a hang glider. They both fly, but that is where all similarity ends. In terms of speed, power, and utility, there is no comparison.

Even though this may seem like exaggeration, it's not. Remember that my boss had taught me that selling life insurance required an average of three one-hour appointments to sell a single policy. Remember that even when I used his persuasion technique I was still only able to sell three policies in five months.

On the other hand, by using the communication techniques I learned from my two mentors, I was able to sell life insurance policies in less than two minutes. In fact, in the space of a few years I sold nearly 1 million life insurance policies to consumers without a single face-to-face meeting with one client. I sold every policy with two-minute television commercials. This feat was so incomprehensible that when the leading life insurance companies were questioned by the media about the kinds of numbers we were reporting, they stated on the record, "That's impossible!" They too were suffering from the kind of past programming that we talked about in our first session.

Equally amazing, these techniques worked just as well when it came to selling any kind of product. I used them to sell millions of videotapes, books, electronic devices, day planners, cosmetics and personal care products, educational products, and fitness and weight-loss products. They also enabled me to recruit major celebrities as spokespeople for my projects, including Tom Selleck, Charlton Heston, Chuck Norris, Michael Landon, Cher, Jane Fonda, Kathie Lee Gifford, John Ritter, Patricia Heaton, Della Reese, and 80 others. Most important, they became the key to effectively and persuasively communicating on a personal level with my wife and children. I did not create or perfect any of these techniques. The greatest communicators throughout history have used them, and I simply learned them from my mentors.

The Difference between Persuasion and Manipulation

Whenever I begin to speak about effective and persuasive communication, there are always a number of people who react to the word *persuasive* because they view it as a form of manipulation. So it is important that I differentiate the two. While I love the art of persuasion, I hate the use of manipulation. Manipulation is using any means necessary to motivate or force someone to do something that fulfills your desire or need. Whether it's in their best interest or not, the focus of manipulation is getting others to do what you want them to do, regardless of what's best for them. Adolph Hitler was not only persuasive, he was without a doubt one of the greatest manipulators the world has ever seen. He was able to manipulate the people of an entire nation into doing things that they would have never dreamed of doing a decade earlier.

Persuasion, on the other hand, is communication that guides people's minds and emotions past all obstacles, enables them to understand what you are saying and feel what you are feeling, and ultimately motivates them to take the course of action that you believe is in their best interest or for the common good. If, on the other hand, you simply want them to do something that is in your best interest and not theirs, persuasion is transformed into manipulation.

Unfortunately, mastering the art of effective and persuasive communication will equip you to become an expert manipulator. These techniques are so powerful and so effective that they can be used improperly to manipulate. Therefore, it's critical that you be careful how you use them. My hope is that you have the right ethics, judgment, and concern for others and that you take care not to use these techniques to manipulate. Once again, true persuasion is communication that guides people's minds and emotions past all obstacles, enables them to understand what you're saying and feel what you're feeling, and motivates them to take the course of action that is in their best interest or for the common good.

Important Definitions

Manipulation: **Using any means necessary to motivate or force someone to do something that fulfills your desire or need, regardless of whether or not it's in his or her best interest.**

Effective communication: **Communication that enables a person to understand what you are saying and feel what you are feeling.**

Persuasive communication: **Effective communication that motivates a person to do what you truly believe is in his or her best interest or for the common good.**

The Big Mistake that Buries Great Ideas, Obscures Good Intentions, and Derails Personal Relationships

Every day men and women have great ideas for their jobs, for their marriages, and for their families. They are motivated by the best of intentions. Unfortunately, their ideas are ignored or rejected—not because they're bad ideas, but because they are ineffectively communicated. When people have an idea or want something, they usually say it in whatever way it comes to their mind. They "shoot from the lip." They haven't taken the time to prepare to say things in a way that will enable their listener to clearly understand what they're saying, feel what they're feeling, and be motivated to act accordingly. The chance of effectively and persuasively communicating when shooting from the lip is about the same as hitting a running and jumping jackrabbit with a slingshot while you're running in the opposite direction. No matter how good your thought or idea might be, there are nine major communication barriers that can prevent your hearer from understanding what you are saying and feeling what you are feeling. If your communication doesn't break through or jump over these barriers, your hopes will be dashed as your speaking falls on deaf ears. No wonder marriage experts report that communication is the number one problem in marriages.

Breaking Through the Barriers

There are nine potential barriers that can prevent your listeners from receiving and responding to your communication. If you consider these barriers as you prepare for your conversation, you will be able to use the communication techniques you will learn in the next session to eliminate or overcome these barriers should they arise. The barriers are:

1. **The listener's frame of reference.** This includes listeners' opinions and feelings; their preconceived notions and biases; their personal agendas; their misconceptions; their past hurts, disappointments, and failures; their hopes and goals; and their fears.
2. **The listener's ego.** Your listeners may think they're smarter or better than you in general or in a particular area of expertise.
3. **Gender differences.** Thoughts and words that are as insignificant as pebbles to men can be as significant as giant boulders to women. Things that women can see as clearly as neon signs can be totally invisible to men. Most men are left brain dominant and most women are right brain dominant, making the male-female communication barrier even greater.
4. **Personality types.** The four personality types give, receive, and respond to communication in totally different ways. They are also motivated by entirely different factors.
5. **Semantics (different definitions).** If you use the exact same word to 10 different people, it may well be interpreted 10 different ways. (If you say, "She's cheap," do you mean that she embraces low moral standards or that she's thrifty?)
6. **They'd rather be speaking than listening.** Our words are often missed because listeners are busy thinking about what they are going to say instead of listening to what is being said.

7. **Opposing opinions.** As you start a conversation, listeners may quickly have an opposing opinion (their own or someone else's) come into their mind and silently argue with what you are trying to say.
8. **Time.** Timing creates all sorts of problems with communication. First, the listener's mind is somewhere else the moment your conversation begins. Second, listeners may not think this is the right time to be talking with you. Third, they may feel anxious because you need more time than they can afford to give. In other words, they become more interested in freeing up their time than hearing what you have to say.
9. **You.** There may be a number of things about you that your listener has a problem with. It may be your personality, your manner, your communication style, or the perceived validity of your expertise or opinion.

Laying the Foundation for Effective and Persuasive Communication

Before you learn the specific techniques for effective and persuasive communication, you must first lay a solid foundation on which these techniques will rest. Without the right foundation, these techniques will still work 60 to 70 percent of the time. But with the right foundation, they will work nearly 100 percent of the time. Before you panic and think this is too hard or complicated, realize that this foundation need not be laid for all of your conversations. It is only necessary when you have something to say that you consider important, and you want it to be clearly understood, felt, and positively responded to. This foundation is made up of four components: an approach of honor, an attitude of consideration, a full perspective, and a thorough preparation.

An Approach of Honor. The first component of this foundation is a commitment to show honor and respect to the person you hope to persuade. Unfortunately, failing in this component derails the potential for effective communication more quickly and more often than any other factor. There are dozens of ways to dishonor your listener, and when you inject even one of those ways into your dialogue your listener can instantly withdraw his or her mind and heart and disengage from anything you are saying.

Nonverbal actions such as rolling your eyes, shaking your head, pointing your finger, or any other action that shows condescension, disgust, disappointment, boredom, impatience, or inattentiveness are dishonoring.

Negative verbal reactions such as "Yeah, right," or "Give me a break," or the use of sarcasm are all dishonoring. Using blanket statements such as "You always do that," or "You never do that," is dishonoring. Interrupting, changing the subject prematurely, or simply discounting what the other person is saying is dishonoring. If you remember nothing else, remember this: *When you dishonor your listener—whether it's your spouse, your child, your boss, your peers, or your friends—you and you alone are defeating the goal of your communication.* On the other side of the coin, there are a number of things that you can do that convey honor and respect to your listener; and not doing those things can convey the feeling that you do not honor or respect them. Here are a few suggestions.

1. **Timing.** When you have something important to talk about, ask listeners to pick a time that best fits their schedule rather than expecting them to bend their schedule around yours. If you want to talk right away, and they say it's not a good time, honor their concern instead of forcing the issue. Let them know the amount of time you will need, and make a commitment not to take any more time than is mutually agreed on.

2. **Listening.** During the conversation, rather than instantly giving your point of view, listen attentively to theirs. Don't interrupt, and don't instantly correct any misstatements. Don't quickly change the subject from what they are talking about to what you want to talk about. Wait until they feel you've really heard what they wanted to say before you move on to what you want to say. As you listen to them, keep your attention visibly focused on them.

3. **Response and Validation.** Make sure you respond to what they say and validate their legitimate feelings, opinions, and concerns before moving into your agenda. If they say something that is incorrect, rather than abruptly correcting them, you might say, "I can see why you might think that, but you should also know that . . ." Anytime you take notes on what they say, or positively comment on specific things they say, you show them that you believe their opinion is worthwhile, and they will feel respected and honored.

An Attitude of Consideration. Many times people reject what we say, not because they disagree with it, but because they are reacting to an offensive attitude that we are projecting. It's easier to have or convey a condescending attitude toward our listeners than it is to convey one that is considerate of their opinions, feelings, and self-esteem. When they perceive that you are being condescending or inconsiderate, they will throw up their defenses and close their spirit and mind to you and your point of view. Their focus will be on how fast they can exit your presence. Unfortunately, we are often condescending and inconsiderate to the most important people in our lives, namely our spouses and our children. This lowers their self-esteem and fuels their fear, frustration, hurt, anger, and ultimately their resentment toward us. Spouses, parents, bosses, and people whose personality types are either that of a lion or a beaver have to work very hard to not convey condescension. They need to work equally hard to convey honor, respect, and consideration, especially to their family members.

A Full Perspective. We automatically approach every conversation from our frame of reference. The problem is that if we don't understand our listener's frame of reference, we are likely to crash headfirst into that barrier as we're just starting our conversation. Anytime you have something important to communicate or something that you want to persuade others to do, it is critical that you first understand their frame of reference either before you enter the conversation or before you begin to make your important points. If you can't gain a clear understanding of your listeners' perspective before you start the conversation, get it as early in the conversation as you can. The best way to learn their frame of reference on any issue or in any situation is to ask them. What do they think about the issue? How do they feel about it and why? If you are not able to ask them prior to the conversation, ask someone else who might have firsthand knowledge of what they think about that issue.

Yesterday on one of my projects, two would-be partners became so frustrated with each other that they became extremely angry and almost walked away from the project altogether. The cost of doing so would have been enormous for each of them. I believe this will be the single greatest business venture either of them will ever experience in their lifetime—a venture that will likely earn them tens of millions of dollars. One of the two was experiencing enormous financial pressures that the other was unaware of. The second was experiencing a devastating personal situation that the other had no understanding of. Because I understood both of their frames of reference, I was able to act as an intermediary and resolve their differences before they both lost the opportunity of their lives. Had I not understood their frames of reference, I would not have been able to do this, and the consequences could have been devastating for both.

One of the most effective ways to gain a clear understanding of another person's point of view is to use a method of conversation that Dr. Gary Smalley calls *drive-through talking.* How many times have you placed an order at the drive-through window of a fast food restaurant and had to go back and forth with the person inside? He or she repeats your order and doesn't quite get it right, and then you repeat it back to him or her, trying to correct the misinterpretation. You keep repeating and re-repeating your order until he or she finally gets it right. If you use this same method when you are trying to reach a clear understanding of what you and your listeners think and feel, it can produce a crystal-clear understanding of thoughts and feelings. Here's how it works. First, your listeners tell you what they think or how they feel on the issue, and then you repeat back to them what you think they said. They are then very likely to correct any misconception you may have. You then repeat back again what you think they just said, and they will either say, "That's right," or they'll give you further illumination or correction. In a matter of moments you will not only understand what they said, they will know that you value them enough to have patiently worked with them to gain that understanding. Next, reverse roles. You explain your thoughts and feelings and they repeat back to you what they think you said. If they don't get it quite right, you correct their misconception. They repeat back what they think you just said. You continue the process until you each are confident that you really understand what the other is saying and feeling.

A Thorough Preparation. A simple rule to follow is: The more important the issue that you want to communicate, the more preparation you need to do beforehand. Learning your listeners' frame of reference is the first step. What are their opinions; their likely objections or excuses; their desires, hopes, and goals; and their fears and frustrations? For important conversations, presentations, or written communication, write out your presentation in outline form, listing all of your key points, and rehearse it. On pages 119 to 120 I give a detailed description of how to prepare for an effective and persuasive verbal or written communication. Using this format for preparing for important conversations or sales calls will increase your success rate hundreds of times over. However, putting this much preparation into an unimportant conversation would be a waste of your most precious and limited resource—your time.

The Critical Elements of Effective and Persuasive Communication

Now that you understand the components that make up the foundation of effective and persuasive communication, let's shift our focus to what actually needs to be accomplished to communicate effectively and persuasively. Remember that communication is only effective when it enables the listener to clearly understand what you are saying and feel what you are feeling. While this sounds simple, it really isn't. We often think people understood what we said, and they think they understood what we said—and yet minutes, hours, or days later we discover they said or did something that showed that they did not understand what we said. It may be that their mind was somewhere else during the conversation and they weren't really focused on our words. It may be that there was a problem of semantics. For example, I once told one of my partners that I was concerned about a project. He thought I meant that I was a little nervous about it. What I really meant was that I was deeply troubled and nearly panicked about it. Big difference!

There are dozens of ways that our words can be completely misunderstood. And when it comes to written communication, the chances of misunderstanding are even greater because of the lack of inflections and nonverbal body language. So the first goal of effective communication, whether verbal or written, is to implant into the listener's mind a clear and precise understanding of what you mean. The good news is that the communication techniques that you are going to learn in the next session are going to accomplish that goal perfectly.

The second goal of effective communication is to implant your feelings into the heart or emotions of the listener. While this is not important when you are talking about something insignificant or an issue where your feelings are minimal, it is critically important when you feel strongly about something or you are trying to persuade someone to think or act in a particular manner. Usually, the more important the issue, the more your feelings will be involved, and the more critical it will be to implant those feelings into the hearts of your listeners. The more they feel what you are feeling, the more effective and persuasive your communication will have been. Feelings are a product of the right side of the brain. Therefore, to convey your feelings to a listener, you must activate and engage the right side of his or her brain. I have only found one communication technique that does just that. It is without a doubt the single most powerful communication technique ever employed. Gary Smalley calls this technique *emotional word pictures,* and every great communicator throughout history has mastered its use. This will be the third technique you will be mentored in during our next session.

The Four Challenges to Effective and Persuasive Communication

In 1976, I left job number nine to join my mentor in a start-up venture. We had acquired the marketing rights for an acne medication, and everything we owned and ever hoped to own was riding on this one project. If it failed, we could both lose everything we had. If it succeeded, we would be in business together. My assignment was to write and produce a two-minute commercial that would persuade television viewers to get up from their sofas, go over to the telephone, dial an 800 number, and order our product. During the course of writing the commercial I realized that I faced four challenges. As it turns out, these are the same four challenges everyone faces when they want to persuade someone to do something. If I could overcome these challenges in two minutes of communication, then my project would succeed. If I couldn't, it would fail. I used the three techniques you are going to learn in the next session, and the result was record breaking; 25,000 people per week (for 20 consecutive weeks) were persuaded to order my product from that two-minute commercial. Imagine selling $1 million of product a week by using only two minutes of communication with the buyers! That's the power of these three techniques.

Challenge 1: Grabbing the Listener's Undivided Attention

Any time you initiate communication, whether verbal or written, at the very outset the minds of your listeners or readers are somewhere else. As you or your letter enters their presence, their minds don't instantly stop thinking about whatever they've been thinking about. They don't instantly think, "Oh boy, look who's here, I can't wait to hear what he's going to say." You are an intruder into their thoughts of other things. They may be thinking about the argument they had with their spouse last night, something someone said in the hallway a few minutes earlier, a phone call that they will have to make in an hour, or a meeting they need to prepare for. But one thing is for sure; they are not thinking about what you're thinking about. So the first challenge is to grab their undivided, undistracted attention and bring it into the moment, focused precisely on what you are going to communicate.

Challenge 2: Holding Their Attention Level High throughout the Communication

Once you gain your listeners' undivided attention, you normally begin to lose it within 30 to 60 seconds. You won't lose it entirely, but it will ebb and flow throughout the communication, depending on their own distractive thoughts and the distractions from their surroundings. This creates the second challenge to effective and persuasive communication, namely retaining your listeners' undivided attention and keeping their attention level high throughout the communication. You are going to have to do something to keep them focused, or to at least draw their focus back into the conversation when you are making your most important points. How many times have you started talking and in a matter of moments the person you are talking to interrupts you and starts talking about something completely different? You think, "What the heck are you thinking about?" Guess what—it's not their fault. You're not holding their undivided attention. You've lost them. But there's a simple technique you are going to master that will keep their attention level high. It will be as captivating with your boss as it is with your peers and customers. In fact, at home it will be just as enticing with a toddler or a teen as it is with your spouse. It's one of the most effective communication techniques I use, and it works every single time I use it.

Challenge 3: Imparting and Implanting Understanding and Feeling

Imparting and implanting understanding and feeling into the mind and heart of the listener is the third challenge to effective and persuasive communication. We have already touched on it because fulfilling this challenge is the best description and definition of effective and persuasive communication. If your listener or reader doesn't understand what you are saying and feel what you are feeling, then your communication has not been truly effective and persuasive. Notice also that it's not good enough to simply impart understanding and feeling, but rather, it must be implanted! Imparting implies the act of transmitting the information and emotion, while implanting it actually enables it to penetrate the thoughts and feelings of your listeners and take root in their minds and hearts. The effective use of emotional word pictures will handle this formidable challenge with ease.

Challenge 4: Influencing Their Will to Make the Right Choice for the Right Reason

Influencing the recipient's will to make the right choice for the right reason is the essence of true persuasion. For communication to be effective, it must be two-dimensional—that is, it must penetrate the recipient's understanding and emotions. For communication to be persuasive, it must be three-dimensional. It must implant understanding into listeners' minds, it must implant emotions into their hearts, and it must influence their will to embrace a belief or take an appropriate action.

What makes this challenge even more difficult is avoiding the use of manipulation. You can force a person's will to bend to yours by the manipulative use of threats and fear or the use of emotional demands and pleas. Impatient bosses (not to mention impatient parents and spouses) often manipulate other people's will by quickly resorting to these controlling tactics. Although such tactics may accomplish the short-term goal of getting people to do what you want them to do, in the long term they are destructive to your listeners and to your relationship with them. Their use lowers people's self-esteem, demotivates them, and fuels resentment, distrust, and rebellion. True persuasion, on the other hand, influences people's will to receive and take ownership of a belief and motivates action from within rather than via outside pressure. People make the right choice for the right reason and feel good about it. This not only achieves the short-term goal, it motivates people for the long term and strengthens the relationship rather than sabotaging it.

As you begin to recognize communication barriers and learn to lay the right foundation for effective and persuasive communication, you will see an immediate difference in the way people respond to you and the communication of your thoughts, opinions, and ideas. Most critically, laying the right foundation prior to your important conversations and presentations will enable the communication techniques you'll learn in our next session to be effective and persuasive nearly 100 percent of the time.

Actions for Traction

WHERE THE RUBBER MEETS THE ROAD

1. Write down some of your ideas, opinions, hopes, or goals that have been rejected by your boss, your contemporaries, or your spouse.
2. Write some of the barriers from pages 89 to 90 that likely contributed to the rejections you listed.
3. When you experienced those rejections, list which of the four foundational components from pages 90 through 93 were lacking that may have contributed to those rejections.
4. If you have any important issues that you hope to communicate in the next several weeks, list each of them.
5. For each important issue that you have listed, write down the barriers from pages 89 to 90 that are likely to stand in your way.
6. For each important issue that you have listed, write down your ideas on how to apply each of the four foundational components to that coming conversation or presentation.
7. Think back on any situation, either personal or professional, in which you either attempted or desired to persuade someone to do something that was important to you, and then answer the following points.
   a. Describe the situation.
   b. What could you have said or done that would have shown a greater degree of honor or value to the person you desired to persuade?
   c. Describe the person's frame of reference as it related to you and the situation or issue (personality type, opinions, past experiences, concerns, etc.).
   d. What could you have done to have more clearly understood the person's frame of reference?
   e. Were you a good listener?

SESSION 6

Using Your Master Key to Open Any Door

Using Three Techniques to Become a Masterful and Persuasive Communicator

Your Master Key Is Worthless if You Don't Know How to Use It. As I mentioned in our last session, three techniques enabled me to persuade 25,000 people a week to order my first product. Was this just a fluke, or was I really on to something? As it turned out, it was no fluke! Since that first campaign in 1976, I have used these same techniques in every commercial and infomercial I have written on dozens of products and services. In all, I've used these techniques to persuade more than 25 million people to call an 800 number to order over $2 billion worth of our products and services. Equally important, I have used these techniques just as effectively to help build wonderful relationships with each member of my family and with lots of friends.

Fact: If your listener doesn't focus on what you are saying, doesn't clearly understand what you are saying, and doesn't feel what you are feeling, it's your fault!

The first technique, called *hooking,* overcomes the first challenge to effective communication in that it grabs the person's undivided attention instantly. The second technique, called *salting,* overcomes the second

The Ninth Law of Extraordinary Success

It's the speaker's sole responsibility to grab a listener's undivided attention, hold his or her attention, impart a clear understanding of what's being said, and implant what is felt into his or her emotions.

challenge to effective communication, because it can be used to hold your listener's attention level high throughout the entire communication. It can also be used to instantly raise or refocus the listener's attention on your most important points. I've already alluded to the third technique, called *emotional word pictures,*" which overcomes the third challenge to effective communication because it imparts and implants understanding in people's minds and feelings in their emotions. This technique also deals with the fourth challenge to persuasive communication because it implants your feelings into the heart or emotions of your listeners. When they understand what you're saying and truly feel what you are feeling, in most cases they will be persuaded to do whatever is appropriate. Even if they're in the minority who haven't been persuaded, they have been moved ninety-nine and two-thirds yards down the football field. Moving them that last 12 inches is relatively easy when you follow the specific steps that I will give you later for preparing an effective and persuasive presentation.

Hooking a Person's Undivided Attention

Imagine that it's a warm summer day and you've just finished doing some yard work. Your spouse calls out to you that lunch is ready. You turn toward the house, focus your eyes on the kitchen, and start walking. You immediately start thinking about taking your first bite of a big juicy hamburger. Meanwhile, your neighbor is in back of you on the other side of your fence, and he's trying out a new fishing rod. On his first practice cast, his hook comes flying over your fence and over your head and firmly hooks your nose. What happens? Are you still thinking about that hamburger? Are your eyes still focused on the kitchen window? Are you still moving in the same direction? No, no, and no. The moment you are hooked, your mind instantly leaves your thoughts of the hamburger, you spin around toward the direction of your neighbor, and all you can think about is that hook—nothing else matters. You are not thinking about the storm clouds coming in from the west, the birds in your trees, or the party you are going to tonight. One hundred percent of your attention is focused on that fisherman, his hook, and your movement in his direction. This is exactly what a good verbal or written hook does to people's mental focus. It doesn't matter where they are, what they are thinking about, or in what direction they are moving. A good hook instantly changes everything. It instantly takes people's minds out of their thoughts, changes their direction, and refocuses 100 percent of their attention on you and what you are about to say. Through the years I have found that there are three types of hooks that always grab a person's undivided attention.

1. A Strong, Captivating Statement

I'll never forget the day I wrote my first television commercial. It was in June of 1976 and I was 27 years old. The moment I finished writing it I jumped into my car and quickly drove over to my mentor's house. When I arrived at Bob's home, we sat at a table outside on his patio. My heart was racing as I handed him the script. (Remember, everything we had in life and everything we hoped for was riding on the effectiveness of this one commercial.) As he silently read the script, I was hoping to see him break into a smile and become as excited about it as I was. My heart sank as I saw a look of concern in his eyes. When he finished reading, he looked up at me and said hesitatingly, "It's good . . . I like it . . . but it's missing one thing . . . it has no hook." I was devastated. I had worked on this commercial for three days, and instead of a high five, I got a look of disappointment and a comment about what it didn't have. Then, with my tail between my legs, I asked him, "What's a hook?" He told me that a hook was something that right at the very top of the commercial would grab the attention of the viewers we were targeting. He handed the script back to me and I looked at the opening paragraph. He was right. There was nothing at the top that was going to grab the attention of the potential buyers of our acne product.

I instantly thought back into my past. In high school I had terrible acne and was deeply embarrassed every time a new crop of pimples appeared on my face. I went to the dermatologist every week and was tortured by ultraviolet light treatments that burned my skin and the lancing of each new pimple with his razor-sharp scalpel. As I thought about the embarrassment and pain that acne inflicted upon me nearly every week of my years in high school, I thought, "What would have stopped me dead in my tracks and grabbed my attention if I heard someone talking about acne in a television commercial?" Then it came to me. I asked Bob if I could borrow his pen and I quickly wrote two sentences at the top of the script and handed it to him. He read the two lines and broke into a smile. He looked up at me and said, "Now that's a hook! It's perfect!" If you never had acne, the two lines I wrote would mean absolutely nothing to you. But if you did have acne, or if you had a child who did, these two statements would have grabbed your undivided attention. Here's how I started that commercial: "Acne is painful, both physically and emotionally. I don't care if you're an adult or a teenager; acne causes embarrassment and anxiety." Bob was right, it was a hook, and in 20 weeks 1 million people were grabbed by that hook, called our 800 number, and ordered $20 million worth of our product.

So the first kind of hook is a strong statement that will captivate the attention of the particular person or group of people you are communicating with. Be sure to tailor the statement to the specific interests, concerns, needs, or desires of that specific person or group.

2. A Personal Reference

The second kind of hook is a personal reference—that is, using the name, image, credibility, or words of someone whom your listener knows, appreciates, respects, or has an interest in. Think back to a time when you were at a party or in any kind of crowded gathering. Perhaps you were talking with someone or were by yourself in your own little world. Then someone you really liked walked into the room. You didn't even see the person, but you heard his or her voice. What happened next? You instantly turned around to see where the person was. As soon as your eyes located him or her, you instantly felt good. Whether it was a friend, someone from work, or even your spouse, as soon as you heard the person's voice you instantly looked his or her way because you knew him or her. That represents the same power of introducing into your communication a personal reference who is known to your listener or reader.

There are hundreds of ways you can use this with anyone. With your teenagers, it might mean referring to something one of their friends or parents of their friends did or said. With a boss, it could mean a reference to his or her boss, someone in your industry that he or she respects, someone he or she has talked a lot about, or even what his or her most respected or hated competitor has said or done.

How do I use a personal reference in a television commercial when I have no knowledge of the specific people who are viewing that commercial? I use celebrities that most of America's population is very familiar with. In fact, people often feel like they know these celebrities because they've watched them in movies or on television for years. The key is picking a celebrity who has credibility with the target audience for the type of product he or she is endorsing. For example, in 1991 I used Michael Landon as a spokesperson for an educational product. My target was parents of grade school, high school, and college students. For years my target market had watched Michael on family-oriented shows like *Bonanza, Little House on the Prairie,* and *Highway to Heaven.* Consequently they felt like they really knew him and that he had a sincere concern about children and their education. So when he appeared on television and started talking about education, no matter what they were doing, they instantly looked at their TV set and thought, "Oh, that's Michael Landon. What's he saying?"

For my first acne commercial, I used Pat Boone and his daughter Debby. They were the ones who had originally introduced me to the product and I simply tapped into their story. You might think, "What credibility would Pat Boone have with acne sufferers and their parents? He probably never had a single pimple." If this was your thought, you would be right. He never did have a problem with pimples, but his four daughters did, and that became the next statement in the commercial. After the opening two statements that provided the hook, the credibility statement was, "Now I'm one of the lucky ones; I never had a skin problem; but I do have four daughters, and in our house they've tried all kinds of medications, and nothing ever really seemed to work . . . did it, Deb?"

In 1976, nearly every mom and dad in America knew who Pat Boone was and rightly believed that he would never tell a lie. So just seeing him at the very beginning of the commercial was a strong hook in itself. They heard his voice and instantly focused their attention on what he was going to say. His hook statements grabbed the undivided attention of all acne sufferers and their parents, and signaled non–acne sufferers that they need not pay any attention to this commercial and that they could retreat back into their thoughts. So this commercial really opened up with two hooks, a personal reference and a strong, captivating statement tailored to the target audience.

How effective is such a personal reference? It's been the single greatest key to our company's record-setting commercials. I've used Jane Fonda on a treadmill and Chuck Norris and Christie Brinkley on our Total Gym. I've used Cher on hair care, Ali McGraw and Meredith Baxter on cosmetics, Richard Simmons on weight loss, and the list goes on and on. I use celebrities that viewers feel they know or have an interest in, which causes them to instantly pay attention to each commercial when it appears on their television set.

3. A Specific Question

The third and strongest hook is a specific question. General questions such as, "How are you doing?" "How was your day?" or "How are you feeling?"

are not hooks at all! A listener can answer a general question and never come into the present. If I ask you how you are feeling, you can answer, "Fine," without even disturbing your current train of thought. You can keep thinking about an argument you had earlier in the day, or about something that's going to happen tonight. I haven't brought your mind into the present and into our communication. To be an effective hook, a question must be very specific and require an answer that will hook your mind away from your previous thoughts and refocus it on our conversation. It must be a question for which you have to think about the answer before you speak.

For example, if I ask you, "What did you have for breakfast today?," you can't keep thinking about the argument you had with your spouse this morning, or the phone call you have to make an hour from now. Instead, you have to bring your mind into the moment and actually think about what you ate for breakfast. My hook has successfully taken your mind out of the past or future and hooked it right into the moment and into our conversation. I've got your undivided attention.

If you are wondering, "What does my listener's breakfast have to do with what I'm going to say?" the answer is, your opening hook doesn't need to have anything to do with what you're going to say. It may, but it doesn't have to, because your goal for the opening hook is simply to turn the people's minds to a different direction and bring them out of wherever they are into the present and into your communication. If you can use a specific question that's also relevant to what you are going to say, that's even better, but it's not critical.

I use this kind of hook in my television shows all the time. For example, with a recent show that I filmed with Chuck Norris and Christie Brinkley, right at the top of the show I had Christie ask the questions, "If you could have any kind of body you want, what kind of body would you have? Would you have the body of a gymnast, the sleek body of a ballerina or dancer?" Chuck then asks, "Or, how about the body of a body builder or a world-class athlete?"

What happens when they ask those questions? Since nearly everyone wants to improve his or her body in some way, these questions grab their mind away from whatever they're doing, whether they're doing the dishes, walking through the room, or channel surfing. They instantly think, "What kind of body do I want?" They're hooked.

I opened one show with Cher asking the question, "Have you ever looked in the mirror at your hair and wanted to cry?" Female viewers instantly thought back and answered the question in their minds. They were hooked, and we launched a hair care line that became a $100 million winner almost overnight.

Of the three hooks, which do you think would be most effective at grabbing your undivided attention: a strong statement, a personal reference, or a specific question? Each situation will be different. Which of the three do you think you would be most comfortable using? Whether you use one or a combination of two or three, these hooks will be your key to capturing the undivided attention of your listener or reader right at the beginning of your communication.

Now that you've used a good hook to grab your listeners' undivided attention, the next challenge is to hold their attention level high throughout the entire conversation or presentation. Placing hooks throughout your conversation will help keep their attention focused; however, the best technique for meeting this challenge is what I call *salting.*

Salting Your Conversation to Keep Your Listener's Attention Level High

It's important to realize that a person's attention span is like a roller coaster. It goes up, levels off, turns away, goes down, turns another way, goes back up, and then goes back down. Left to its natural track, it would continue this kind of roller coaster pattern throughout a conversation, presentation, meeting, or written communication. While it's okay for your listener's attention level to rise, fall, and wander a little during the less important moments of your conversation, it's not okay for it to be doing so when you are making your important points. The salting technique will allow you to accomplish three objectives. For brief conversations, it will allow you to keep your listener's attention level high and totally focused throughout the entire conversation. For longer conversations or presentations, it will allow you to refocus your listener's attention and raise it to a higher level every time you want to make an important point. And for presentations that include numerous important points and two or three critical points, it will enable you to raise a listener's attention level to an even higher peak for those critical points.

For two years I have been working on a book entitled *The Richest Man Who Ever Lived: His Breakthrough Strategies for Wealth and Happiness.* In this book I mentor readers in the understanding and application of the insights and strategies articulated by Solomon in the biblical book of Proverbs. All of the strategies that I am presenting to you in our sessions find their roots in the book of Proverbs. One of the proverbs featured in my book is Proverbs 15:2, "The tongue of the wise makes knowledge acceptable." When most people speak or write, they only transmit information or knowledge. Solomon teaches that wise men and women go one giant step beyond that. They present their knowledge or information to their listeners in a way that makes it acceptable. In other words, they present it in a way that makes the listener desire the information and that makes that information understandable and usable to the listener. The salting technique makes your listener want to hear what you are going to say before you even say it! The next technique we're going to look at (emotional word pictures) makes your information understandable and usable to the listener. Was Solomon ahead of his time or what!

Have you ever heard the adage, "You can lead a horse to water, but you can't make him drink"? That adage may be true for you, but it's totally false for me. I can lead any horse in the world to water and make him drink 100 out of 100 times. All I have to do is feed him a few oats beforehand and put lots of salt on the oats. Salt has the same effect on you. Think of how you feel after you've had your first few handfuls of popcorn in a movie theater. Within moments you're reaching for that soda or water you've placed in the seat's cup holder. Why? Because salt makes you thirsty. And that's what this communication technique does to your listeners: It makes them thirsty to hear what you're about to say. So you always use this technique right before you make an important point. Or, if you notice that your listeners are starting to lose focus, you throw a little salt into your conversation to make them thirsty again. The more salt you add, the more thirsty they will become for the information you are going to hand them.

How do you salt your conversation? *Simply stated, you create curiosity about what you are going to say before you say it.* For example, when I tell you that there's a way you can grab anyone's undivided attention, whether they are your three-year-old daughter, your teenage son, your spouse, your boss, your banker, or your customer, I am salting you about the hooking technique before I actually reveal the technique.

Recently I was in a meeting with Patricia Heaton, the costar of the television show *Everybody Loves Raymond.* I was presenting a new product that I wanted to recruit her to be a spokesperson for, along with Chuck Norris. The product was the nation's first truly family-safe Internet service provider, called MAX.com. Before I told Patricia about the distinctive benefits of this product, I wanted to make her thirsty to hear them. I knew that she was the mother of four boys. I said, "Patty, the moment your children log on to the Internet they are live targets entering the sights of

Internet pornographers. There are four things they do to make sure they will get to your sons, and your current parental controls will not protect your children from these four things. But before I tell you about that, let me show you something . . ." Patty leaned toward me and said, "Wait, wait . . . what are the four things?" She didn't want me to go one step further into the presentation until I had revealed these four tactics of pornographers. I had only given her a little bit of salt, but it made her desperately thirsty and she wanted to hear the information immediately. She was ready to receive the four important points I wanted her to hear and remember. If she hadn't become thirsty from that first statement, I would have added another salty statement, such as, "Today pornographers have come up with ways to reach kids as early as eight years old, and using these four tactics they can have any teenager addicted to pornography within a matter of days. And that's an addiction that therapists tell us is as hard to break as crack cocaine." However, the first sprinkle of salt made her so thirsty for the information that I saved these salty statements for later in the presentation. By the way, she joined our team and will be featured with Chuck in our national TV campaign for MAX.com.

When it comes to salting, here's one important rule to remember: Only use as much salt as you need. Don't oversalt. Too much salt is irritating and offensive. If it's overused in a conversation or presentation, it can become ineffective. So the first place you want to use salt is preceding the important points you're going to make. Beyond that, you should use it if you notice your listeners' attention level starting to drop. You can salt them with a question, a description, or even an analogy or story.

Another example of how I recently used salt in one of my commercials was with Christie Brinkley telling viewers, "According to recent medical studies at Tufts University, there is now proof that there is one simple thing you can do for a few minutes a day that will absolutely reverse the 10 major signs of aging." Are you curious yet? If not, I'll add a little more salt. "This one thing can increase your energy level by more than 100 percent, increase your strength by more than 200 percent, greatly enhance your sex life, lower your blood pressure and cholesterol, raise your metabolism, lower your risk for cancer and heart disease, add years to your life, and make the years ahead a lot more enjoyable." If you're still not salted enough, put this book down and go take a nap. If you are thirsty for the answer, I'm talking about strength training, and the Tufts studies revealed you only need to engage in it for 20 to 30 minutes at a time, three to four days a week.

Now that you have successfully grabbed your listeners' undivided attention with a hook, and kept their attention level high and focused with salting, you are ready to move on to the third and most difficult challenge to effective and persuasive communication; enabling your listeners to clearly understand what you are saying and feel what you are feeling. The only technique I have ever found that effectively meets this challenge is the use of emotional word pictures.

Using Emotional Word Pictures to Implant Understanding in the Listener's Mind and Feeling in the Listener's Emotions

Now we get to the third and most powerful technique that I've ever used. As I said earlier, it's been used throughout the centuries. Jesus used this technique over and over again, not to manipulate people but to help them clearly understand what he was saying and feel what he was feeling.

Ronald Reagan was a pro at it. When Reagan took office in 1980, America was at an all-time low in morale and spirit. At the time, we were drowning in runaway inflation of about 12 percent. Lending interest rates were at 21 percent and mortgage rates were above 16 percent. Our unemployment rate was over 8 percent. The Christmas before Reagan took office, President Carter told us that we were entering a new age—the age of austerity. In his speech telling us why he was not lighting the lights on the White House Christmas tree, he said that we would never go back to the prosperity our nation had enjoyed in the 1950s and 1960s, but rather, we were entering the age of sacrifice. We were going to have to learn to live with all these different things, including long gas lines, high oil and energy prices, and so on. I was devastated. I was 31 years old, our business was barely four years old, and with the cost of money being so high, we were struggling just to meet payroll.

Then Reagan took office. By using emotional word pictures, he convinced an entire population that our best years were ahead of us, not behind us. He changed the spirit of America. All off a sudden we believed there was hope. By the time he left office, the inflation rate and the lending and mortgage rates had been cut in half. Unemployment had dropped below 6 percent, oil and energy prices had dropped back down, and there were no gas lines. President Carter's age of austerity had only lasted two years and had been replaced by the greatest economic boom in American history. That's the power of emotional word pictures. They had been used to change the spirit of an entire nation.

Your brain is divided into two parts; the left hemisphere, which is the analytical side, and the right hemisphere, which is the feeling and visual side. Emotional word pictures are so effective because they stimulate the right side of the brain. They convey a very clear visual picture and stimulate your feelings about the subject being discussed.

What Is an Emotional Word Picture?

An emotional word picture is a word, a statement, or a story that creates an instant picture in listeners' minds that clarifies what you are trying to say and implants a feeling into their emotions. It can be as simple as a single word or a statement, or it can be as complex as an analogy or even a short story.

For example, in the first chapter of this book, I said that our dreams were like destinations on a map of America, and that when it comes to pursuing dreams most adults are only equipped with shoes. They give up on their most cherished dreams because they are too distant to reach with a short, comfortable walk. Then I said that I was putting a brand-new 415-horsepower Porsche Turbo Carrera in your garage, one that could take you to your most distant dreams in a matter of hours. In this session, I told you that your Porsche's master key would not only unlock your car and start its engine, but that it could unlock any door in your world. All of these analogies are word pictures. I have been using them throughout our sessions to clarify concepts and impart understanding. Emotional word pictures go one step further. They relate to you in a more personal way and therefore impact your feelings.

Recently I was thinking back on September 11th, one of the most tragic days in American history. If I were to ask you how many people were actually killed on that terrible day, you probably couldn't give me the exact number. And yet, every single digit in that number represents a human life: a mom or dad, husband or wife, son or daughter who was taken away from a family. However, none of us can remember the exact number because numbers only stimulate the left side of our brain.

On the other hand, if I ask you where you were when you first heard of the towers being hit, you can instantly picture where you were and have no trouble recalling that. If I ask you to remember what it looked like when that second jet crashed into the south tower, you can easily visualize that. If I asked you how you felt as you watched the news reports throughout the day and evening, you can easily remember your feelings. Disbelief, grief, anger, and fear were probably just a few of the emotions you experienced. The fact that you can so easily recall all of this is a demonstration of the power of the right side of the brain. It's the right side that evokes feelings, and it's awesome that there is a communication technique that can actually appeal to that side of our brain. And that is just what emotional word pictures do. In fact, I've found seven things that emotional word pictures can accomplish that make them worth their weight in gold.

Why Emotional Word Pictures Are So Effective

1. **Like a hook, they can instantly grab and direct a person's attention.**

2. **They have the power to change a person's thinking and beliefs.** They literally have the power to change a person's life.

3. **They can breathe life into any communication.** Hopefully you're finding our sessions interesting and enjoyable. And one of the factors that is making them interesting and enjoyable is that instead of just giving you a bunch of words that are hard to understand and remember, I'm giving you pictures and stories that you can instantly visualize in your mind, making our communication come alive.

4. **They actually lock understanding and feeling into a person's memory, sometimes for life.** Sixty-two years after the fact, my 86-year-old mother could recite in great detail everything she experienced on December 7, 1941, the day Pearl Harbor was attacked by Japanese aircraft. It was just as fresh in her mind as it was when it happened. I was alive when John Kennedy was shot, and I can tell you right where I was and what I was doing. I can tell you my first thoughts and exactly what I said to the people who were with me. That was 40 years ago, and I was only 14. Yet I can remember it as easily as I can remember the events of last night.

5. **They provide a gateway to deeper relationships because they enable the listener to actually feel what you're feeling.** Emotional word pictures can take us to a deeper level of intimacy with those we care most about because they enable us to experience each other's most intimate feelings and thoughts.

6. **They can enable you to correct or reprove someone's behavior or attitude in a way that can be more easily received without negative consequences.** How many times have you tried to correct those you care about, only to have them react against you? They become defensive and even get angry. When you use the right emotional word picture, you can give effective correction that will enable them to receive it rather than react to it. It can change the way they feel, the way they behave, and even their attitudes.

7. **They provide the only communication method that can bridge the chasm between right brain–dominant individuals and left brain–dominant**

individuals. Women are forever wondering how they can tell a man something 10 times and he still won't get it. The answer is that they are trying to communicate their right-brain feelings to left brain–dominant men. Eighty to 90 percent of women are right brain dominant, and 80 to 90 percent of men are left brain dominant. Using emotional word pictures is the only way to stimulate the right side of the brain of a left brain–dominant male. When a woman uses a good emotional word picture to communicate how she feels, her man will finally "get it." And when he truly feels what she feels, his behavior will finally change for the best.

A Typical Example of the Power of Emotional Word Pictures

Let me give you a real-life example. For more than 30 years, my best friend (other than my wife) has been Jim Shaughnnessy. Jim was single for most of his adult life. At the age of 40 he fell in love with an angel named Patty Plant. They dated for five years, but Jim's independence and business endeavors, which took him all over the world, made it incredibly difficult for him to make the commitment to get engaged. Patty was Jim's dream come true. She was a living doll physically, and, more important, she was wonderfully loving, kind, and compassionate; fun and sweet; and thoughtful and considerate. All of Jim's close friends were rooting for Patty and getting frustrated with Jim's reluctance to tie the knot.

One day Patty sat down with Jim and used an emotional word picture. It was so powerful that for the first time in five years Jim actually felt what his inaction had made Patty feel like. This former All-American football player was literally moved to tears. Patty didn't have to wait any longer. They got engaged that day and were married in a matter of weeks.

This wasn't manipulation. In fact, before she used the word picture Patty said, "I just want you to know that if it takes forever, I will wait for you. I'm never going to look to anybody else. You are the man I want to marry."

In his senior year in high school, Jim was one of only two first-team All-American football players from Pennsylvania. Thirty-five of America's finest universities offered Jim full football scholarships. Turning down the biggest football powerhouses, Jim signed with Arizona State University at the urging of his coach. Unfortunately, he played behind a college All-American running back and spent a lot of time on the bench. At the time, football was Jim's whole life. He knew that he was every bit as good as the first-string player, and to his dismay and frustration, he remained on the bench game after game. When his coach would play him, Jim would perform wonders. In fact, his career average of 6.9 yards per carry still stands as an unbroken record at Arizona State.

When Patty wanted Jim to understand what she was feeling, she came up with the perfect word picture. She said, "Jim, can you remember how you felt in those games where you knew you could be out there gaining yards and winning games, and yet Frank Kush kept you on the bench? How did that make you feel?"

As Jim started to talk about it, Patty would ask him specific questions that made him dive even deeper into his feelings. He talked about it for nearly a half an hour. He even got teary-eyed as he talked about his hurt and frustration.

Then Patty said the magic words. "Jim, I have been sitting on the bench waiting to get in and play for five years. I want to be your wife. I want to do all the things a husband and wife do, without reservation. I want to have children with you. But month after month, year after year, you've kept me on the sidelines. I'm on the bench! I'm not in the first string of your life."

Wow! Jim was blown away. This emotional word picture not only made him feel what Patty had been feeling, it had a second effect. It made him remember how good he felt when he actually got off the bench and started playing in the game. So he thought, "I've kept her on the bench and she's been feeling like I felt. Now I'm going to take her off the bench and put her in the game, and I'm going to get in the game, and we are going to have the best time of our lives." They were playing the game together. Jim told me, "It made everything exciting and fun as we began to plan our wedding and honeymoon." That was 12 years ago, and I can tell you that 12 years and three kids later, Jim and Patty are one of the happiest couples I have ever known.

For women, emotional word pictures are the key to gaining understanding from any man—whether a customer, a boss, an employee, or your husband—and to helping him feel what you're actually feeling. Men, it's just as important to you, too. There are times when the women you work with or the woman you live with can't identify with many of the things you experience. They sincerely think they understand, but they really don't feel it. An emotional word picture can instantly enable a woman to feel what you are feeling and consequently can move her from one opinion to another. This is the one and only communication technique that builds a bridge from the mind of a typically left brain–dominant male to the mind of a typically right brain–dominant female.

Six Steps to Creating Effective Emotional Word Pictures

There are six steps to creating effective emotional word pictures in important situations. You can use them spontaneously in any communication. You can instantly think of an analogy or a picture that will help the person understand what you're saying. When you have something really important that you want to communicate, then you should take these six steps to create an effective emotional word picture.

1. **Set a specific time to create the word picture.** Don't try to go into an important situation and just come up with one spontaneously. That's really hard to do, and you might communicate the wrong thing. Patty had set aside a few hours to plan her word picture for Jim. If you have something that you consider to be important to communicate with anyone, set aside a specific time to actually create that effective word picture.

2. **Think about the other person's interests.** The more you tailor the word picture to the other person's frame of reference, the more effective your word picture will be. Patty had grown up in Indiana, where basketball was king, but an emotional word picture about basketball would have left Jim scratching his head, and they still might be single.

3. **Create your word picture from one of the following inexhaustible sources.**

- The passions, hobbies, or interests of the other person you're communicating with. If he or she is a golfer, you might come up with a good one involving golf. If he or she is a workaholic, you might use one that involves his or her passion for work.
- Memorable events from the person's past, or present events that he or she is currently involved in.
- Everyday objects that the person is familiar with. For example, one day my five-year-old son's bicycle was wedged between my brand-new car and the wall of our garage. Determined to get his bike out of the garage, he muscled it past my car with his metal handlebar gouging a long, deep scratch across its door. The next day at work, I told the story to my partners, all of whom had expensive cars and could easily relate to my feelings of shock and dismay. A month later, one of my partners said, "Remember how you felt when Sean ran his bike against the door of your car?" Of course that instantly brought back those unforgettable feelings. He went on to say, "Well, something you did yesterday made me feel those same feelings." My response?

I said, "Holy mackerel! What did I do?" This was a great word picture because I remembered exactly how I had felt. It not only enabled me to feel what my partner was feeling, it made me want to do whatever it would take to relieve his feelings. He had my ear, my attention, my heart, and my commitment to do whatever it would take . . . all from that one simple word picture.

- Images from nature, such as oceans, lakes, streams, mountains and so on. I live on a mountain that is truly awesome. I used to live on the beach in Malibu. If my partners want to use a word picture from nature, they can draw from the beach or the mountains and enable me to instantly visualize and feel what they are feeling.
- Imaginary stories that picture the points you want to make. You can create your own story and get the other person to actually enter into that story so he or she is picturing the different points.

4. Practice using a word picture before you actually share it with the person. Once you've created it, say it in front of a mirror. If you can rehearse it with someone else without violating the confidence of another, do it. But if you run the risk of revealing something personal or hurtful about the person you're going to communicate with, only rehearse it by yourself.

5. Pick a convenient time with minimal distractions to communicate your word picture. If you are dealing with a customer, if possible, take him or her out for coffee, lunch, or dinner where the chances of being interrupted or distracted are reduced. This is also true at home. If the kids are up and making noise, that is not the time. If the phone is ringing or your spouse is exhausted, don't do it then. Pick a time when distractions will be minimal and the energy level is going to be adequate.

6. Without overusing them, be persistent and soft in using emotional word pictures. Too much of a good thing can make the good thing less meaningful and effective. Use emotional word pictures to communicate those issues that are truly important to you. Use simple one-word or one-sentence analogies to communicate less important issues. Also, be careful not to have a condescending attitude as you present a word picture. Solomon wrote, "A soft answer turns away wrath, but grievous words stir up anger." A condescending or overbearing spirit will cause your listener to react to your attitude rather than respond to your word picture.

Using the techniques of hooking, salting, and emotional word pictures will ensure that your listeners will understand what you mean and feel what you feel. You will have effectively communicated. In many cases, once listeners feel what you are feeling they will be persuaded to take the action you were hoping they would take. And in the few cases where they aren't moved to action, you will have moved them ninety-nine and two-thirds yards down the field toward your goal of persuasion. Getting them to move that last 12 inches will be accomplished by doing two things. First, you must appeal to one or more of the three greatest motivating factors in human nature, and second, you must adequately prepare a persuasive presentation before you deliver it.

Using the Three Greatest Motivating Factors to Recruit the Will

According to psychologists, there are three major factors that motivate people to act. They are: (1) the desire for gain, (2) the fear of loss, and (3) the need to love and be loved. When people clearly understand what you are saying and truly feel what you are feeling, if they are still not motivated to act in the way that you believe is in their best interest, you then need to focus your appeal on one or more of these three factors. The easiest and usually the most effective appeal is to the desire for gain. Nearly every commercial or infomercial I have ever written focuses upon viewers' desire for gain. My fitness products focus on their desire for a better physical condition and a better-looking body. My cosmetic products focus on their desire for gaining a more attractive and youthful-looking face. My educational products appeal to parents' desire for their children to learn more in less time with less stress and get better grades.

Through the years, I've had a lot of people present ideas and products to me to try to recruit my involvement in their projects. Believe it or not, at the core of their appeal has been how much they will gain from my participation in their project, rather than how much I will gain. That is the exact opposite of appealing to your listener's desire for gain and is not a motivating factor at all. When you are trying to persuade anyone to do anything, it is critical that you focus upon what he or she will specifically gain by taking the action you are requesting.

The second motivational factor is the fear of loss. When a bank commercial reminds you that the bank's accounts are insured by the federal government and that money market funds are not, the commercial is appealing to your fear of loss. As parents, we appeal to this fear regularly by threatening the loss of privileges. As spouses, we appeal to this fear with obvious and lightly veiled threats. More times than not, this is a form of manipulation rather than persuasion. Appealing to the fear of loss is only a legitimate focus of persuasive communication when it accurately reflects a legitimate negative consequence. My father was a bomber pilot in World

War II. Before each mission, he and the other pilots would receive a briefing on their mission from the mission commander. Each briefing would include strict instructions with stern warnings that would strike fear in the hearts of the pilots. This was not manipulation, because not heeding those warnings could cause the death of the pilots and their crews. Anytime a warning accurately reflects consequences that have a reasonable chance of occurring, the appeal to fear of loss is a legitimate form of persuasion rather than manipulation. The "Hold on to Dear Life" campaign that urges people to use their seat belts is a legitimate appeal to the fear of loss, because the consequences portrayed happen every day to people who fail to use seat belts and child restraints. So, when consequences warrant, this is a strong motivating factor that can be appealed to. Just be careful not to use it recklessly to motivate a quick reaction. To do so is to manipulate rather than persuade.

The third motivational factor is the desire to love or be loved. Here again, it is critical that your appeal to this factor be a legitimate appeal rather than a manipulative one. Unfortunately, this factor is more often used for manipulation than for legitimate persuasion. When someone says, "If you really loved me, you would let me . . .", this is usually nothing more than manipulation. However, if a person says, "I want to love you more deeply, but to do so I need you to be totally honest," this is a legitimate appeal to the desire to be loved, because the person has accurately portrayed a genuine requirement that he or she has in order to engage in a truly loving relationship. Of course, when jewelry store advertisements imply that you will be more loved if you give a diamond bracelet to your spouse for Valentine's Day, they are using your desire to be loved in a manipulative way.

When preparing for an important conversation or presentation, review your points and determine if you have clearly and adequately appealed to any of these three motivational factors. If so, should the appeal be strengthened or softened? Are you using a persuasive appeal or a manipulative one? These are questions that should be answered before you engage in the conversation or deliver the presentation. This brings me to the second step of ensuring the persuasiveness of your conversation or presentation, namely, preparation.

Preparing a Persuasive Presentation

Remember from our last session that the fourth component in laying the foundation of effective and persuasive communication is preparation. The simple rule is, The more important the issue that you want to communicate, the more preparation you need to do beforehand. On pages 119 to 120 you will find a guide for preparing a logical and persuasive presentation. On pages 121 to 130 you will find a presentation worksheet that is ideal for this.

You should also remember that the more you use the communication strategies, skills, and techniques that we have looked at during these past two sessions, the more proficient you will become in using them to communicate effectively and persuasively. Like any skill, these skills may seem a little awkward or difficult initially. But the more you use them, the easier they will become, and ultimately, not only will you master these skills, they will become second nature to you.

A note of caution: If you apply all of the skills and techniques we have looked at and are still not able to persuade your listener to act on your idea, realize that it may be the result of two possibilities: (1) Your idea may not be the best answer for the individual situation and you may need to go back to the drawing board to improve and revise the idea; or (2) your listener may have problems or issues that go beyond the scope of your idea—problems as simple as his or her ego or poor values and priorities, or as deep as perversity and prejudice.

You could have made the most effective and persuasive presentation in history in an effort to convince Adolf Hitler that his vision for the Third Reich was wrong—that it would not lead his nation into glory, but rather into oblivion and the needless deaths of millions of his countrymen. However, he still would not have been persuaded to act otherwise. Not because his ideas were better than yours, but because his ideas grew from an evil nature that was centered in his very core. He was driven not by a desire for what was best, but rather by an evil arrogance and bitter hatred that were ingrained into the fiber of his personal makeup. People often act not according to what they believe to be best, but according to personal values, drives, and prejudices.

Fortunately, this will not be the case with most of the people we deal with. The tools that I am placing in your hand will provide you with all the power you need for effectively and persuasively communicating with normal people in normal situations. My hope is that you will use these power tools wisely and skillfully.

Actions for Traction

WHERE THE RUBBER MEETS THE ROAD

IMPORTANT DEFINITIONS

Hook: A strong captivating statement, personal reference, or specific question that instantly grabs a listener's undivided attention.

Salt: A statement, question, or story that creates curiosity about what you are going to say before you say it.

Emotional word picture: A word, statement, or story that creates an instant picture in listeners' minds that clarifies what you are trying to say and implants a feeling into their emotions.

1. Describe any situation, personal or professional, in which you either attempted or desired to persuade someone to do something that was important to you.
2. Write out several different hooks that could have been used to grab the person's undivided attention.
3. Write out statements or questions that could have been used as salt to keep the person's curiosity high throughout your conversation or written presentation.
4. Write out one or more emotional word pictures that could have been used to enable your listener or reader to better understand what you were saying and feel what you were feeling.
5. Write how you could have appealed to one or more of the three greatest motivating factors (fear of loss, desire for gain, or desire to love or be loved).

— Bonus Section —
Preparing a Logical and Persuasive Presentation

This section shows you the steps for creating a persuasive oral or written presentation. Following this section are the presentation worksheets that are included in the preprinted vision mapping journal. You can also order them from my Web site (www.stevenkscott.com) or from my office at (800) 246-1771. If you do not want to order one of our preprinted vision mapping journals, please feel free to copy the worksheet format on pages 121 through 130.

Preliminary Steps

1. Describe your listeners or readers.
2. Make a list of their needs or desires that are relevant to your idea or product.
3. Make a list of their concerns or fears that are relevant to your idea or product.
4. State why or how your idea or product fulfills their relevant needs or desires better than any other idea or opportunity available.
5. State why or how your idea or product resolves their concerns or fears better than any other idea or opportunity available.
6. List and then prioritize every objection or excuse they may have for resisting or rejecting your idea or product or the action you are asking them to take.
7. Write down how your idea or product overcomes each individual objection or excuse.

Preparing the Presentation

1. Make sure everything you write or say in your presentation treats your listener with honor and respect and avoids condescension.
2. When appropriate, appeal to at least one or more of the person's three greatest internal motivating factors (desire for gain and fear of loss that your idea or product affects).
3. Write a presentation that follows this structure:
   - Create an opening that will immediately grab the listener's attention with as strong a hook as you can create. (Use an emotional word picture if appropriate.)

- Describe the problems your idea or product is going to solve.
- Salt the presentation with curiosity-building statements or questions as often as you need to keep the individual's undivided attention.
- Use emotional word pictures to make your most important points crystal clear and unforgettable. Use your idea or product benefit list and your answers to objections and excuses to form the body of your presentation.
- Use testimonials of others who have benefited from similar ideas or from your product. If this is a sales presentation, use the testimonials of satisfied customers, industry experts, or other credible sources to increase the credibility of your product and your claims.
- Use comparisons to other ideas, products, or prices to build a perceived value of the idea or product that far exceeds what you are proposing or the selling price of your product.
- Close the presentation with a quick summary (when time allows) of the benefits of your idea or product. Give a risk-reward comparison, a clear-cut reason for action, and finally, a call to action.

Presentation Worksheet

1. Describe the person you are presenting your idea or product to, and list their desires or needs that your idea or product will fulfill:

Description of Listener

____

____

____

____

____

____

____

____

____

Desires or Needs Your Idea or Product Fulfills

____

____

____

____

____

____

____

____

____

____

____

From *Vision Mapping Journal*, © Steve Scott 2003.

Presentation Worksheet, continued

2. State why your idea or product fulfills these needs BETTER than any other idea or product available to your listener/reader.

Idea or Product Advantages & Benefits

____
____
____
____
____
____
____

2A. How does your idea or product appeal to your listener's "Desire for Gain" or "Fear of Loss"?

Desire for Gain

____
____
____
____
____
____

Fear of Loss

____
____
____
____
____
____
____

From *Vision Mapping Journal*, © Steve Scott 2003.

Presentation Worksheet, continued

3. List and prioritize every possible objection and excuse a person could use to avoid accepting your idea or product.

Objections & Excuses

From *Vision Mapping Journal,* © Steve Scott 2003.

Presentation Worksheet, continued

4. List and prioritize how your idea or product overcomes each objection or excuse.

Objection:______________________________________

____

Answer:____

____

____

Objection:______________________________________

____

Answer:____

____

____

Objection:______________________________________

____

Answer:____

____

____

Objection:______________________________________

____

Answer:____

____

____

Objection:______________________________________

____

Answer:____

____

____

From *Vision Mapping Journal*, © Steve Scott 2003.

Presentation Worksheet, continued

5. Create an opening that INSTANTLY "grabs" the listener's undivided attention, using as strong of a hook as you can create.

Opening Statements or Questions

____

____

____

____

____

____

____

____

6. "Set Up" the problem or problems your idea or product is going to solve.

Problems That Will Be Solved

____

____

____

____

____

____

____

____

From *Vision Mapping Journal*, © Steve Scott 2003.

Presentation Worksheet, continued

7. "Salt" the presentation with curiosity building statements or questions as often as you need to raise your listener's attention level.

Salting Questions or Statements

____

____

____

____

____

____

____

____

____

____

____

____

____

____

____

____

____

____

____

____

From *Vision Mapping Journal,* © Steve Scott 2003.

Presentation Worksheet, continued

8. Using "Emotional Word Pictures" to make your most important points crystal clear and unforgettable, take your most important benefits and answers to objections and illustrate them with word pictures.

Word Pictures That Illustrate My Most Important Points

From *Vision Mapping Journal,* © Steve Scott 2003.

Presentation Worksheet, continued

Word Pictures That Illustrate My Most Important Points

From *Vision Mapping Journal,* © Steve Scott 2003.

Presentation Worksheet, continued

9. Use testimonials of others who have benefited from your idea or product.

Possible Testimonials

____

____

____

____

____

____

____

____

10. Use comparisons to other ideas, products or prices to build a "perceived value" that far exceeds the cost of the idea or product.

Comparisons or Perceived Value

____

____

____

____

____

____

____

____

From *Vision Mapping Journal*, © Steve Scott 2003.

Presentation Worksheet, continued

11. Close with a quick summary of the most important benefits, a risk/reward comparison (minimizing the potential risk and maximizing the potential gain) and a clear cut reason for action or call to action.

Close

From *Vision Mapping Journal*, © Steve Scott 2003.

SESSION 7

With This Technique You'll Superachieve; Without It You Won't!

Gaining a Precise and Empowering Vision of What You Want to Achieve

Your Porsche Has the Most Advanced GPS System in the World, but You Have to Download the Software. You have reprogrammed your onboard computer. You have used the key to unlock its door and start its engine. But if you don't know where you're going, it will not take you anywhere. Fortunately, your Porsche came equipped with an incredible global positioning satellite (GPS) system. All you have to do is load your destination and map software, and this system will take you to each of your dreams in record time.

A friend of mine once offered me his vacation home in Hawaii. It was a palatial estate with its own private beach and acres of tropical gardens. The house alone had 15,000 square feet. It was one of the most beautiful slices of paradise I have ever seen. Imagine that I offered you a two-week, all-expenses-paid vacation for two in Hawaii at my friend's estate. The vacation would include two first-class tickets to Hawaii, the use of my friend's $200,000 red Ferrari convertible, and $1,000 a day in cash for spending money. But that's not all. When you get there, you'll find an envelope on the kitchen table with your name on it. Inside the envelope you will find $1 million in cash—and it's all yours! Now, there's only one catch: I'm only going to give you all of this if you can find my friend's home on your own. If you can't find it, you reimburse me the $3,000 for the airline tickets and you're on your own during your stay in Hawaii: no house, no car, no expense money, no million dollars.

Your first question might be, "What's the address?" If my answer was, "I already told you, it's in Hawaii," your next question would be, "Well, what island is it on?" I would answer, "One of the seven." Now you would probably get a little frustrated and ask, "How on earth am I supposed to find it?" I would answer, "Just go to Hawaii and start looking. I'll give you a whole day to find it." With only one day to search the coastline of seven islands, not having a clue as to what this estate looks like and not having any address or map to get there, what would be your chances of actually arriving at the right address in the limited amount of time that you are given to find it? Zero!

Knowing that you're going to have to pay your own way if you don't find my friend's estate on the day you arrive, would you even try to find it? Of course not! Even with $1 million waiting for you, you still wouldn't try, because no matter how great the reward, there's absolutely no chance you're going to be able to find that one specific house in the limited amount of time available to you.

What do you need to know to raise your chances of winning? First, you need to know which island the estate is on so you can schedule a flight to that particular island. Second, you need a specific address. Third, you need a detailed road map with a clear set of directions to get you from the airport to the house.

Now, suppose I tell you that I'm going to give you a very precise set of directions that will take you from the airport over several highways and then through a half-dozen back roads, directly to the gates of the estate. I'll also give you the six-digit code to open the gate, but I will only tell you the address, directions, and six-digit code once. Would you try to memorize everything or would you write it all down? The good news is, with all of the directions in your hand, it will only take you 30 minutes to get to the house and win your trip and collect the million dollars once you leave the airport. What are your chances of success now? Virtually 100 percent. In a matter of minutes, your chances of success have gone from 0 percent to 100 percent. Your impossible destination not only became possible, it became a sure thing.

Well, guess how more than 97 percent of America's adults journey through their days, weeks, months, years, and, sadly, through their entire lives? When it comes to pursuing their dreams, they don't even know which island those dreams are located on. They don't have a single address. They don't have a map to follow to get there. And unfortunately, the amount of time they have to achieve their dreams is a lot more limited than they think. How about you? The fact is, if you don't have a clear picture of your destination and a precise, detailed map to get there, you will never arrive. You will not achieve any significant dreams, and it won't matter how hard you try and or how great the reward may be.

Hopefully you're starting to get the picture. If you would take the time to get the directions and write them down to win a two-week vacation, how much more important is it to get the addresses of your personal and professional dreams and create a road map to achieve all of those dreams in time to enjoy them? How much more important is your career than a vacation? How much more important are your relationships with your spouse, your children, and your friends? And yet, chances are you are part of the 97 percent of America's adult population who have never created a specific road map and timetable to achieve your dreams in each of the most important areas of your life.

Master Strategy 7—Gaining a Clear and Precise Vision of What You Want to Achieve

How powerful is this master strategy? When John was 17, he went to work as a bookkeeper for a dry goods store in Cleveland, Ohio. His salary was $4 per week. After a few weeks on the job, he gained a vision for starting his own business. For three years he saved and borrowed everything he could. Then he recruited a partner, and with less than $2,000 they started their own dry goods trading business. That same year, the first oil well in America was drilled, and for the next three years John watched Cleveland businessmen begin to make significant amounts of money by setting up small oil refineries. He and his partner decided to invest $4,000 into setting up a small refinery, and they recruited a third partner to do just that. As the oil industry began to boom, chaos reigned supreme. And yet, according to one author, in the midst of all of the chaos John "had a clear vision of where the industry was going, and the key role his company could play in it" (*John D. Rockefeller: The Heroic Age of American Enterprise*, C. Scribner's Sons, 1941).

Notice that John did not have a head start in this new industry—in fact, he was a latecomer. He did not have a size advantage either, as his refinery was one of the smallest in Cleveland. He didn't have the deep pockets or the backing of a group of angel investors to gain a financial advantage. In fact, he was running everything on a shoestring budget. All John had was a clear vision of where the industry was headed and the key role his company could play in it.

Which Would You Choose?

Now, think about this. If you were beginning a business in an emerging industry in its infancy stage, and you had the choice of (1) the financial backing of investors with deep pockets and a war chest of millions of dollars or (2) nothing more than a few thousand dollars, two partners, and a clear vision of where the industry was going and the key role your company could play in it, which would you choose? You, and everyone else I know, would select the first choice. I would too. But we would all be wrong. For as important as financial depth is, nothing is more powerful than a person with a clear and precise vision.

Back to our story. John also proved that nothing is more powerful than a man with a clear vision. Within a few short years, John D. Rockefeller had become the richest man in the world. His company, Standard Oil, owned 25 percent of all of the oil wells in the United States, 80 percent of the oil refineries, and 90 percent of the oil pipelines. Contrast John's story of a man with a vision and little financial backing with that of the dot-com companies of the nineties. They had billions of dollars in financial backing and no true vision. John D. Rockefeller ended up with the most valuable company ever created, and the dot-coms ended up with companies that vaporized almost as fast as they were formed.

As you read the biographies of the world's most successful people, you'll see this same lesson repeated again and again. As I mentioned in our third session, Ray Kroc was a 52-year-old salesman of milkshake machines. The machines he sold could mix five milkshakes at a time. The average coffee shop would typically order one machine, and large restaurants might order two. When Kroc received an order for eight machines from one restaurant, he couldn't wait to get to San Bernardino, California to see what kind of restaurant would need enough machines to make 40 milkshakes simultaneously.

When Ray first arrived at the tiny octagonal restaurant, he was surprised by its small size, and he was shocked to see a line of people coming out of the restaurant and wrapping completely around the building and through the parking lot. In his autobiography, *Grinding It Out* (Regnery, 1977), he

The Tenth Law of Extraordinary Success

Extraordinary achievement is impossible to attain without a clear and precise vision and a detailed plan to achieve that vision.

wrote, "That night in my motel room I did a lot of heavy thinking about what I'd seen during the day. Visions of McDonald's restaurants dotting crossroads all over the country paraded through my brain."

In a single day, Kroc had gained a clear and precise vision of what this one little restaurant could become, and he couldn't stop thinking about it. On the other hand, even though the McDonald brothers (the restaurant's founders) had experienced firsthand the phenomenal success of their restaurant, they did not have a clear vision of what that restaurant could become. They didn't even believe in Ray's vision, so they were thrilled to sell all of their formulas, their menus, their name, and the worldwide franchising rights for only $2 million. Empowered by his vision, Ray Kroc created the most successful restaurant operation in history, building over 25,000 McDonald's restaurants worldwide. His vision not only produced an incalculable fortune for his family for generations to come, it produced billions of dollars of wealth for his franchisees and shareholders.

What Are Your Dreams?

A while back I was speaking at a convention and I asked an audience of 3,000 people, "What are your dreams?" Instead of hands springing up all over the auditorium, the only thing I saw was 3,000 faces with blank looks. After the meeting, as I was signing books, I would ask each individual, "What are your most important dreams?" There was always a minute of awkward silence as each person would race through the recesses of his or her mind trying to think of an answer. After a minute or so, each would give me a very general dream. "I want to be successful." "I want to be a millionaire." "I want financial independence so I can quit my job." The people would smile as they gave their answers, as if they had finally come up with the answer to a pop quiz. But their smiles quickly turned to looks of bewilderment when I asked, "How are you going to achieve that dream?" These people were not uneducated or illiterate. Most were college graduates, and many had advanced degrees. A few were top-level engineers and scientists that worked for NASA. And yet not one had clearly defined his or her dreams and mapped out a course of action to achieve them.

How about you? What are your dreams? If you could have anything you want, what would it be? Would you want extraordinary success, riches, a fulfilling marriage, an ideal body, a long life, or maybe all of the above? What do you really want?

Now, regardless of your answer, I would like you to show me your written plan to achieve your most important dreams. You don't have a plan?

Side-by-Side Comparison

How People Pursue Significant Dreams in the Most Important Areas of Their Lives

Drifters	Pursuers	Achievers	Superachievers
Dreams are undefined or nonexistent. Hopes are vague at best.	Dreams are vague or generic. No specific "addresses," no plans, no timetables, but lots of hopes.	Dreams are vague, but short-term goals are defined and have target dates. Vigorously pursue and often achieve short-term goals in a timely manner.	Big dreams, clearly defined with detailed map of intermediate goals and timetable with target dates for each task, goal, and dream. Vigorously pursue and achieve dreams and often revise dreams upward.

Well don't feel too bad; that just means you're in the same boat as the 97 percent of American adults who dream, but never achieve their most important dreams.

"Where There Is No Vision, the People Perish." (Proverbs 29:18)

King Solomon had a worldwide reputation as the wisest man in the world. Kings and queens from far and near paid him fortunes to receive his counsel. In the biblical book of Proverbs, Solomon wrote, "Where there is no vision, the people perish." To Solomon, a vision was not something mystical, vague, or abstract. It was a precise and clearly defined objective or goal. The wisdom of this statement is enormous. Solomon says that when people do not have a clear and precise vision for what they want to achieve in any given area of their life, they will begin to experience the dying process in that area. This dying process isn't physical, but rather a mental and emotional process. If you have no vision in your marriage, your parenting, your job, your business, your career, or any particular project, you will begin to lose your drive, your motivation, your commitment, your energy, and ultimately any hope of significant achievement or happiness in that area or endeavor. That's the bad news.

The good news is that as true as this proverb is, its converse is equally true; *where there is vision, the people live!* In other words, gaining a clear and precise vision for what you want to achieve in any given area or project will

The Eleventh Law of Extraordinary Success

Vision infuses life into any project or endeavor, and the lack of vision infuses the dying process.

result in the infusion of life into that area or project. New life means more drive, greater motivation, stronger commitments, increased energy, and true fulfillment. Amazingly, vision brings this kind of life into any endeavor to which it is applied, from a project at work to your career in general; from your relationship with your spouse to your relationships with your children. Gaining a clear and precise vision is critical to achieving extraordinary outcomes. Without a vision, instead of extraordinary achievement, there is only death and the perishing process.

What Is This Kind of Vision?

If you were planning to take a three-week vacation and drive across America, would you just point your car in any direction and begin your trip with no destination in mind, or would you pick out your destinations before you started your trip? Of course you would pick out your destinations before you started your trip. Why? Because you would know that you've only got three weeks, and you would want to make the absolute most of your trip. Once you have picked out your destinations, would you get a road atlas and map out the highways you are going to take to each of those destinations? Of course you would. Why? Because you want to take the best routes so you can arrive at each destination without getting lost or sidetracked along the way. Would you try to figure out what days you want to arrive at each destination and how much time you want to spend at each one? Of course you would. Why? Because you want to have enough time to visit the places that you consider the most important to see and do the activities that you want to do most, and you know that you only have three weeks to do it all. Would you even consider taking the trip without a detailed map in your car? Of course not! That map is the key to achieving all of your goals for that vacation.

What's More Important?

What's more important to you, a three-week vacation or a career in which you achieve all the personal fulfillment and financial goals you desire? What's more important, a three week vacation or a fulfilling marriage in which you and your spouse have all of your deepest physical, emotional, and spiritual needs met? What's more important, a three-week vacation or the happiness and well-being of your children? The answers to all of these questions are obvious. And yet, if your answer to my first question, "What are your dreams?" is as general and vague as those given by the attendees at the convention, then that tells me that you would treat a three-week vacation as a much higher priority than these far more important areas of your life. You create a clear and precise vision for your vacation, with all of the destinations and routes mapped out and scheduled. But with the most important areas of your life, all you have done is pointed your car in a general direction and driven blindly on the most important journeys of your life.

What Are Visions, and How Do You Get Them?

For our purposes, we are not going to concern ourselves with Webster's definition of a vision. Instead, we will focus on what Solomon meant when he used the word. For Solomon, a vision was a clearly defined dream, idea, goal, or objective and a plan detailing the specific steps that must be taken to achieve it.

Important Definition

Solomon's vision: **A clearly defined dream, idea, goal, or objective and a plan detailing the specific steps that must be taken to achieve it.**

Henry Ford had a promising career as an engineer with the Edison Electric Company. While working at Edison he became enamored with the new craze of the wealthy—horseless carriages. Encouraged by Thomas Edison's example and words, Ford built a prototype automobile in his humble garage. He became obsessed with the potential that he saw, and quit his job and went to work for the newly founded Detroit Automobile Company. While every auto manufacturer in the world was turning out cars that were only affordable to the very rich, Ford acquired a vision to create an automobile that would be affordable to everyone. His superiors at the Detroit Automobile Company did not share his vision and insisted that he focus on designing cars for the proven market—the very rich. Forced to set his vision aside, Ford went through the dying process that Solomon described. He lost his motivation, his energy, his commitment, his creativity and productivity, and ultimately his job.

When he started his own company the following year, Ford set his focus on his original vision—to create an automobile that was so inexpensive that it could become a commodity every family in America could afford. At the time there were 250 auto manufacturers in the United States and many more throughout Europe. These manufacturers produced anywhere from 12 to 300 cars per year. Fueled by his vision, Henry Ford developed innovative manufacturing techniques that enabled him to mass-produce cars at a rate that dwarfed all other manufacturers. Within a few years, while most of his competitors were turning out less than 1,000 cars per year, he was producing 1,000 cars per day! By 1928, one out of every two cars in the world was a Ford.

Now, if you're still not convinced of the power of gaining a vision, let's look at the invention of the electric light bulb. Scientists and engineers with degrees in mathematics, physics, and chemistry had been trying to create an electric light bulb for more than 50 years. These men were backed by the finest scientific institutions in the world, and they still couldn't do it. Thomas Edison, on the other hand, had only completed three months of formal education. By his own admission, he was not adequately trained in any of the sciences or in mathematics, and did not have the genius IQ of a scientist. Yet he achieved his goal of creating a practical and affordable electric light bulb in less than three years. How did he do it? By using the exact same process that you are about to learn and by applying one additional strategy that you will learn in a future session. Amazingly, he used this same strategy to create more than 1,000 breakthrough products for which patents were issued. His inventions created whole industries, including sound recording and motion pictures. Equally important, he created each invention in record time. How? In every case he started the process with a clear and precise vision of what he wanted to achieve.

Here's one more important point. Of these men—Edison, Ford, Kroc, and Rockefeller—not one trusted his own memory. They all recorded their visions in writing. From the very beginning they would write out their vision on a page or two and describe how they wanted to accomplish that vision, including the specific steps they would have to take. They also attached target dates to each task or step they wanted to accomplish.

Writing Out Your Visions—Is It Really That Important?

If history's greatest superachievers found it necessary to define and map out their dreams in writing, what makes you or I think we can do it without putting this information in writing? Think back to the Hawaiian vacation offer we talked about earlier. How important was it that you write down the address and all of the directions to find the estate in order to win the free vacation? It wasn't just somewhat important, it was critical! Had you simply tried to remember the address, the directions, and the six-digit gate code, there is no chance that you would have succeeded in finding the estate and getting through the gate in the limited amount of time you were given. And then there was the three-week driving vacation. You would never start a cross-country trip without first determining your desired destination and consulting a clearly defined road map. How much more important is your life? How much more important are your marriage and the futures of your children? How much more important are your career and business pursuits? Do you want to be just a meaningless statistic on a census bureau report, or do you want to have a life in which you and those you love are truly productive and fulfilled? Or do you want to be among the 97 percent of adults who start every year at nearly the same place they started the year before? They walk toward distant dreams, often going in circles until they finally give up on those dreams. Do you want to be like them, or would you rather climb into your Porsche Turbo Carrera and drive toward your dreams at 180 miles per hour with all of the destinations and maps downloaded into your GPS system? That's the difference mapping out your dreams can make in your life.

Vision Mapping—Your Porsche's GPS System

It doesn't matter how well equipped your Porsche may be or how much horsepower its engine can produce: Without a destination and a road map, it will never take you to a distant destination. You've got to define your destinations and create maps to get to each one, and we are going to take the first step in that process right now. I call this process *vision mapping.* It is one of the most powerful concepts that you're going to learn, and it will provide a foundation on which other master strategies will be built.

For the remainder of this section and for our next session you will need the second loose-leaf notebook we talked about at the end of the first session. We'll call it your vision mapping journal. If you prefer a preprinted journal with all of the necessary tab dividers and printed forms, you can order one from my assistant at (800) 246-1771 or from my Web site, www.stevenkscott.com. You can also achieve the same results with your own loose-leaf notebook and tab dividers. However, the preprinted journal keeps everything neater and allows you to map out your dreams more quickly and easily.

Important Definition

Vision mapping:

1. **Defining and describing your dream or vision in writing.**
2. **Converting that vision or dream into a set of specific goals.**
3. **Converting each goal into a set of specific steps.**
4. **Converting each complex step into a specific set of tasks.**
5. **Setting target completion dates for each task, step, and goal.**

Vision Mapping–The Preliminary Steps

Although the vision mapping process itself only involves five steps, there are several preliminary tasks you need to complete before you begin this process.

1. **Make a list of the most important areas of your life.** Everyone is different on this one. I've known some people who list as few as two important areas, and others who list as many as 12. My list is made up of seven important areas: my relationship with God; my relationship with my wife; my relationship with my children; the health, happiness, security, and fulfillment of my family; my health; my business pursuits; and my extracurricular activities.

Although I have seven important areas, you might have more, or you might have less. The number doesn't matter. What's important is that you simply create the list, long or short, of the most important areas of your life.

2. **Prioritize your list.** Once you visually see the list in front of you, go ahead and prioritize that list. But put the items in the order that truly reflects your heart and mind, rather than reflecting what you think they should be or what you think other people would want them to be. For example, maybe the spiritual area of your life is your number seven priority. Don't list it as number one because you want your wife and everybody else to know that you're a spiritual person; put it on the list where it truly belongs. Remember that this journal isn't for anybody else, it's just for you. You don't need to ever share its content with anyone. It's your private road map and nobody else's. So it's critical to be honest in each of these areas.

3. **With tab dividers, create sections in your notebook for each important area.** The first page of each section should be titled "Dream Index," and will become the list of your specific dreams for that particular area. For example, here are my current lists from my business pursuits section and my extracurricular section.

Example: Business Pursuits and Projects—Dream Index

1. Write and produce a new Gary Smalley show.
2. Write and produce a new Total Gym show.
3. Write and produce a show for launching MAX.com.
4. Write and produce a show for launching Aqua Max.
5. Write and produce a show for launching Zero F.

Example: Extracurricular Activities—Dream Index

1. Complete the writing of *Mentored by A Millionaire.*
2. Create a book focusing on the wisdom and strategies articulated by Solomon in the biblical book of Proverbs.
3. Write a made-for-television comedy entitled *Dirty Tricks Incorporated,* with Aaron and Chuck Norris.
4. Write a science fiction novel entitled *Total Eclipse.*

Don't try to prioritize your list as you are creating it, because that can complicate your thought process. However, after you have created your list for any section, then prioritize those dreams by simply placing a letter next to each numbered dream. Your top priority will get the letter A, your second priority will get the letter B, and so on

I know that all of this seems simple, and you may wonder if it's really going to do that much for you. Remember, these are only the preliminary steps for creating a road map to each of your most important dreams and projects. In our next session we are going to go step by step through the process itself. I promise you that when you do this exercise and create your own vision mapping journal, you will become empowered to achieve more of your dreams in less time than you could ever imagine. Dreams that you might otherwise abandon or those that would normally take a lifetime to achieve might well be achieved within a matter of months. Remember, Edison achieved in less than 3 years that which hundreds of scientists had failed to achieve in 50 years!

We are not interested in just improving your productivity level by 20 or 30 percent or helping you to slightly improve your marriage or relationship with your children. We want to increase your success infinitely in every important area of your life. That is the goal of our mentoring sessions, and achieving breakthrough results will be the natural outcome of using this process and every strategy and skill that you will learn in our sessions.

I would like to close this session with a true definition of extraordinary success. In our first session we looked at all of the false standards of measurement that are out there—occupation, job title, income level, and so on. Those are not accurate measurements of success. They are measurements of progress, to be sure, but they are not measurements by which you will ultimately judge your life. Extraordinary success in any area of your life is measured by the degree and the quantity of meaningful and fulfilling accomplishments you are able to achieve in a limited amount of time that reflect your most prized personal values. If you become a billionaire, but your family life is terrible, your extraordinary success in business has not produced extraordinary happiness and fulfillment in your life or the lives of those you love most. If your children become rebellious and do all sorts of things that are destructive to their own lives and the lives of others, then what kind of extraordinary success have you really experienced?

By many of the world's false standards, Mother Teresa would be judged a total failure. She probably had a bank account that was less than those of your children. She didn't have a job title. She didn't have a fancy office to work out of. Yet, when she came to the end of her life, I can promise you that she was happy and fulfilled with what she had achieved.

So that's our focus. Let's always keep our eye on what true success is. If it doesn't reflect your own values, goals, and dreams, then there's nothing fulfilling about it.

Actions for Traction

WHERE THE RUBBER MEETS THE ROAD

The following exercises should be performed in the notebook you've titled "Vision Mapping Journal." Preprinted vision mapping journals are available in bookstores or by visiting my Web site (www.stevenkscott.com) or calling my office at (800) 246-1771.

1. Using your section dividers, create one section for each of the most important areas of your life. Number and place the sections in order of their importance.
2. Beginning with your first and most important section, make a list of your dreams for that area.
3. In each section, create and title one page for each dream you've listed in that section. This exercise is the first stage of the vision mapping process. You will be adding information to each of the pages as you complete the exercises at the end of each of the remaining sessions.

SESSION 8

A Vision without a Map Is Worthless!

Turning Visions into Reality through the Vision Mapping Process

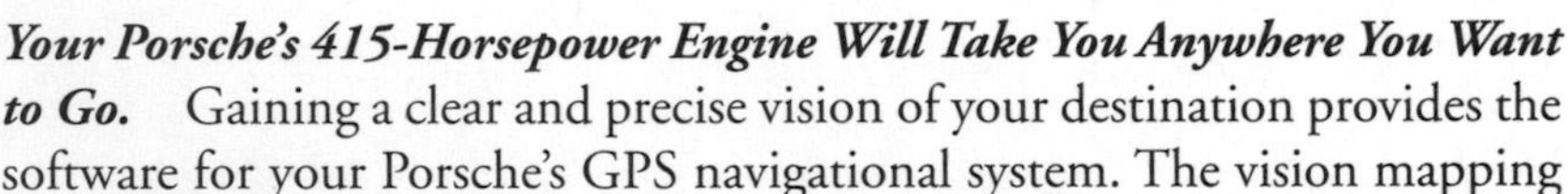

Your Porsche's 415-Horsepower Engine Will Take You Anywhere You Want to Go. Gaining a clear and precise vision of your destination provides the software for your Porsche's GPS navigational system. The vision mapping process is your Porsche's powerful engine that will provide all of the power you need to reach your most important dreams.

Ray Kroc gained a clear and precise vision for taking the McDonald brothers' tiny restaurant and putting it on street corners all over America. John D. Rockefeller gained a vision for a company that would dominate the oil refining and distribution business. Thomas Edison gained a vision for creating an electric light bulb and lighting every home, office, and factory in America.

Three men, three visions; and three out of three saw their visions transformed into reality. Every year, millions of adults gain a vision for something they really want, either personally or professionally. And yet, less than 1 percent of those people actually see their visions transformed into reality. What's the difference between these three men (a milkshake machine salesman, a 10 cent an hour bookkeeper, and a first-grade dropout) and 99 percent of America's adult population?

Imagine for a moment that you had a vision of something you really wanted, and it was located at a destination 3,000 miles away from your home. Imagine that there was a nice straight, wide-open freeway to that destination, with no speed limits. If the only way you could achieve your dream was to walk to it, chances are you wouldn't even try. Walking eight hours a day, seven days a week, it would take at least six months of walking to arrive at your destination.

If, on the other hand, you were allowed to use your new Porsche Turbo, your 415-horsepower engine would enable you to average 160 miles per hour. You could reach your destination in less than a day. While most adults are relegated to walking to their dreams, an elite few drive to them. The walkers rarely get more than a few miles toward their personal and professional dreams before they either replace them with easily attainable dreams or give up dreaming altogether. On the other hand, those with 415 horsepower at their disposal not only start the journey to their distant dreams, they complete it with plenty of time left over to pursue more dreams. The vision mapping process is the engine that supplies all of the power you need to drive to each of your dreams in an acceptable amount of time.

Master Strategy 8—Using the Vision Mapping Process of Setting and Achieving Goals

For nearly 30 years people have been bringing their products and ideas to my partners and me with the hope that we would use our marketing expertise to launch their products in our television marketing campaigns. Jane Fonda came to us with her idea for a nonmotorized treadmill. Cher and Christie Brinkley wanted to us to develop and market skin care and hair care products. Richard Simmons wanted us to work with him to create and market a weight loss program and a series of workout dance videos. And these are just a few of the celebrities who have approached us. There have also been hundreds of others whose names you wouldn't know. They all had visions of what they wanted to achieve. Some of those visions were vague, and some were more clear and precise. But merely having a vision was not enough.

One makeup artist had turned her vision into a product, but in eight years had only sold a few cases. Richard Simmons' weight loss plan consisted of no more than a one-page typewritten instruction sheet and a plastic bag with a few pieces of cut-up construction paper inside. A friend of mine was a Baptist minister who for 10 years had wanted to write a book on marriage to help marriages all over America, but had done nothing about it.

They all had visions, but they had only been walking in circles (many for years) with no power to actually reach those distant dreams and turn them into reality. As I met each one of them and listened to their visions, I would ask a number of questions. Their answers would give me all of the information I needed to go back to my hotel room and use the vision mapping process. In each case this process became the 415-horsepower engine that provided the power for transporting each of the people to their most cherished dreams. The vision mapping process transformed the makeup artist's one product into a product line of 160 products and sales of $300 million. It turned Richard Simmons' cut-up pieces of construction paper into his Deal-A-Meal weight loss program and his *Sweatin' to the Oldies* videos, a business that generated hundreds of millions in sales. This process turned the Baptist minister into one of the world's best-selling authors on relationships. His 15 best-selling books and 18 best-selling videos have been purchased by millions of people. Millions of marriages around the world have been saved and revitalized because of his work. And these are just a few of the dozens of cases in which I have used the vision mapping process to empower people to achieve their "impossible dreams."

Last year a neighbor came to me with a vision for providing a truly family-safe Internet service for families all over the world who are concerned about protecting their children from pornographers and other predators who so effectively use the Internet to entrap young people. I loved his vision, but he had no map. Using the vision mapping process, we have now created what I believe will be the most welcomed Internet service ever offered to concerned parents. My friend and partner Chuck Norris, and Patricia Heaton, the costar of *Everybody Loves Raymond,* will be the international spokespeople for this new service called MAX.com.

The Triple-Barreled Power of the Vision Mapping Process

The vision mapping process will empower you to achieve three powerful benefits in your life that nothing else will. First, it will enable you to transform vague, blurry, or abstract dreams into perfectly clear, well-defined visions. Second, it will make your impossible dreams possible and your possible dreams probable. Without this process, most of your dreams would remain only dreams. Third, this process will enable you to expand your dreams and achieve them much more quickly than you would have been able to without vision mapping.

In our last session you completed the two preliminary steps for vision mapping by defining the most important areas of your life and then listing and prioritizing your current dreams for each of those areas. These two preliminary steps give you the general location of your dreams, the distance to them, and how important it is for you to achieve each particular dream. Don't worry about how many or how few dreams you have currently defined in each area. Whether you have defined a single dream or 20, it doesn't matter. As you move through the months and years ahead, some of your dreams that aren't a high priority will fall by the wayside. You won't even be interested in pursuing them. Other dreams that you have not yet envisioned will come into view and ultimately gain a high priority. Your vision mapping journal is a fluid lifetime book. It's going to be with you the rest of your life, and as your dreams change you are simply going to redefine those dreams in writing and put them into the right priority.

Step One–Convert Dreams into Specific Goals

The first step of the vision mapping process is to convert a dream into specific goals. If you have one of our preprinted vision mapping journals, you can turn to the tabbed section entitled "Goals," and you'll find pages that are titled "Dreams to Goals." If you do not have one of our journals, you can create your own page (following this template.) Create one of these pages for each one of your dreams.

To help illustrate each step of this process, I am going to walk you through two of my personal vision maps step by step. The first example will be my third dream from my business pursuits and projects, "Write and produce a show for launching MAX.com." The second example will be taken from my extracurricular activities. It is the second dream I listed in that area, "Create a book focusing on the wisdom and strategies articulated by Solomon in the biblical book of Proverbs."

Example 1: Dream—Write and Produce a Show for Launching MAX.com

Specific Goals that Must Be Accomplished

1. Contract celebrity endorsers.
2. Write show.
3. Determine shooting locations and sets.
4. Schedule production dates.
5. Shoot principal photography.
6. Shoot second-unit photography.
7. Offline edit.
8. Online edit.

Dreams to Goals

Dream #:__________ Dream:____________________________

Goals

1. ____________________________

2. ____________________________

3. ____________________________

4. ____________________________

5. ____________________________

6. ____________________________

7. ____________________________

8. ____________________________

9. ____________________________

10. ____________________________

11. ____________________________

12. ____________________________

13. ____________________________

14. ____________________________

15. ____________________________

From *Vision Mapping Journal,* © Steve Scott 2003.

Dreams to Goals, continued

Shooting For The Moon Revision/Revised Goal (when applicable):____________________________

My Key Strengths:____________________________

My Key Weakness:____________________________

Outside Resources Needed to be Recruited:____________________________

Current or Potential Obstacles or Roadblocks:____________________________

Creative Alternatives or Outside Resources to Overcome Roadblocks:____________________________

Partners or Mentors Needed: ____________________________

In this first step, we take the dream and break it down into the general goals that must be accomplished to achieve that dream. As you can see from this example, there are only eight goals that need to be accomplished anytime I write and produce a show. However, achieving each of those goals requires the completion of a number of specific steps. The second example focuses on my dream of writing a book about the strategies I have used over the years from the biblical book of Proverbs. As you can see in that example, there are only five goals that I need to accomplish to achieve that dream. From these examples you can see that this first step of the vision mapping process is simply a matter of converting your dream into a group of general goals that need to be accomplished to fulfill that dream.

Example 2: Dream—Create a Book Focusing on the Wisdom and Strategies Articulated by "The Richest Man Who Ever Lived," from the Biblical Book of Proverbs

---

Specific Goals that Must Be Accomplished

1. Write a treatment describing the scope of the book and summarizing each chapter.
2. Circulate treatment to publishers.
3. Negotiate distribution deal.
4. Write first draft of book.
5. Edit book and complete final draft.

Step 2–Convert Goals into Specific Steps

The second step of the vision mapping process is to convert each goal into the specific steps that need to be taken to achieve that goal. If you have one of our preprinted vision mapping journals, you can turn to the tabbed section entitled "Steps," and you'll find pages that are titled "Goals to Steps." If you do not have one of our journals, you can create your own page (using the template on the following pages.) Create one of these pages for each one of your goals.

The second goal for my dream in the first example is to write the show. I've written more than 800 television commercials and about 50 infomercials, and as you can see, writing a show involves more than just sitting down with my laptop and typing out a script. I broke this specific goal into 14 steps.

Goals to Steps

Dream #:________ Dream:________________

Goal #:________ Goal:________________

Steps	Target Date
1.	
2.	
3.	
4.	
5.	
6.	
7.	
8.	
9.	
10.	
11.	
12.	
13.	
14.	
15.	

From *Vision Mapping Journal,* © Steve Scott 2003.

Goals to Steps, continued

Shooting For The Moon Revision/Revised Goal (when applicable):________________

My Key Strengths:________________

My Key Weaknesses:________________

Outside Resources Needed to be Recruited:________________

Current or Potential Obstacles or Roadblocks:________________

Creative Alternatives or Outside Resources to Overcome Roadblocks:________________

Partners or Mentors Needed:________________

Example 1: Dream—Write and Produce a Show for Launching MAX.com

Goal 2—Write Show

Specific Steps that Must Be Taken

1. Compile background information on dangers of the Internet.
2. Compile information on parental controls offered by the major Internet service providers including AOL, MSN, Earthlink, and Juno.
3. Identify weaknesses and failings of parental controls of the major Internet service providers including AOL, MSN, Earthlink, and Juno.
3. Create and prioritize list of benefits and strengths of MAX.com.
4. Differentiate and contrast MAX.com's strengths with weaknesses of AOL, MSN, Earthlink, and Juno.
5. List objections and excuses consumers might have to subscribing to MAX.com.
6. List answers to each objection and excuse.
7. Create outline for Show.
8. Create outline for interior commercials.
9. Write draft of script.
10. Read through draft with Chuck Norris.
11. Read through draft with Patricia Heaton.
12. Rewrite final draft.
13. Read through final draft with Chuck Norris.
14. Read through final draft with Patricia Heaton.

In the second example, the first goal of creating a book on the wisdom and strategies of Proverbs is to write a treatment that my literary agent can circulate to publishers. Normally my treatments are only 30 to 40 pages long. But, as you can see, achieving this simple goal requires taking seven steps. Completing the first two steps required several hundred hours of research, while completing the sixth and seventh steps was much easier, requiring only about 40 hours of work.

Example 2: Dream—Create a Book Focusing on the Wisdom and Strategies articulated by "The Richest Man Who Ever Lived," from the Biblical Book of Proverbs

Goal 1—Write a Treatment Describing the Scope of the Book and Summarizing Each Chapter

Specific Steps that Must Be Taken

1. Organize the teachings in the book of Proverbs into specific categories based on the strategies, skills, and techniques that they teach.
2. Organize categories according to their practical application for personal and professional pursuits.
3. Determine which categories to include in book.
4. Organize categories into chapters.
5. Outline each chapter.
6. Write a one- to two-page sample and summary of each chapter.
7. Write a three- to seven-page executive summary.

As you can see from these examples, vision mapping is a fairly simple process once you decide to simply allocate the time to do it. If you are thinking that this is good for business pursuits but not necessarily relevant for the personal side of life, you are wrong. It's just as important and effective in personal areas as well. For example, if one of your dreams is a more fulfilling relationship with your spouse, here's how this process could be applied to that dream.

Example 3 (Hypothetical): Dream—A More Fulfilling Relationship with My Spouse

Goals

1. Do whatever I am able to provide my spouse with a relationship in which his or her most important needs (physical, emotional, spiritual, financial, etc.) and desired dreams are fulfilled.
2. Have my spouse meet my most important needs and dreams for our relationship.

Next, you would convert these goals into specific steps.

Goal 1—Do Whatever I Am Able to Provide My Spouse with a Relationship in Which His or Her Most Important Needs (Physical, Emotional, Spiritual, Financial, etc.) and Desired Dreams Are Fulfilled

Steps

1. Discover from my spouse and from other experts (counselors, authors, etc.) what are his or her most important needs and desired dreams.
2. Determine the best ways to meet each of those needs and fulfill those desired dreams.
3. Create a plan for meeting those needs on a regular basis and for timely fulfillment of those dreams.
4. Begin meeting those needs consistently and become proactive in pursing his or her dreams using the vision mapping process.

Goal 2—Have My Spouse Meet My Most Important Needs and Dreams for Our Relationship

---

Steps

1. Clearly define in writing my most important needs and dreams for our relationship.
2. Use the presentation worksheet to create a presentation of my needs and dreams.
3. After discovering my spouse's needs and dreams and working out a plan with him or her for fulfilling those needs and pursuing his or her dreams, set aside a time to present my needs and dreams.
4. Begin actively working with my spouse to have my needs met and pursue my dreams for our relationship.

Step 3–Convert Complex Steps into Tasks

As you can see from our three examples, this process takes a little time and effort, but look at the end result. You've already determined the precise location of your dream. Next, by breaking your dream into specific goals, you've determined your intermediate destinations for your journey. Then, by breaking each goal into specific steps, you've outlined the major highways you need to take to move from where you are right now all the way to your final destination—the achievement of your dream. However, there is still one step left. If you live in a western suburb of Philadelphia, and your dream is located at the entrance to Disneyland in Anaheim, California, knowing the major highways between Philadelphia and Anaheim is

Steps to Tasks

Dream #:__________ Dream:____________________

Goal :__________ Step:____________________

Tasks | Target Date

1.______________________________

2.______________________________

3.______________________________

4.______________________________

5.______________________________

6.______________________________

7.______________________________

8.______________________________

9.______________________________

10.______________________________

11.______________________________

12.______________________________

13.______________________________

14.______________________________

15.______________________________

From *Vision Mapping Journal,* © Steve Scott 2003.

Steps to Tasks, continued

Shooting For The Moon Revision/Revised Goal (when applicable):______________________________

My Key Strengths:______________________________

My Key Weaknesses:______________________________

Outside Resources Needed to be Recruited:______________________________

Current or Potential Obstacles or Roadblocks:______________________________

Creative Alternatives or Outside Resources to Overcome Roadblocks:______________________________

Partners or Mentors Needed:______________________________

not enough to get you from your driveway to the entrance of Disneyland. You need to know all of the local streets to take you from your driveway to the highway; all the local streets you will need to take to transverse each city and town; and each local street that will take you from the Golden State Freeway right to the entrance of Disneyland. In the vision mapping process, this step is done by converting any complex step (a step that requires more than one task to be completed) into the specific tasks that need to be completed to take the step.

If you have one of our preprinted vision mapping journals you can turn to the tabbed section entitled "Task," and you'll find pages that are titled "Steps to Tasks." If you do not have one of our journals, you can create your own page (following the template.) Create one of these pages for each one of your complex steps.

In the first example, I convert my first step into eight tasks that will need to be completed for me to take that step. Now I know exactly what has to be done, and all that's left is to schedule the time for me or someone else that can be delegated to fulfill each stated task.

Example 1: Dream—Write and Produce a Show for Launching MAX.com

Goal 2—Write Show

Step 1—Compile Background Information on Dangers of the Internet

---

Specific Tasks that Must Be Completed

1. Look for articles on the Internet about usage studies by age group.
2. Look for articles on the Internet on sexual exploitation of children through the Internet.
3. Look through news media archived reports on Internet exploitation.
4. Research facts on adult Web site traffic; studies on adolescent traffic to adult Web sites, violence Web sites, gambling Web sites, and so on.
5. Research the teenage targeting of pornographic e-mails and chat rooms.
6. Research governmental studies on the subject.
7. Research media reports on the subject, including *Dateline, 20/20, 48 Hours, 60 Minutes, The John Walsh Show, USA Today,* Cox Newspapers, and AP.

8. Create a sheet of the facts and highlights of studies and reports researched.

In the second example, taking the first two steps for achieving the goal of writing a treatment, I organized the strategies contained in the book of Proverbs into 46 categories. To take the third step toward achieving this goal, I needed to convert that step into five tasks.

Example 2: Dream—Create a Book Focusing on the Wisdom and Strategies Articulated by "The Richest Man Who Ever Lived," from the Biblical Book of Proverbs

Goal 4—Write a Treatment Describing the Scope of the Book and Summarizing Each Chapter

Step 3—Determine Which Categories to Include in Book

Specific Tasks that Must Be Completed

1. Prioritize the categories according to those that I believe readers would be most interested in learning.
2. Show categories to my agents and ask them to prioritize them according to what they would like to read.
3. Show the categories to friends in various jobs and professions and ask them to prioritize them according to what they would like to read.
4. Show the categories to women (married, single, and divorced) who are homemakers and ask them to prioritize categories according to what they would like to read.
5. Study results of these four tasks, and make the final decision on which categories to include in the book.

Step 4–Set Target Completion Dates for Each Task, Step, and Goal

As you can see, once your steps have been converted into specific tasks, you now have a detailed map to help you travel from where you are right now to the final achievement of your goals and dreams. There's only one thing left to do—create a schedule. Most people would never start a trip without a planned schedule. To do so would usually mean that you would never be able to accomplish everything you want to achieve in the amount of time

> ***The Twelfth Law of Extraordinary Success***
>
> Dreams without clearly defined goals, and goals without clearly defined steps, will never be achieved expeditiously or efficiently, and will rarely be achieved at all.

you have available. The same is true with the pursuit of our dreams and projects. When you try to schedule the pursuit of your dreams, there are only two important rules. First, you start from the bottom up. That is, you assign target dates for tasks first, then for the completion of each step, then for the completion of each goal, and then for the final achievement of the dream. If you are working on a goal or project that has a preset deadline, then you start at the top with the completion date of the project or goal and then work down, assigning target dates to each goal, step, and task. The second rule is, be flexible and realistic. Don't assign target dates that are so hard to hit that you are likely to miss them. And if you see that you're falling hopelessly behind on a target date, either recruit help from others or move your target dates back.

Do I Really Have to Go into This Much Detail in Writing?

This is the one question I am always asked anytime I teach the vision mapping process. The answer is absolutely yes and absolutely no! If you have an important dream that you really want to achieve in a reasonable amount of time, the answer is yes. If you're pursuing a relatively unimportant or easily achieved goal, the answer is no. To put this much effort into the pursuit of an easy or unimportant project or dream would be a waste of time. However, for any dream or project that is important to you and is not easily achieved, using this process is critical.

Another question I'm asked is, "What happens if I don't convert a goal into steps?" If you don't break a goal into specific steps, you won't take the steps; and if you don't take the steps, you won't reach the goal. Achieving a goal without breaking it into steps is no more likely than reaching the top of your roof on a ladder without rungs. If you don't write down your goals, steps, and tasks, you will not consistently visualize them. And visualization, as we learned earlier, is critical to achievement. Are you thinking, "But I have achieved lots of goals without writing them down or breaking them into steps"? If so, I would agree that lots of people achieve simple and easy goals without writing them down or breaking them into steps. However, had you applied the vision mapping process to those same endeavors, you would have achieved much higher goals in much less time. You don't need a stepladder to climb to the top of a wall that is only two feet high. But try to climb over a 12-foot wall without a ladder! Remember that the whole reason you and I are engaged in our mentoring sessions is not to slightly improve your life, but rather to raise your achievements and fulfillment to extraordinary levels.

In our next session we're going to look at the turbocharger for your Porsche's engine. This source of power is the difference between the acceleration of a golf cart and your Porsche. In baseball lingo, it's the difference between a walk and a grand slam. When you apply this turbocharger to the vision mapping process, it will enable you to reach destinations you haven't yet dreamed of, and you will reach them faster than you've ever imagined. It's the strategic secret of the world's most successful people. Amazingly, this strategy is not only not taught in high school, college, or graduate school, the very opposite strategy is taught at all levels of education and by most motivational speakers and trainers. And yet, every superachiever I have ever known or studied has used this breakthrough strategy. You will too. But before we look at it, take a break and get started on the exercises in the "Actions for Traction" section.

Actions for Traction

WHERE THE RUBBER MEETS THE ROAD

1. If you haven't already done so, starting with the most important area of your life and your most important dream in that area, create a page entitled "Dreams to Goals." On that page, write down all of the specific goals you can think of that need to be accomplished to achieve that dream. After you have completed setting the goals for that dream, move on to the next dream in that area, and follow the same routine for each of your dreams in each important area. You can tackle one dream at a time, or start on as many as are truly important to you.
2. For each goal that you have stated, create a page entitled "Goal to Steps." On each "Goals to Steps" page, write down all of the steps that need to be taken to achieve that goal. Once again, start with your highest-priority dreams.
3. For each step that you've listed, create a page entitled "Step to Tasks." On each of these pages, write down the specific tasks that need to be accomplished to take that step. After you have listed all the tasks necessary to complete a particular step, assign a target completion date for each task.
4. Look through all of the tasks necessary to complete each step of each goal, and circle the ones that you cannot achieve on your own due to your lack of know-how, resources (time, talent, or money), adequate ability, or personality traits.
5. For each circled task, write down the type of person, company, or outside resource you need to recruit to accomplish that task. Later you'll learn the specific strategies and techniques you'll need to use to recruit those outside resources.

The Secret Strategy of the World's Most Successful People

Dreaming Bigger than You Can Possibly Achieve

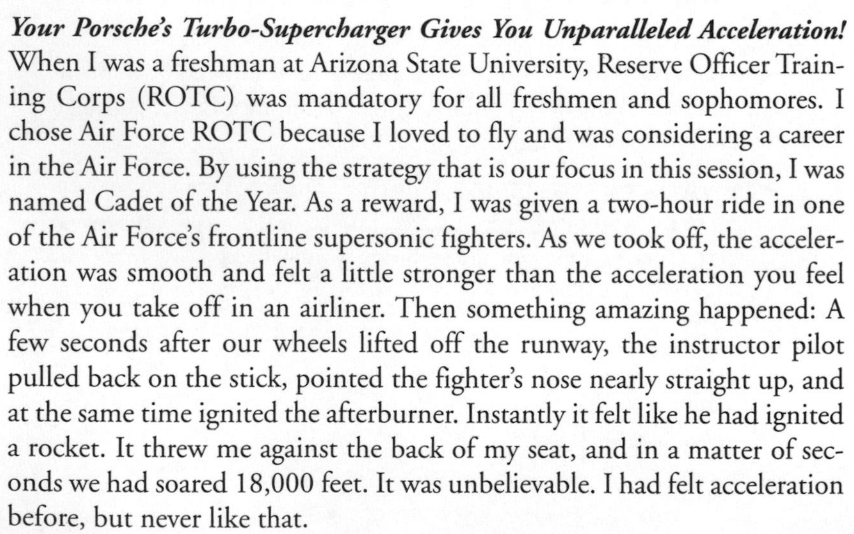

Your Porsche's Turbo-Supercharger Gives You Unparalleled Acceleration! When I was a freshman at Arizona State University, Reserve Officer Training Corps (ROTC) was mandatory for all freshmen and sophomores. I chose Air Force ROTC because I loved to fly and was considering a career in the Air Force. By using the strategy that is our focus in this session, I was named Cadet of the Year. As a reward, I was given a two-hour ride in one of the Air Force's frontline supersonic fighters. As we took off, the acceleration was smooth and felt a little stronger than the acceleration you feel when you take off in an airliner. Then something amazing happened: A few seconds after our wheels lifted off the runway, the instructor pilot pulled back on the stick, pointed the fighter's nose nearly straight up, and at the same time ignited the afterburner. Instantly it felt like he had ignited a rocket. It threw me against the back of my seat, and in a matter of seconds we had soared 18,000 feet. It was unbelievable. I had felt acceleration before, but never like that.

The Porsche in your garage has a turbo-supercharger that is so powerful it provides acceleration like that fighter's afterburner and can power you toward dreams so lofty that until now they have been far beyond your field of vision. Even though your Porsche can take you to any of your current dreams without this turbocharger, with its power you will set your sights on far greater dreams than you have ever imagined. More important, you will actually achieve these loftier dreams more quickly than you would have otherwise achieved much lesser dreams. That's what master strategy 9 is all about. It is the strategic secret of the world's most successful people. I'm not talking about the top 3 percent, but rather the top one-hundredth of 1 percent.

As I mentioned in our previous session, before Thomas Edison decided to attempt inventing a practical electric light bulb, far more intelligent scientists had spent more than 50 years trying to do the same thing. At the time Henry Ford started his own automobile company, there were already 250 other automakers in the United States, all with substantial head starts. By the time Bill Lear decided to attempt to build a practical small jet aircraft for corporate use, aerospace giant General Dynamics had already given up on the idea because they had determined that building a prototype would cost over $100 million. They had also determined that there was no significant market for expensive corporate jets anyway.

Now think for a moment about each of these examples. If more qualified scientists had been working on the invention of an electric light bulb for over 50 years without success, how long should it have taken someone with no formal education to invent one? Certainly no less than 50 years, and a far more reasonable answer would be more than 50 years.

When Henry Ford started his auto company, each of the other 250 American automakers were turning out 12 to 300 cars per year. What would have been a reasonable production goal for Ford to set? A reasonable goal would have been the hope of producing a lot more than the slowest manufacturer and a little less than the most productive manufacturer. Perhaps a goal of 150 cars per year would have been just right. If he wanted to be number one, Ford might have set a goal of 400 or even 500 cars a year. Certainly, 650 cars a year (more than double the most productive manufacturer) would have been an extraordinary goal, and 1,000 cars a year would have been outlandish. In fact, Ford's competitors would have labeled that kind of number an impossible dream. If you had been Henry Ford, what kind of goal do you think you might have set?

How about Bill Lear? If the world's best aeronautical engineers at General Dynamics had determined that it would cost $100 million to build a prototype of a small corporate jet, what kind of cost should Bill Lear have shot for? And since General Dynamics had determined that such corporate jets would be so costly that corporations would not be able to afford them and therefore there would be no market, what kind of market should Lear have set his sights on?

Master Strategy 9—Dreaming Bigger than You Can Possibly Achieve

Thankfully, none of these men merely set their sights on reasonable and achievable goals. Edison set his goal of inventing the light bulb in an impossible time period of three years or less, and did it in less. Ford set his goal at putting a car in every garage in America, and within a few years, instead of hitting the impossible dream of 1,000 cars per year, he was building 1,000 cars a day! Even though Bill Lear had invented the car radio and the autopilot, he didn't have $100 million to spend on a prototype of a corporate jet. He didn't even have $20 million. He set his sights on building a prototype for the impossible number of $10 million, and he did it for less!

One of the Greatest Falsehoods Ever Sold

One of the greatest falsehoods ever propagated by motivational speakers, writers, and educators is the crippling concept found at the heart of their teachings on the subject of goal setting. In a nutshell, these well-intentioned experts tell us that we should only set reasonable and timely achievable goals. They are afraid that if we set goals that are too lofty, we won't achieve them, which may cause us to give up on those goals and ultimately abandon the goal-setting process altogether. Their reasoning is correct when goal-setting programs fail to incorporate several critical elements, such as partnering, reprogramming, overcoming the roadblocks of lack of know-how and limited resources, and overcoming the fear of failure. However, when these elements are an integral part of goal setting, as they are in the vision mapping process, such fears are unwarranted. Setting goals that are reasonable and achievable will severely limit and ultimately cripple an individual's ability to achieve extraordinary results.

If your only hope is to experience a moderate to good improvement in an area of your life or in a particular endeavor, then setting reasonable and achievable goals will help you do just that. However, that is all you'll achieve. Edison, Ford, and Lear achieved their impossible dreams because they discovered the nuclear power of dreaming bigger than they could possibly achieve.

Recently, I was working on a project with the number one corporate trainer in the Franklin Covey organization. During the past 18 years, this man has trained managers and executives of every single company in the Fortune 500 in the areas of time management and personal productivity. As I began to explain this strategy, he was a little defensive at first. Then the light went on. Once he got it, he *really* got it. Excitedly, he said, "This changes everything . . . *everything!*" He asked, "Do you realize that this runs completely contrary to what we teach and to what every motivational speaker that I've ever heard teaches? I have never heard anyone say what you are telling me now."

On the surface, the vision mapping process appears to be similar to other goal-setting programs in that it is a process in which dreams are converted into definable goals, which are converted into specific steps, which in turn are converted into detailed, achievable tasks. But the surface is where all similarity to other goal programs ends. Beneath its surface, at its very core beats a completely different heart—one that empowers its user to achieve levels of success he or she hasn't even conceived of. It literally changes everything! It will raise the focus of your vision from the road directly in front of you to the stars in the heavens. It changes your dreams from the attainable to the impossible. It raises the bar of each of your goals and creates steps that seem impossible to take. I call this process *shooting for the moon,* and it embodies our ninth master strategy: dreaming bigger than you can possibly achieve.

Shooting for the Moon—the Secret Strategy of the World's Most Successful People

Shooting for the moon is the central strategy that changed everything for me. It enabled me to increase my annual income, not by 30 or 40 percent, but by 70,000 percent! It enabled me to write, direct, and produce television shows that have sold billions of dollars of products, even though I had no previous experience or training in writing, directing, or producing television shows. But this process not only turned everything around for me, as I began to look at the lives of other people who had achieved their impossible dreams, it was this specific strategy that had successfully launched each one of them to the moon and the stars. When Steven Spielberg and I met up 18 years after we had graduated from high school, I discovered that he too had shot for the moon on every project he had ever taken on. Every single person

> ***The Thirteenth Law of Extraordinary Success***
>
> No one has ever achieved extraordinary success without shooting for the moon. Everyone who has ever achieved their "impossible dreams" has done so by shooting for the moon.

Side-by-Side Comparison

How People Use Goal Setting to Achieve What They Want from Life

Drifters	Pursuers	Achievers	Superachievers
Do not use a real goal-setting process. They simply do what comes naturally to try to achieve only what they think they are capable of achieving.	Set general goals occasionally but usually do not convert their goals into specific steps with clearly defined tasks.	Use conventional goal-setting process. They set goals that are reasonable and achievable in a timely manner. They achieve their moderate goals.	Combine the vision mapping process with shooting for the moon to set extraordinary and impossible goals, and achieve them.

who has ever achieved extraordinary outcomes or their impossible dreams has done so by using this strategy.

As powerful as this strategy is, it is unused by 99.99 percent of the adult population. Why? First, it is not taught in colleges, graduate schools, motivational courses, or success seminars. Second, its very opposite is taught at every educational and professional level. Third, without utilizing the other 14 strategies we are focusing on in our sessions, shooting for the moon is an impotent strategy, no more powerful than wishful thinking or daydreaming. But, when used in conjunction with the other 14 strategies, its power is both life altering and history making.

The Critical Difference between Ray Kroc and the McDonald Brothers

The McDonald brothers were happy with their $100,000 a year income from their hamburger stand and decided to give franchising a try. After selling two franchises, one in Phoenix and one in Sacramento, they determined that there wasn't enough money in franchising to make it worth their while. After his first glimpse of their tiny operation, Ray Kroc gained a true vision for what that operation could become. As he began to tell the McDonalds his dream, they shrank back and said, "We tried franchising, and it's really not that big of a deal. It doesn't make that much money. In fact, our franchisees are struggling." Even though he was 52 years old at the time, Kroc dared to dream bigger. He had an impossible dream and decided to shoot for the moon. Later, the McDonald brothers were happy to sell their interest to him for less than $3 million. They thought that they were making a killing. Today, years after Ray Kroc dreamed the impossible and shot for the moon, their share, had they kept it, would be worth billions instead of millions.

Important Definition

Shooting for the moon: **The process of defining dreams and setting goals that are extraordinary to impossible for a person to achieve on his or her own. This process is powerless without utilizing the other master strategies, but it is fully empowered when used in conjunction with the other master strategies.**

How Does Shooting for the Moon Work?

Shooting for the moon starts at the beginning of the vision mapping process. Instead of defining dreams and setting goals that are reasonably achievable, you envision dreams and set goals that are seemingly impossible for you as a lone individual to achieve, but that reflect what you would want in that situation if you could achieve any outcome, regardless of how possible or impossible it may seem. For example, when I start a new project, the first thing I have to do is create a list of potential celebrity spokespeople who would be best suited for that project. An approach that would be consistent with a normal goal-setting program would be to list only those celebrities who I knew I had a good chance of recruiting, and who would be affordable within the production budget that had been allocated. If I followed that approach on any project, the result would be a very short list of mediocre celebrities. Instead, I shoot for the moon. I think, "If I could have anyone in the whole world presenting this product, who would it be?" That number one person becomes the top person on my list, regardless of how remote the chance may be of signing him or her or being able to afford his or her monetary demands. Then I think, "If I can't get that person, who would be my second choice?" That person becomes the next person on my list. I keep building the list until I finally get down to people that I know I can afford and I know I can recruit. These are at the bottom of my list.

When I begin my recruiting effort, I start at the top and don't go down to the next person on the list until I've been turned down by the one at the top. In 27 years of recruiting over 90 celebrity endorsers for my various projects, I haven't had to go down to the lower part of the list with all of the affordable and attainable names that I knew I could get, even once! On the other hand, many times I have recruited the person at the very top of the list even though there was no possible way that I could afford him or her or should have been able to recruit him or her. That's how I got Cher for my hair care products; Michael Landon, John Ritter, and Hugh Downs for my educational products; and Chuck Norris, Christie Brinkley, and Jane Fonda for my fitness products. Using the shooting for the moon process, I was even able to recruit President Reagan, Charlton Heston, and Tom Selleck to appear in my commercial for my favorite political magazine. Not only was this the first time a sitting president appeared in a television commercial, it was also the first time that Charlton Heston appeared in a television commercial, and the one and only commercial that Tom Selleck appeared in since gaining his fame. Even more impressive, they all appeared in the commercial for free! Had I used the conventional goal-setting approach taught by educators and motivators, in my 27 years of television marketing I would have never recruited a single major celebrity, and instead of selling billions of dollars worth of our products and services, I would not have sold even a hundred dollars worth.

To be accurate, I must admit that using a conventional goal-setting approach of setting achievable, reachable goals will significantly improve your job performance. It could double your income in a fairly short amount of time. It could improve your marriage and friendships. However, if you use the shooting for the moon approach of dreaming bigger than you can possibly achieve, the changes and improvements will be far greater than significant: They'll be staggering. Instead of improving your relationships, you will revitalize and even revolutionize them. Instead of doubling your income, you can launch it to levels you've never imagined. When I started on my tenth job after college, my salary was $10,000 a year. If I had used the conventional approach to goal setting, I might have doubled my income to $20,000 within a year or two. But because I began to shoot for the moon, starting with my very first project, instead of merely doubling my income, within a year I had increased it by 15 times to $150,000 a year. Within a few years I was making over $1 million a year, then over $2 million, and then over $7 million. From the time I started using the shooting for the moon approach, my income has increased not by a few hundred percent, but by more than 70,000 percent! This increase wasn't achieved by applying the shooting for the moon approach to a goal of increasing my income, but rather by applying it to each of my projects. Using this approach, my partners and I were able to start brand-new companies from scratch and build them into companies generating sales of more than $100 million each. While most of these companies ultimately achieved sales between $100 million and $200 million, one achieved sales of $300 million and another will soon pass the billion-dollar mark.

In Which Areas of Life and on What Kind of Projects Should This Approach Be Applied?

The shooting for the moon approach can be applied to any dream, goal, or project in your life, whether personal or professional. It should be applied to any dream, goal, project, or endeavor that you consider important. When my oldest daughter was in junior high, she dreamed of her softball team becoming the league champions even though the previous year they had compiled the worst record in league history (all losses and no wins). Using this approach and the vision mapping process, her softball team was miraculously transformed from the worst team in league history to the league champions with all wins and no losses!

As a freshman at Arizona State University in 1966, I signed up for Air Force ROTC. At that time, ROTC was mandatory for all male freshmen and sophomores. Because the corps had 40 platoons and only 39 officers qualified to command those platoons, I was given the opportunity to command the fortieth platoon. It was made up primarily of disgruntled misfits, most of whom were close to failing the course. The other 39 platoons were composed of students with much better attitudes and grades, and were commanded by third-year officers.

At first my goal was simply to avoid total failure with this group of 30 freshmen and sophomore cadets. Then I decided to shoot for the moon. I set my sights on winning the annual drill competition. In the history of Air Force ROTC, no underclassman had ever been given command of a platoon, much less won this competition. I created a vision map and began to implement the steps and tasks that were necessary to achieve that goal. Instead of treating my platoon members in the normal condescending fashion, I decided to treat them as partners. I was able to implant my vision in their minds, and the result was mind boggling. When the competition rolled around, out of the 40 platoons, we scored high enough to compete in the finals with the other top 3 platoons. Halfway through this final competition I was ordered to halt my platoon's performance, while the other three were allowed to continue. I was later told that our performance was so extraordinary that the judges felt that letting us continue would be too humiliating to the other three platoons and their commanders. Out of a possible 300 points, we received a record-shattering 287. The second-place platoon had been awarded only 167 points. As a result of our performance,

I was named Cadet of the Year and was offered a full three-year Air Force flight scholarship and given the ride of a lifetime in a supersonic F-100 fighter. All of this because I had decided to shoot for the moon.

How Do You Apply the Shooting for the Moon Approach to Achieving Your Dreams and Goals?

Seeing the results of using this process in ROTC, I began applying it to other projects as well, with the same kind of success. Unfortunately, I didn't start applying it to my business projects until I partnered with my mentor on my tenth job. Since using it on our very first project and seeing the resulting success, I have applied it to every business project I have ever pursued. That doesn't mean I've hit the moon on every project; I haven't. But, when you shoot for the moon, even if you miss, you're still high. As I studied the lives and biographies of others who had achieved their impossible dreams, every one had used this method. So the question becomes, how can you apply this approach to the most important dreams, goals, and projects in your life?

It Starts with a Choice. Anytime we approach any endeavor that requires an effort, we have to make a choice: In baseball lingo, do we just want to avoid a strikeout and get on base ("a walk's as good as a hit"), do we want to get a hit, or do we want to swing for the fence? When I was first starting to play little league baseball, I remember my coach yelling to me as I walked toward the batter's box, "Remember, Scotty, a walk's as good as a hit." He was hoping that I would be more concerned about just getting on base rather than getting a hit. Unfortunately, his perception that a walk was as good as a hit was a false perception. Yes, a walk would get me to first base, but that's all it would do. A hit, on the other hand, would get me to first base and maybe farther. But that's not all a hit would do. It would start the adrenaline flowing in my teammates and in me. It would encourage me to take stronger and better swings the next time I came up to bat. It would signal my teammates that the pitcher wasn't nearly as fast or scary as they thought he was. As it turned out, there were a lot of benefits that a hit produced that a walk did not. Even though they both get you to first base, a hit gets you there feeling a lot better about yourself and at the same time expands your horizons and raises your chances of getting on base more often than a walk does. So, all things considered, a walk isn't even close to being as good as hit. Equally true, a base hit's not as good as a double, and nothing is as good as a home run.

Now as basic as this is, the sad truth is that most people come up to the plate in life just trying to get on base. They truly believe that a walk is as good as a hit. They just don't want to strike out. If they set any goals at all, they only set ones that are so easily achieved that there is almost no chance of failing.

Babe Ruth was inarguably one of the greatest baseball players who ever lived. While most baseball fans know that he set records for the most home runs hit in one season and the most home runs hit in a career, they may not know that these were just two of the many records he set. For example, even though he only pitched in two World Series, he established a phenomenal pitching record in the 1918 World Series that stood for 43 years, outlasting his home run records. And yet for generations the name Babe Ruth, has been synonymous with one thing: home runs—lots and lots of home runs! When the Babe was first sold to the New York Yankees, the Yankees didn't even have their own baseball field. They played at the Polo Grounds, the home of the New York Giants. Even so, the first year Ruth played for the Yanks, over 1 million people showed up to see the "Sultan of Swat." They didn't turn out in droves just to see him hit singles or doubles; they came to watch him hit home runs. Prior to his entry into baseball, home runs were a fairly rare occurrence. The American League record for the most home runs hit in a single season was 16. The Babe broke that record in 1919, while he was still a pitcher for the Red Sox, by hitting 29. That year he pitched 20 games, winning 13. The next year, as a Yankee, was the first year he didn't pitch. That year he hit 54 home runs, a feat that was beyond anyone's wildest imagination. The next year he hit 59, and the Yankees could then afford their own stadium.

Babe Ruth did one thing that separated him from any other player of his day. Every single time he came to the plate, he made a choice. He wasn't just going to meet the ball. He wasn't just going to try to get on base. Every single trip to the plate he was going to do one thing. He was going to swing for the fence. He wanted to hit that ball so hard that from the moment of its contact with the bat, he and everyone else in the stadium would know that the ball was going to sail over the fence. He loved rounding third base to the cheers of a roaring crowd. Every time he hit a home run, the crowd cheered, his teammates all jumped up and excitedly met him as he came across the plate, and he felt great. His home runs motivated his team to play better than any team in baseball. No matter how hard they were trying, after he hit a home run they tried even harder. That's what home runs do: They not only get us all the way around the bases, they motivate everyone around us to do better than they thought they could.

So the shooting for the moon approach on any given project begins with the choice to swing for the fences rather than just trying to get to first base. In a marriage, it means choosing to swing for a great relationship rather than settling for an acceptable one. It means choosing to meet your spouse's greatest emotional, physical, and mental needs, even if that means learning a lot more than you currently know. At work, it means choosing to set and achieve goals that are way beyond your expectations and the expectations of those above you. In any important area of your life, for any important dream, goal, project, or endeavor, it means raising your sights way beyond the limits of your own capabilities or personal resources. But even though this approach starts with a choice, that's only the first step. We not only want to shoot for the moon, we want to hit it! The shooting for the moon approach is a five-step process. In our baseball analogy, it's to no avail to simply swing for the fences if you haven't developed the skill and employed the techniques to actually hit the ball in the process.

After making the choice to shoot for the moon, the second step is to return to each vision map that you have created for achieving any important dream, goal, or project, and revise upward those stated dreams, goals, or projects to reflect that choice.

The third step is to list the roadblocks or obstacles that could prevent you from hitting the moon on each of your revised dreams, goals, or projects. These may be obstacles to achieving a dream or goal or even completing a single step or task needed to achieve a goal. Such obstacles will include your lack of resources (time, talent, or money) and your lack of know-how. You already know from our previous sessions that the key to overcoming these obstacles is identifying, recruiting, and effectively utilizing the right kinds of partners, counselors, advisors, mentors, experts, financiers, and so on. There are two more obstacles that we haven't yet addressed, but we will in Sessions 11 and 12. These are your conscious and subconscious fear of failure and your conscious and subconscious avoidance of criticism. Unless these are effectively dealt with, they too will cause you to set goals that are much lower than those you should be setting.

After you have listed the potential obstacles that could prevent you from hitting the moon in a given dream, goal, or project, the fourth step is to identify the type of outside resources you will need to recruit to overcome each obstacle. After you have identified the type of resource needed, you then need to follow the steps given earlier for identifying and recruiting the specific partners you will need. The fifth step is to actually recruit the needed outside resources and to begin to complete the tasks and steps that you have clearly defined in your vision map.

Summary of Steps for Shooting for the Moon

1. **Make the choice to shoot for the moon in a specific dream, goal, project, or endeavor.**
2. **List the obstacles or roadblocks that may prevent you from hitting the moon on that specific dream, goal, or project or that might keep you from completing specific steps or tasks that are necessary to complete to achieve a goal.**
3. **Identify the types of partners or outside resources you will need to recruit to overcome any of the obstacles you have listed.**
4. **Identify the specific individuals or resources you will try to recruit.**
5. **Recruit the partners or resources needed and begin to complete the steps and tasks you have listed on your vision map.**

In 1975, Paul Allen read about a small company in New Mexico called MITS that had created a $400 microcomputer for hobbyists and electronics enthusiasts called the Altair 8800. It had no keyboard or screen and had to be patched into a teletype machine to serve any practical purpose whatsoever. Paul called his high school buddy, Bill Gates, who was attending Harvard at the time. He proposed that they work together to create an operating language for the Altair 8800. Even though they didn't have the processor itself, they decided to shoot for the moon and call the head engineer of MITS and tell him they had created an operating language for his microprocessor. He invited them to Albuquerque to demonstrate it. Now that they had his interest, they began an all-out effort to actually create the language they had promised. After working at a feverish pace for about eight weeks, they thought they had it done. Even though they didn't know if it would work, Allen flew to New Mexico and nervously met with the company's executives. To everyone's delight, the language worked and MITS agreed to purchase a license to use the language at a royalty rate of $30 per computer. Bill dropped out of Harvard and along with Paul moved to New Mexico to start a new company they called Micro-Soft. (They later dropped the hyphen and changed it to a single word, and moved to Seattle.)

But this was not the only time Bill and Paul shot for the moon. When IBM decided to enter the personal computer market in 1980, they knew they would need an operating system to run their PC. Instead of potentially spending a year or two developing an operating system on their own, this $30 billion giant decided to see if they could find an outside source that already had an operating system that could be customized to their machine. They had heard about the wonder boys in Seattle who had created languages for various microprocessors and summoned Gates and Allen to a meeting to discuss the possibilities. Even though Microsoft's annual sales had now grown to $4 million, their only products were operating languages. They had never attempted to create an operating system.

Shortly after the meeting had begun, Bill and Paul were asked if they had an operating system that could be customized to operate IBM's PC. They were told that the system would need to be operational within 90 days. Before Paul Allen could tell them that Microsoft didn't have an operating system, had never created an operating system, and couldn't possibly create one within 90 days, Bill decided to shoot for the moon. He answered, "Yes!" Even though Paul was shocked and dismayed by Bill's answer, he nodded. Bill signed an agreement to deliver the operating system prior to the 90-day deadline.

Had Gates been accustomed to only operating in the comfort zone of his company's expertise and capabilities and in the mode of only setting achievable, reachable goals, his answer to this pivotal question would have surely been, "No, we do not have an operating system, we're not in that business, and even if we were, creating one in 90 days would be impossible!" Microsoft's entire destiny would have been forever changed. It would have remained a small to medium-size company, ultimately achieving sales of $25 million to $50 million per year. But Bill didn't answer no. He shot for the moon and said yes, even though there was absolutely no possible way he could achieve that goal and fulfill his commitment. But saying yes wasn't the only way he shot for the moon. In return for committing to deliver an operating system within 90 days, Bill demanded that Microsoft would retain total ownership of the operating system, and that IBM would receive a non-exclusive license to use it. How could a tiny $4 million company expect the $30 billion giant to succumb to such an audacious demand? Once again, Gates was simply shooting for the moon. But Bill Gates not only shot for the moon, he hit it. Although IBM executives were taken back by the demand, they agreed to it because they surmised that IBM was venturing into the hardware business where they believed the big money was. Who cared if they left a few pennies on the table? As far as they were concerned, there was little money to be made in the relatively insignificant industry of software.

Bill not only hit the moon in gaining these concessions, he also hit the moon by actually delivering the operating system within the 90-day deadline. How? The exact same way you are going to hit the moon when you shoot for it. Bill, Paul, and their executive vice president Steve Ballmer identified and recruited an outside resource. A small nearby company, Seattle Computer Products, had created an operating system for a PC (called 86-DOS) that could possibly be tailored to operate IBM's PC. Allen purchased a license to use 86-DOS without letting the company know who he was going to use it with. Microsoft engineers then tailored this operating system to the IBM PC and delivered it within the 90-day deadline. Shortly before IBM introduced its PC to the world, Allen purchased all rights to 86-DOS from Seattle Computer Products for a paltry $50,000.

The fact that Gates had negotiated a nonexclusive license with IBM meant that the sales of his MS-DOS would not be limited to the PCs sold by IBM, but rather could also be licensed to every other maker of personal computers in the world. IBM had purchased a golden egg, but Gates owned the goose that would soon begin to lay millions of those golden eggs all over the world. Like every other superachiever, Gates didn't just shoot for the moon once or twice, but instead made shooting for the moon both a habit and a way of life.

Shooting for the Moon in Your Personal Life

Although you may now have a grasp of how to apply the shooting for the moon approach to your professional life, it's equally important to understand how it can be applied to the personal side of your life.

Years ago I used to counsel young couples in my home. One evening a woman I was counseling (we'll call her Jenny) told me, "My husband's just driving me crazy. I want to stay in the marriage, but I'll tell you, he's wearing me down. He criticizes everything I do. No matter what I do, it's never good enough. I just can't get him to stop criticizing me." I asked her, "If you could achieve anything you want with him, what would it be?" She answered, "I just want there to be less criticism." Now that's an achievable, reachable goal. Reduce the criticism. That's all she wanted out of her marriage.

I said, "That's a nice dream, but let's go for one a little better than that. How about if we say that he completely ends all criticism?" She instantly replied, "Well, that will never happen." I said, "Okay, so we're getting closer. So that's an impossible dream?" She answered, "Yes." I then said, "How about we go one step further. Not only will he not criticize you, but he will actually begin to praise you. He'll not only say encouraging words, he'll actually do things that are really encouraging to you." She said, "Tom?"

I answered, "Yes, Tom." She said, "Impossible!" I said, "Great, we're almost there. How about this: He will not only want to praise and encourage you, he'll want to become the best possible husband and fulfilling your deepest needs will become his number one priority in life." She said, "That will never happen." I said, "Great. Now we're shooting for the moon, and that will become your impossible dream."

In a matter of minutes we had taken her initial dream and revised it upward until she was truly shooting for the moon. The new dream was that her husband would make meeting her deepest emotional, spiritual, and physical needs his number one priority. She wanted a spiritual husband and at the time he was an atheist. How impossible was that! How would she ever have her husband meet her spiritual needs when he didn't even believe in God? We took an achievable, reachable dream and turned it into a truly impossible dream. With this dream, Jenny was not only swinging for the fence, she was swinging for the parking lot.

Six months later, she and her husband were attending a meeting in my home. With tears in her eyes she said, "I feel like I'm Cinderella. I am the happiest married woman I've ever known. I am so grateful for Tom." Tom said, "I feel like I am the luckiest guy in the world to be married to Jenny. She is everything I've ever wanted in a wife and I can't believe how long she had to put up with all of the stuff I've put her through." Today, nearly 30 years later, they are still one of the happiest married couples I've ever known.

A Teacher in One of Texas's Poorest Towns Sees the Power of Shooting for the Moon

Last week I read another amazing story that demonstrates the incredible power of shooting for the moon. Elsa, Texas, is one of the poorest communities in America. In this town only 15 miles from the Mexican border, 75 percent of the households earn less than $10,000 per year. Many of the town's high school students live in shacks with no electricity or running water. After earning his master's degree in 1991, Frank Guajardo, the son of a Mexican field hand in Elsa, returned to his hometown to teach English in the high school. Frank challenged some of his honors students to apply for admission to Ivy League colleges. To help implant his vision, he raised $12,000 to take nine students in borrowed vans on a tour of a number of the top Ivy League schools. His vision found fertile ground, and that fall five of the nine were accepted into America's most elite colleges. Guajardo's vision continued to grow, and to date 51 of his high school's graduates have made it into our nation's top universities. Last year 65 percent of the seniors of Edcouch-Elsa High School continued their education at the college level. By using our master strategy of effective partnering, Guarjardo has shot for the moon and hit it in other ways as well. In 1997, he created the school's year-round Llano Grande Center for Research and Development, where students are better prepared to enter college and succeed. He's even raised the center's annual funding of $500,000 per year.

Does this process work? Absolutely yes! But it only works when it's used in conjunction with the other master strategies we've talked about and those we will talk about in our remaining sessions. I've seen it work in nearly every venue imaginable. I've even seen it work in the area of weight loss. I've seen men and women who were 100 to 200 pounds overweight lose all of their excess weight and regain bodies they thought were forever lost—all because they used the vision mapping process and the shooting for the moon approach.

As I mentioned earlier, the single most important strategy for actually hitting the moon when we shoot for it is the strategy of effective partnering. The second most important strategy for hitting the moon is the one we will focus on in our next session. It is the strategy that enabled Thomas Edison to create more breakthrough inventions than any other human being in history. It will provide tremendous power to your swing, and it will result in a much higher percentage of hits and home runs.

Actions for Traction

WHERE THE RUBBER MEETS THE ROAD

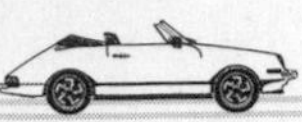

Summary of Steps for Shooting for the Moon

a. Make the choice to shoot for the moon in a specific dream, goal, project, or endeavor.

b. List the obstacles or roadblocks that may prevent you from hitting the moon on that specific dream, goal, or project or that might keep you from completing specific steps or tasks that are necessary to complete to achieve a goal.

c. Identify the types of partners or outside resources you will need to recruit to overcome any of the obstacles you have listed.

d. Identify the specific individuals or resources you will try to recruit.

e. Recruit the partners or resources needed and begin to complete the steps and tasks you have listed on your vision map.

1. Review each of your most important dreams that you've defined in your vision mapping journal, and revise those dreams upward, shooting for the moon.*
2. Make any changes necessary to revise your goals, steps, and tasks for those dreams.
3. Use the steps listed in the preceding summary to identify the obstacles and recruit the partners you will need to overcome those obstacles in order to hit the moon on each of your most important dreams.

*If you have our preprinted vision mapping journal, you'll see that the first section under the title is "Shooting for the Moon Revision." Use that space to revise your dream upward. You'll also notice on the back side of the "Dream to Goals" page, the "Goals to Steps" page, and the "Steps to Tasks" page a section for revising your goals, steps, and tasks in light of the shooting for the moon revision of your dreams.

SESSION 10

The Billion-Dollar Difference . . . Better than Winning a Lottery!

Edison's Techniques Turned My Million-Dollar Loser into a Billion-Dollar Winner!

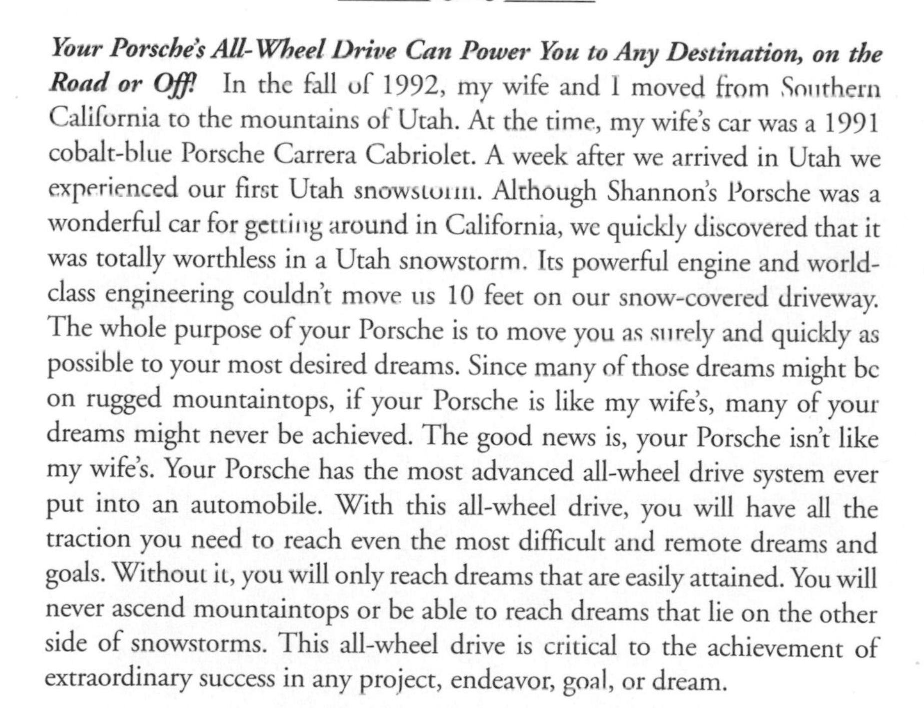

Your Porsche's All-Wheel Drive Can Power You to Any Destination, on the Road or Off! In the fall of 1992, my wife and I moved from Southern California to the mountains of Utah. At the time, my wife's car was a 1991 cobalt-blue Porsche Carrera Cabriolet. A week after we arrived in Utah we experienced our first Utah snowstorm. Although Shannon's Porsche was a wonderful car for getting around in California, we quickly discovered that it was totally worthless in a Utah snowstorm. Its powerful engine and world-class engineering couldn't move us 10 feet on our snow-covered driveway. The whole purpose of your Porsche is to move you as surely and quickly as possible to your most desired dreams. Since many of those dreams might be on rugged mountaintops, if your Porsche is like my wife's, many of your dreams might never be achieved. The good news is, your Porsche isn't like my wife's. Your Porsche has the most advanced all-wheel drive system ever put into an automobile. With this all-wheel drive, you will have all the traction you need to reach even the most difficult and remote dreams and goals. Without it, you will only reach dreams that are easily attained. You will never ascend mountaintops or be able to reach dreams that lie on the other side of snowstorms. This all-wheel drive is critical to the achievement of extraordinary success in any project, endeavor, goal, or dream.

In 1995, my partners and I launched a new cosmetics company featuring Kathie Lee Gifford as our spokesperson. On that particular project we made three critical marketing mistakes, and the result was disastrous. In a matter of months we lost millions of dollars and came very close to losing our business. By the end of the year we had only enough money to produce and test-market one last project. We had several products we were looking at, and my partners asked me the $64,000 question: "Of the products we're looking at, which one would Steve Scott choose?" They were willing to bet everything we had left on my choice. As I looked at the possibilities I said, "If I can recruit Chuck Norris and Christie Brinkley to serve as our spokespeople for the Total Gym, that is the project I would pick. If I can't recruit them, I would pick a different one." They agreed with my choice and I set up meetings with Chuck and Christie. Chuck had been using his Total Gym daily for 18 years and really believed in it. Christie had never seen one and needed to try it to see if it would do everything we said it would. As it turned out, she loved it. To our delight, both Chuck and Christie agreed to be our spokespeople, and I wrote and produced an infomercial that I thought would be a grand slam home run.

After a private screening of our new show, my partners became as excited about it as I was. It looked like our business and our livelihood would be saved. However, we all knew that our love for the infomercial was of little relevance. The only thing that really counts in our business is how television viewers respond to our infomercials when we broadcast them. Simply stated, do lots of viewers get up from their sofas, walk to their telephones, and order our product, or do they simply watch the show and think, "That's not for me"? On the weekend of September 7, 1996, the initial airings of our first Total Gym infomercial were broadcast on several national cable stations and a handful of local stations. To our dismay, the results were only mediocre and not good enough to merit a national rollout. It looked like our company was going to go out of business, and my partners and I were facing the possibility of losing most or all of our personal assets as well. But then something incredible happened. We used a particular process that turned a devastating strikeout into the all-time grand slam home run of our lives—one that would ultimately produce over $1 billion in Total Gym sales. The process itself can be stated in two words: *creative persistence.*

True Persistence—It's Not What You Think It Is

A professor of entrepreneurship at UCLA was once asked, "What do successful entrepreneurs have in common?" Her answer was, "Tremendous tenacity . . . they just don't give up." Although she was absolutely right, most people have a dangerous misconception of what tenacity or persistence is. They associate it with the adage, "If at first you don't succeed, try, try again." This concept of persistence is like hitting a brick wall, falling down, then getting back up and hitting it over and over again. That is not persistence, it's stupidity. Unfortunately, this often-quoted adage can be deadly if you don't make significant creative changes with each new try.

At an air show in my teenage years I watched a stunt pilot in his biplane attempt a low-altitude loop. He dove toward the ground to build up his speed to 180 miles per hour, then pulled up about 50 feet above the ground and soared upward into his loop. At the top half of the loop, his engine sputtered. Instead of aborting the loop and simply rolling out of it, he continued through the top half of the loop and pointed the plane back toward the ground. His engine sputter had only caused him to lose 50 to 100 feet in altitude at the top of the loop, and he thought that he could persist his way through the remaining half of the loop. Unfortunately, he missed completing his pullout by about 20 feet and crashed into the ground at nearly 160 miles per hour. His tenacity in his attempt to complete the loop had taken his life. How tragic that was, when a simple creative alternative would have saved his life. All he had to do was roll out of the loop, land, do a quick mechanical check on his engine, and perform his loop an hour or two later. Instead, he persisted right into the ground. Did persistence kill the pilot, or a misconception of persistence? The answer is, He was killed by a commonly held yet deadly misconception of persistence.

Critical Distinction

What persistence is not: **When failure is contemplated, persistence is not simply a matter of staying the course no matter what. When failure is experienced, persistence is not simply refusing to give up and then trying the same thing over and over again, but with more effort, intensity, or frequency.**

What true persistence is: **When failure is contemplated, true persistence makes the necessary midcourse corrections to reduce risk and increase the possibility of success. When failure is experienced, true persistence analyzes various elements or factors that may have caused or contributed to that failure and then designs and tries creative alternatives that might result in significant improvement and ultimate success.**

As I've looked at my own experience over the past 30 years and studied the biographies of many of the world's most successful people, I've come to realize one absolute truth: Those who achieve extraordinary success in any endeavor, whether personal or professional, have developed the skill to creatively persist. They analyze the possible causes of their failures and then add the element of creativity to their persistence by designing and implementing creative alternatives that reduce, eliminate, or reverse the negative affects of the causes of their failure. The greatest example I have found is that of Thomas Edison. He typically experienced more failures in a year than most people experience in a lifetime. He certainly experienced thousands more failures than any inventor in history. However, because he had developed a specific skill that combined his techniques for spawning creativity with his techniques for producing persistence, he persisted through thousands of failures to create more successful breakthrough inventions than any inventor or group of inventors in history. This skill not only worked for Edison, it has worked miraculously for me as well. I call this skill *creative persistence.*

Side-by-Side Comparison

How People Deal with Problems, Setbacks, and Potential or Realized Failures

Drifters	Pursuers	Achievers	Superachievers
Quickly change course, retreat, or give up and move on to the next project.	If they see hope of overcoming the problem or reversing a failure, they try harder, making additional attempts to succeed, before giving up.	Try their hardest to overcome problems and setbacks and power their way through failure to succeed in one way or another. They only surrender to failure when they know they cannot succeed.	Approach each important project expecting problems, setbacks, and potential failure to block their path to success. They utilize their partnering skills to draw on the creative input and resources of others to creatively persist through each problem until they succeed one way or another. If they discover that a project is a "three-legged horse," they "shoot it" rather than race it.

Creative Persistence—Edison's Ultimate Secret for Success

Unfortunately, creative persistence is not an inborn trait. There is one of the four personality types for whom persistence comes a little easier than it does with the others, and that is the lion. For the strong lion, the drive to persist is a part of his or her nature right out of the womb. While this inherent drive makes it easier for lions to implement the skill of creative persistence, like the other three personality types, they must first learn this skill before they can apply it. Once they learn it, their natural drive to persist makes the consistent application of this skill easier. For the other three personality types, the natural drive to persist is not an inborn trait. That's the bad news. The good news is that creative persistence is a learnable skill, and regardless of one's personality type it can be developed and consistently applied by anyone to his or her professional and personal pursuits. It's no more difficult to learn and implement this skill than it is to learn and implement the other skills we have focused on, such as hooking, salting, emotional word pictures, or vision mapping. Even strong otters whose personality type leans toward abandoning hardship rather than persevering can choose to learn and apply creative persistence. In fact, the two strongest otters I have ever known are Jim Shaughnessy and Henry Marsh. Both were able to learn and apply this skill to their athletic pursuits in their early youth. The result? Jim became an All-American football player and Henry became a world-champion distance runner and a four-time Olympian. In fact, Henry's American record has stood for more than 25 years.

Why the Skill of Creative Persistence Is Critical to Your Success

Right now you might be thinking, "Why on earth do I need to develop the skill of creative persistence? Life isn't that hard." The answer is, you don't

> ***The Fourteenth Law of Extraordinary Success***
>
> Extraordinary success can never be achieved without encountering extraordinary roadblocks, setbacks, and failures. These can only be overcome through creative persistence.

need creative persistence to achieve mediocrity, maintain the status quo, or experience moderate improvement. However, if you want extraordinary success in any area of your life, whether at work or at home, then this skill is critical. Why? In one of my earlier books I gave three insights that say it all. (1) You never need persistence to go downhill, but you always need it to go uphill. (2) Every extraordinary achievement and worthwhile dream can only be found on a mountaintop and can never be found on a valley floor. (3) Worthwhile dreams can never be achieved without encountering and overcoming strikeouts, criticisms, obstacles, and roadblocks. Creative persistence is the skill that will power you to the top of any mountain and overcome countless strikeouts, criticisms, obstacles, roadblocks, and failures. Creative persistence will provide the winning edge that will be the difference between having a good career and an extraordinary career, a tolerable marriage and a great marriage, or an income that barely pays the bills and an income of extreme abundance.

Even though dreams on valley floors are easily achieved, they are not that fulfilling. However, the fact that you purchased this book and that you've read this much of it tells me that you want a lot more out of life than just a job that only meets your basic needs, or a marriage that merely survives instead of thrives. That being the case, creative persistence is one skill you can't afford to live without.

Master Strategy 10—Using Breakthrough Techniques for Creative Persistence

Imagine that everything you owned, everything your partners owned, and the jobs and livelihoods of all of your employees were at risk and would be lost if you failed to succeed with your one last effort to save your company. Literally everything you had worked for your whole life would be lost in a single event if your last at bat produced a strikeout. That was the position in which my partners and I found ourselves on that fateful weekend in September 1996, when we first broadcast our original Total Gym infomercial. If TV viewers saw our infomercial and ordered the product in large numbers, we would be able to roll out the program into a national campaign that would save our business, our employees, and us from a financial disaster. On the other hand, if viewers didn't respond in adequate numbers, all would be lost with no hope of recovery. If you can imagine yourself in that position, you will understand how we felt going into our test airings. You will also understand why we were shocked and dismayed when only a handful of people ordered our product when the show was first broadcast. The day after the initial broadcasts, doom and gloom filled our hearts and minds. The project we had hoped would save our company was instead pounding the final nail into our collective coffin.

As we sat around our conference table, one partner said, "This show is too good to generate such a low response. Something is wrong. There is a reason why viewers aren't responding, and we just have to figure out what it is. Somehow, we've made a big mistake, and we are missing it. We need time to make changes to the show, broadcast the revised version, and see if anything will bring it to life."

While everyone agreed that this was the course of action we would like to take, there was one major problem. Our contracts with our celebrities only gave us a limited number of weeks to test the infomercial. Once we reached that deadline, any further broadcasts would constitute a national rollout and trigger multi-million-dollar annual guarantees to Chuck and Christie. If we triggered those guarantees and the changes in the show did not improve the viewer response rates, we would face an even greater disaster than we were already facing. This was a risk we couldn't afford to take. We desperately wanted to persist our way through this setback and create a winning show, but our celebrity contracts made persisting a nonoption.

When the Going Gets Tough, the Tough Get Creative!

Thomas Edison has been quoted as saying, "When the going gets tough, the tough get going." But *going* for Edison didn't simply mean *moving.* It meant becoming more committed, more intense, and most of all more creative. And that is exactly what started to happen around our conference table. One partner came up with a simple yet brilliant idea. "Why don't we ask Chuck and Christie to waive their guarantees and let us extend our testing period, and if we find a way to make it work, we can gradually roll the program out nationally?" The only problem was that in our 20-year history of working with more than 80 celebrity spokespeople, not one had ever considered waiving the annual guarantees. In fact, I think it's safe to say that in Hollywood's history no major celebrity has ever waived his or her guarantees. So our first step was to come up with a creative alternative for approaching Chuck and Christie with our unconventional request. Fortunately for us, Chuck waived his guarantee, which reduced our risk enough to enable us to take the next step of the creative persistence process, namely analyzing all of the possible causes of our show's failure to generate a significant response.

Dave Marsh, one of my partners, was the first to focus our attention on our pricing. He came up with a simple, creative change to the way we presented our price in the show. His idea was to present the price in a way that could possibly increase the number of people who called for more information, without reducing the price. We made that simple change to the show and the result was near miraculous: It more than tripled our response rate. Unfortunately, although the number of callers skyrocketed, the percentage of callers who were actually buying our product plummeted. Dave then came up with two creative alternatives that involved our choice of answering services and the scripting for our telephone sales reps. These changes tripled the percentage of callers who purchased the product. Dave's two creative alternatives had taken a million-dollar loser and turned it into the biggest winner of our corporate history. This year the Total Gym will pass the billion-dollar mark in sales, making it the single most successful direct response product in the history of television. That's the awesome power of creative persistence.

Even though this example illustrates creative persistence and its power, it does not adequately demonstrate the specific elements that can make creative persistence an effective strategy for your projects, your endeavors, and the pursuit of your dreams. To accomplish this, we'll turn to Thomas Edison himself, who had nearly perfected the skill of creative persistence by the time he was 16 years old. Later in his life Edison wrote, "The three things that are most essential to achievement are common sense, hard work, and stick-to-itiveness. . . . Unfortunately, many of life's failures are experienced by people who did not realize how close they were to success when they gave up. I have more respect for the person with a single idea who gets there than for the person with a thousand ideas who does nothing." Edison consistently utilized six techniques that provided him with the ongoing motivation and power to creatively persist through thousands of failures and produce enormous payoffs on most of his endeavors.

Edison's Six Techniques for Developing and Implementing the Skill of Creative Persistence

1. Define the Idea or Dream in Writing. The first thing Edison did when he conceived of a new idea, dream, or potential project was to take one page in his notebook and write out his idea succinctly. Normally he would only write a few sentences and never more than a single page. If you have started your vision mapping journal and have defined your most important dreams in writing, you have taken Edison's first step toward creative persistence. However, Edison added one more powerful element to this first step: He would draw a picture of what he thought his idea might look like. Doing this would enable him to visualize his idea. Even if the vision changed, drawing a picture gave him a place to start and would lock a visual image into his mind instead of a set of words. One picture is truly worth a thousand words because it activates both sides of our brain and is almost never forgotten, while words are easily forgotten. Edison once said that when he would take his famous midday naps, he would go to sleep with the image of his idea in his mind and wake up with new improvements for his idea that had come to him during his nap. That's the power of a visual image.

2. Enumerate the Broad Ramifications of Achieving the Dream. The second technique that Edison used demonstrated his true brilliance. After defining his dream or idea, he would then write out all of the broad ramifications of achieving his dream. While defining his idea for the light bulb only required one page in his notebook (a few written sentences and a drawing of what he thought it would look like), his enumeration of the broad ramifications of creating an electric light reportedly filled nine pages. In most cases, I write out the broad ramifications in a paragraph or two. To illustrate this second technique, I'll paraphrase Edison's statement of the broad ramifications of inventing an electric light bulb.

> If I create a practical, long lasting, and affordable electric light bulb, then every home, factory, office building, and farm in America will want to replace their kerosene lamps and gaslights with my electric light bulbs. If every home, factory, office building, and farm in America wants to use my electric light bulbs, then they will need electric power to turn on those lights and keep them on, so I will create the means of generating that power and selling it to them. And since they will be buying my electric power to run their electric lights, they will want to buy electric appliances, tools, and machinery to reduce their labor and increase their efficiency and productivity, and I will invent those electric devices. And if I can provide electric lights, electric power, and electric devices in America, then I can do these same things throughout Europe, Asia, North America, and South America.

Can you see the power of this technique? All of a sudden, instead of just inventing an electric light for the sake of selling a few light bulbs, Edison was using his light bulb as a springboard to control and sell the flow of electric power throughout the world, and create and sell countless electric inventions to a world that would become hungry to use his electric power to make life easier and more productive. The reason this technique brings so much power to creative persistence is because it demonstrates that giving up on an idea creates a loss that is much greater than just losing the idea itself. Although

Edison and his team of researchers failed over and over, he could not abandon his dream of creating a practical electric light in two years, because if he did he would lose the massive opportunity of creating a worldwide market for his electric power and electric tools, appliances, machines, and devices. If he had not enumerated the broad ramifications of inventing a light bulb, he could have easily given up after a few hundred failures and decided to move on to his next invention. But, the broad ramifications of inventing the light bulb provided such an unparalleled opportunity that any time he became discouraged, all he had to do was remember how much he would be walking away from if he failed on this single invention.

When you enumerate the broad ramifications of achieving extraordinary success in any of your projects, goals, or dreams, you will gain a new source of power for persisting through any kind of adversity, setback, or discouragement to achieve ultimate success. This technique is as powerful with your personal dreams as it is with your professional ones. If married couples would enumerate the broad ramifications of having a great marriage and those of an unhappy or failed marriage, the divorce rate in America would plummet. This has always been one of the first steps that I have taken when unhappy husbands and wives have sought my counsel. In nearly every case it has provided them with tremendous motivation and power to creatively persist through adversity and redouble their efforts to make their marriages more successful.

3. Infuse Your Dream into the Hearts and Minds of Others. Edison's third technique for creative persistence is nearly as powerful as the first two. After he would define his dream in writing and enumerate its broad ramifications, he would "infect" key people around him with that same dream. As you know from our earlier sessions, without a vision the people perish, and with a vision comes life, energy, motivation, and commitment. Edison would use the same communication techniques you learned in our fifth and sixth sessions to infuse his dreams into the hearts and minds of other key people around him: his family, his friends, his bankers and investors, and his staff. Whenever he would run out of mental or emotional gas and feel like giving up, those he had infected with his vision wouldn't let him walk away from the dream. One of the great benefits of utilizing the strategy of effective partnering is that whenever one partner feels like giving up on a project or an idea, there are always one or two others who don't want to give up and who provide the motivation or creative breakthroughs to keep persisting until success is achieved. My partners and I have been together for 27 years, and there have been countless times when one or more of us have felt like a project was hopeless. Then another partner would refuse to give up and that refusal would provide the time and motivation to develop creative alternatives that often turned would-be failures into major successes. Years ago I launched a new product with Richard Simmons called Deal-A-Meal. Within 18 months we had achieved gross sales of around $20 million, and I thought we had exhausted the market and it was time to retire the project. One of my partners felt there was still a lot of life left in the product and convinced the rest of us to let him try to get a little more juice out of the orange. His creative persistence paid off. During the next five years, Deal-A-Meal and its aerobic video series, *Sweatin' to the Oldies,* generated more than $130 million in additional sales.

4. Expect Criticism, Problems, and Failures and Predetermine the Right Way to Deal with Them. I normally fly around 100,000 miles a year, so I meet a lot of people on airplanes. It's not uncommon to hear tales of woe about their jobs, their careers, their businesses, or even their marriages. Most have seemed surprised or even shocked by the fact that in their pursuit of success in their projects, goals, or dreams, they encountered harsh criticism, severe adversity, or even failure. The truth is, no worthwhile success in any endeavor is ever achieved without encountering adversity. Since every worthwhile dream lies on the top of a rugged mountain, there is no easy way to get to it. Edison not only understood this fact—he counted on it! He considered criticism, adversity, and failure as necessary to the achievement of extraordinary success, just as exhaling is necessary to breathing. Because Edison expected criticism, he was always prepared for it and *responded* to it rather than reacting to it. Because Edison expected problems and failures, he was always ready for them and never panicked by them. How about you? Do you expect and prepare for criticism, problems, and failures in your pursuit of your dreams? While doing so runs contrary to our human nature, it is critical to the achievement of our dreams. Edison knew it, I learned it, and now you know it. The good news is, when you learn the right way to deal with these natural negative components of achievement, you don't have to fear them at all!

We do have natural reactions to criticism and failure. Unfortunately, our natural reactions are nearly always the wrong reactions. Here are just a few of the wrong ways most of us deal with criticism and failure. First, we may become angry, defensive, discouraged, or depressed. We may pout, withdraw, or deny: "It wasn't my fault, I really didn't make that big of a mistake." We make excuses. We rationalize our failures. Some personality types respond to failure by attacking, blaming others, or even blaming circumstances. Some people become overly introspective and frustrated and view themselves as failures. These are some of the wrong ways that we naturally react to failure. If you identify with some or even all of them, don't feel too bad, because this is how almost everyone reacts to striking out.

So what are the right ways for dealing with our failures or strikeouts? Edison saw three critical components. First, you must accept full responsibility for the strikeout or for your part in it. Second, analyze your strikeout to determine its causes. Third, come back up to the plate with a new approach, determined not to make the same mistakes in your future efforts.

Accept Full Responsibility for Your Strikeouts. You must not blame other people or unfavorable circumstances for your failures. Ted Williams was the greatest hitter in baseball history. One key element of his extraordinary success was his ever-present attitude of personal responsibility. After striking out in a very important game, he was asked by one reporter if the strikeout was his fault or the pitcher's. He answered, "Hey, I'm the one that struck out. It doesn't matter what pitch was thrown to me; it doesn't matter how high, how low, how fast, or how far away it was from the plate. It doesn't matter how hard the wind was blowing or how loud the crowd was screaming. All that matters is, *I* swung the bat and *I* struck out." No wonder he was the greatest hitter of all time.

Analyze the Failure or Strikeout after a Brief Timeout. The second critical component for effectively dealing with failures or strikeouts is to analyze them, looking for their causes, after you have taken a timeout. Anytime you strike out, there is a period of time when you are still feeling a lot of pain from the event. That is the wrong time to try to analyze the causes of that failure. Give yourself a few hours, a day, a week, or even a month after the strike out, so you can look at it with more objectivity and less emotion. Strikeouts always hurt, and until the pain subsides it is hard to be objective. So after you've accepted responsibility for the strikeout, give yourself a little bit of adjustment time. Then and only then, come back, look at the strikeout, and analyze it.

In 1976 I wrote and produced my first direct response television commercial, and thankfully it was a home run. Unfortunately, in the year that followed, three out of every four commercials that I wrote and produced were strikeouts. My success rate for that year was only 25 percent, and I was initially devastated. I spent a lot of time analyzing each of my failures and made sure that I didn't make those same mistakes the following year. My success rate then climbed to 50 percent. Even though that felt better, I was still bothered that one out of every two commercials I produced failed. I continued analyzing every failure and making sure I did not make the same mistakes in the projects that followed. That year, my success rate rose to nearly 75 percent. That year I also discovered that the average success rate for companies in our industry (television direct response marketing) was under 5 percent. Thank goodness I had not heard that statistic earlier.

Had I known that my success rate of 25 percent was five times higher than the industry average, I might not have analyzed my failures, learned from them, and raised my hit rate to the 75 percent level.

Often we fail in a project or an endeavor because of our own blind spots. Then, when we analyze those failures, we may miss some of their most important causes because we are still blind to those same factors. That's why it's critical that we reach outside of ourselves when we are analyzing our failures. After you have completed your own initial analysis, ask those around you what they think went wrong. This may leave you vulnerable because they may point a finger at you and your personal failing in that situation. If that happens, do not become defensive, as that will defeat the purpose of your analysis. More important than your own ego or feelings is your goal of discovering what went wrong and how can you make sure you don't repeat the same mistake on your next project or endeavor. After 27 years in my business, and hundreds of projects and marketing campaigns, each year I still strike out 25 to 50 percent of the time. I still analyze every failure, and I still seek out the opinions of everyone involved.

The need for actively analyzing your failed efforts, projects, and endeavors applies to every area of life—business, financial, and personal. In 1993, 1998, and 2000, I made three bad multi-million-dollar investment decisions that cost my family most of our life savings. Had I effectively analyzed the cause of my bad investment decision in 1993, I would have never made the same mistake again in 1998 and again in 2000. But I did not, and my losses were staggering. After the loss in 2000, I finally saw the two root problems and made a fundamental change that will now keep me from repeating these mistakes in the future.

Relationships expert Gary Smalley also points out that the reason more second marriages fail than first marriages is that men and women repeat the same mistakes in their second marriage that they made in their first. The bad news is, it doesn't end there. More third marriages fail than second marriages for the exact same reason. If men and women would analyze the true reasons their first marriage failed, focusing on the mistakes they made rather than those made by their ex-spouses, they would have a much better chance of not repeating the same mistakes and failing the second time around. Even if your spouse was 99.9 percent responsible and you were only one-tenth of 1 percent responsible, set the focus of your analysis on your one-tenth of 1 percent rather than on their 99.9 percent. The blame game may make your conscience feel better, but it's counterproductive to your goal of discovering causes and not repeating them in the future.

Come Back up to the Plate with an Improved Approach. After failing at anything significant, it is not uncommon for people to think of themselves as failures and make a decision never to take a chance of failing again. In other words, the best way not to strike out is to never come up to bat. This reasoning, whether conscious or subconscious, is a crippling restraint to the pursuit and achievement of extraordinary success. It's important to realize that a single strikeout only ends an at bat. It never ends a career. Said another way, each failure is only one sentence or paragraph in the book of your life. Knowing this, Edison never let a single failure slow him down. In baseball lingo, he would figure out what caused the strikeout and then come back to the plate, swinging better and harder than ever. After you have analyzed your strikeout, it's critical that you too keep coming back up to bat. Each time you will come back smarter and more likely to get a hit or even a home run.

How Do You Handle Other People's Strikeouts? Edison's true genius was demonstrated not only by the way he handled his own strikeouts, but also by the way he dealt with the strikeouts of others. By dealing with the strikeouts of his staff in the right way, he fostered undying loyalty, wholehearted commitment, inexhaustible creativity, unending inspiration, and tremendous productivity. Bob Marsh, my mentor and senior partner, dealt with my strikeouts in the same manner as Edison. Of the 10 bosses I have had since college, Bob was the only one who dealt with my strikeouts in such a positive and motivating way. Consequently, every time I struck out, instead of crying and cowering in my office, I couldn't wait to get back up to bat and take the next swing.

How about you? How do you react when someone you're counting on strikes out? Do you become critical or angry? Do you lecture, advise, criticize, discipline, or overcorrect? My first coach in Little League baseball did all of the above. Every time I struck out he would yell, criticize, or overcorrect. As I would walk back to the dugout I would hear comments like: "When are you going to learn how to hit the ball?" "I can't believe you swung at such a high pitch," or "What were you thinking?" His comments made me fear coming up to bat. In fact, they made me want to walk away from playing baseball. As might be expected, my hitting didn't improve at all that year. The next year my new coach coached me instead of criticizing me, and my batting average soared. The fact is, when people around you strike out, the last thing they need to hear is a lecture or a criticism. They are more upset by their failure than you are, and they need time to recover and adjust.

Here are a few tips for dealing with other people's failures the right way. First, allow them recovery time. Give them a little time for the pain to wear off. Next, listen, comfort, and encourage them. The key word here is *listen,* without giving your thoughts, advice, or criticism. Then, when they are ready, you can help them to begin to analyze their failure. Always start with questions rather than statements or solutions. You might ask: "Why do you think you struck out?" "What do you think you did or didn't do that contributed to that failure?" "What do you think should have been done differently?" It's always good to let them know that you too have made mistakes and failed, and it helps to give them a specific example of one of your failures if you can think of a relevant one that applies to their situation. Last but not least, you should offer your help and partnership. You might say, "You know, when you're ready to talk about it, I'm available," or, "I'll think about it for awhile and if I come up with any good ideas I'll jot them down and we can talk about them."

5. Use Roadblocks, Obstacles, and Failures as Springboards to Develop Effective Creative Alternatives. Edison not only expected obstacles, roadblocks, and failures, he consistently used them as springboards to develop creative alternatives. Remember, the misconception of persistence is hitting a wall, falling down, and then getting up and hitting it again and again and again. True persistence is hitting a wall, falling down, and then developing a creative alternative to get over it, around it, or under it or blow it up. This is a good time to recruit outside resources. Throughout my life there have been hundreds of times when I've hit the wall and could not come up with a good creative alternative to get past it. And yet, 9 times out of every 10, I could find someone else who would provide a creative alternative that would work. There's absolutely no shame in turning to someone else for help in devising creative alternatives. To the contrary, it's usually the wisest course of action.

In filmmaking, once a script has been chosen, the single most important element in the production process is casting. The right cast can turn a mediocre script into a box-office smash. On the other hand, many strong scripts have been turned into mediocre movies because of wrong choices for starring or costarring roles. No one knows this better than Steven Spielberg and Robert Zemeckis. When they were first casting for a film in 1984, they chose an up-and-coming film actor named Eric Stoltz for the lead role. Eric gained critical acclaim for his starring role in *Mask,* in which he played a disfigured boy with a winsome personality. Two weeks into their shooting schedule, Spielberg realized that he and Zemeckis weren't getting the performance from Stoltz that they had hoped for. It wasn't that he was just failing as an actor. Zemeckis's directorial skills could have fixed that kind of problem. It was worse. Spielberg and Zemeckis had simply miscast the part. Stoltz's personality was not right for the character he was playing. Spielberg then made what he called "the hardest decision of my career." He stopped the filming and developed a creative alternative, one so radical it meant he would have to throw away the thousands of feet of film they had shot, along with the millions of dollars they had spent shooting it. He would have to recast the lead role and then start all over. He and

Zemeckis turned to a television sitcom actor who had no previous experience in movies (a major risk in itself). Needless to say, developing this creative alternative, which cost invaluable time and millions of dollars to execute, paid off big. Michael J. Fox's performance turned *Back to the Future* into one of the best comedies ever filmed, and drove it right to the top of the box-office charts.

6. Recognize a Three-Legged Horse, and Take It out of the Race! One out of every three or four projects that my partners and I develop ultimately fails. Prior to a project's failure, we invest months and sometimes a year or two in its development. Our investment by the time we have completed all of our market tests is $1 to $2 million. We have worked hard with an inventor and major celebrities and are emotionally connected to the project and everyone involved. Before we give up on a project, we have creatively persisted through countless creative alternatives. And yet, despite all of our investment of money, work, and emotional capital, there comes a time when we have to say the project is a "three-legged horse," and it's not going to even run a race, much less win it. There have been times when we have foolishly refused to admit defeat and kept throwing good money after bad, making matters even worse.

In business management classes in college, students break up into teams and create a fictitious company and develop every aspect that would be necessary to launch that company and make it successful. Fred Smith's idea for his project was a company that would pick up packages from businesses and for a premium price deliver those packages anywhere in the United States the very next day. His professor took the position that no one would pay the kind of money it would cost to have a package delivered the next day when they could send the package so much more cheaply via the U.S. Postal Service or UPS and have it delivered in a week or less. Fred received a D and was infuriated. He was also motivated to prove the professor wrong, and creatively persisted through hundreds of roadblocks to ultimately create Federal Express. He not only proved his professor wrong, he proved that he was a man of tremendous creative persistence.

After a few years of unparalleled success, Fred had another idea. There was a budding technology called telephone facsimile that enabled companies to send copies of documents to any location in the world that also had an expensive facsimile machine. However, because these machines were very big and very expensive, most businesses could not afford to own or even lease them. Fred's idea was to buy tens of thousands of these machines and place them in office buildings throughout America. Federal Express would then receive a fee every time anyone used his machines to fax copies of their documents. He bought the machines and placed them in office buildings throughout the country. Unfortunately two giant problems rained on his parade. First, most companies didn't see a need to fax documents, and Fred's advertising couldn't convince them otherwise. Second, fax machines started getting a lot smaller and a lot cheaper. Companies that recognized the value of faxing bought their own less expensive machines rather than use Fred's. With this venture, Fred proved that he was not only a man who had mastered creative persistence, he was a man who, once he recognized a project was a three-legged horse, wasn't afraid to take it out of the race and put it out to pasture. He collected all of his machines and discontinued the service. Federal Express lost $1 billion on this project. However, had Fred not pulled out of the market, he would have lost billions more.

How can you recognize when one of your ideas, endeavors, or projects is a three-legged horse? First, when no creative alternative gets it close to the goal line. In the case of the Total Gym, the first creative alternative reduced our risk by removing a celebrity guarantee. The second made a major difference in our viewer response rate. The third and fourth creative alternatives made a huge difference in our conversion rates and made the project a grand slam. However, I've also had projects where the response rates were less than half of what we needed to succeed and each creative alternative we developed only made minor differences. That's the first tip that you may be looking at a three-legged horse. Second, if you and your partners, counselors, advisors, or others involved in a project cannot conceive of any creative alternative that might make a major difference, that is a second sign that it's time to give up. Many businesses and families lose everything because they fail or refuse to recognize that their horses can't run, so they keep pouring their resources into a project, dream, ideal, or goal that should be ended. Finally, every project, goal, and dream should have a realistic deadline and budget for being achieved. That is a critical part of the vision mapping process. Although it may be wise to stretch a deadline a little or expand a budget to a degree, it's usually not a good idea to go significantly beyond a reasonable deadline or over a budget. Bill Lear made lots of money with his inventions of the car radio, the autopilot, and the Lear jet. But he also lost all his money trying to create a modern-day automobile that could run on steam. Although he went way over budget and way past his deadlines, he refused to recognize this three-legged horse.

Actions for Traction

WHERE THE RUBBER MEETS THE ROAD

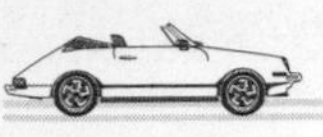

1. In your Vision Mapping Journal, do the following on each of your Dream Pages.
   a. State the broad ramifications of achieving that dream.
   b. Make a list of the people that you want to share your vision with.
   c. List the potential obstacles that could prevent you from achieving that dream.
   d. For each potential obstacle, develop creative alternatives for overcoming the obstacle.
   e. List your lack of resources, know-how, and your weaknesses that could prevent you from achieving that dream.
   f. List the types of partners, mentors, or outside resources you will need to recruit to overcome the limitations you've defined.
   g. Review all of your target dates for achieving your important dreams and consider if they should be revised to follow a marathoner's pace or a sprinter's pace. Any long-term vision may require a long-term commitment and therefore may need a marathoner's pace with extended deadlines.
2. In your Mentoring Notebook make a list of some of your past failures, both at home and on the job. Consider each one and determine if you were trying to run a "three-legged horse," or if you simply failed because of your lack of resources, lack of know-how, or inability to develop creative alternatives.
3. List some of the failures that people around you (at home or at work) have experienced and write down your response or reaction to those failures. Did you lecture, advise, criticize, discipline, overcorrect, or become angry? Or, did you listen, encourage, ask questions, and coach the person through their strikeout? How could you have better dealt with their failures?

SESSION 11

Removing the Single Greatest Roadblock to Achieving Your Dreams

Defeating Your Conscious and Subconscious Fear of Failure

Your Porsche Has a Revolutionary Windshield Clearance System. When I was in college I was invited to spend a weekend in Northern Arizona with some friends. We drove from Phoenix toward Flagstaff in a beat-up 20-year-old car. Thirty miles outside of Flagstaff it started snowing and my friend flipped the switch to start his windshield wipers. To the dismay of everyone in the car, the wipers remained motionless. In a matter of seconds we couldn't see anything other than a snow-covered windshield. The fact that we were moving at about 65 miles per hour made the next few moments even more traumatic. In a matter of seconds my friend had brought the car to a safe stop off of the highway. We remained in that spot for six hours until the snowstorm had passed. Because our view of the highway had been blinded by snow, our progress toward our goal had been brought to a complete halt. Since that experience, snow has impaired my progress on other occasions as well. Once it precipitated a wreck that stopped a cross-country trip 2,800 miles short of my destination. More than once, whiteouts have caused me to miss a highway exit that I was supposed to take. Ten years ago I was rushing my pregnant wife to the hospital to give birth to my son Ryan. We were driving on the freeway in a blinding snowstorm when all of a sudden my visibility was reduced to zero. I decided to try to make an instant exit off the freeway and lost control of my Jeep, plowing into a snowbank. Even with four-wheel drive, my Jeep would not budge. Fortunately, two cars full of young army reservists on their way to a 6 A.M. reserve meeting pulled off the road and came to our rescue.

In the pursuit of success in any endeavor, there is a blinding snow that prevents most people from clearly seeing the roads of opportunity that they need to take to achieve extraordinary success. This "snow" can stop them dead in their tracks just like that snowstorm stopped my college buddies and me. It can also blind people to wonderful opportunities that pass right by them unseen, just as the highway exits that I have missed while driving in a storm. The good news is that your Porsche is equipped with the world's most advanced windshield clearance system. Once you activate it, snow will never again blind your vision and impede your progress. This blinding snow that I am talking about is your conscious and subconscious fear of failure.

Master Strategy 11—Overcoming Your Subconscious and Conscious Fears of Failure

In 1996, Zig Ziglar closed his review of my first book with the statement, "Steve Scott is living proof that failure is an event, *not* a person." In my case he would have been more accurate if he had said, "Steve Scott is living proof that failure*s* are event*s*, not a person," because my failures have been far too many to count. I have had tremendous failures in my investment decisions, dozens of failures in my business projects, and gut-wrenching failures in my personal life. However, because I have used a particular strategy in dealing with my failures, many of them have resulted in later successes that were far more extraordinary than the failures that preceded them. For example, the first fitness product I marketed failed miserably and cost my partners and me a loss of more than $100,000. However, what I learned from that failure concerning the selection of celebrity spokespeople became the key to marketing a second fitness product that generated sales of more than $140 million and a profit of $39 million in

> ***The Fifteenth Law of Extraordinary Success***
>
> Fears of failure blind one's vision to opportunity. Extraordinary success cannot be achieved until those fears are effectively dealt with and vision is restored.

only 26 weeks. Would you be willing to experience a $100,000 failure in order to make a $39 million profit? Unfortunately I became somewhat arrogant after that success and the next two fitness products I marketed failed, and we lost over $1 million. However, the lessons I learned from those two failures provided important insights to marketing my next fitness product, which has generated $1 billion in sales. Using a specific strategy for dealing with my failures meant that each failure provided new insights that contributed to greater and greater successes.

I'm not the only one who has discovered the power of this strategy. As I began to meet others who had achieved extraordinary success, I found out that they too had experienced significant failures and had used this same strategy as a key to growing their extraordinary successes out of the nutrient-rich topsoil of failure. I have worked with Academy Award–winning actors and actresses such as Charlton Heston, Jane Fonda, and Cher; dozens of Emmy Award–winning television stars; and a number of Grammy-winning recording artists, and nearly all of them drove to extraordinary success on a highway paved with failure. I have known people who have made hundreds of millions of dollars and even a few billionaires, and they too have experienced significant and sometimes devastating failures at different times throughout their lives.

While working on his invention of the alkaline storage battery, Thomas Edison and his team tried over 10,000 combinations of various elements without success. Edison was reportedly asked why he continued his vain attempt to create such an invention when his 10,000 attempts had failed and had not produced any results. His answer has become one of his more famous quotes. "Results? Why, man, I have gotten lots of results! If I find 10,000 ways something won't work, I haven't failed. I am not discouraged, because every wrong attempt discarded is just one more step forward." But Edison wasn't the first to realize the incredible worth of failure. Nearly 100 years before Edison was born, the English poet John Keats wrote, "Failure is in a sense the highway to success, inasmuch as every discovery of what is false leads us to seek earnestly after what is true."

Failure Is the Most Often Missed Key to Extraordinary Success

As you may remember from our session on effective partnering, Henry Ford's first venture into automobile manufacturing was a total failure. After two years of blood, sweat, and tears he was summarily fired by the board of directors of the Detroit Automobile Company. Henry Ford echoed Keats's and Edison's sentiments when he said, "Failure is only the

Side-by-Side Comparison

How People Deal With Their Personal and Professional Failures

Drifters	Pursuers	Achievers	Superachievers
Avoid failure at all cost. They rarely fail because they rarely attempt to achieve anything that isn't easily achieved. They are destined to a life of mediocrity or worse.	Fear failure and work hard to avoid it. When they do fail, they either excuse or rationalize their failure or blame it on adverse circumstances or other people.	Fear failure and work hard to avoid it. When they do fail, they accept responsibility and work even harder to avoid failure next time.	Set impossible goals regularly and often fail. They realize that failure is just part of the game, and although they hate failing, they are not afraid of it. They quickly and exhaustively analyze each failure and use the lessons they learn to increase their probability of extraordinary success in the future.

opportunity to more intelligently begin again." He proved that statement true when he began his second automobile company. The mistakes he had made in his first venture provided lessons that became the foundation on which he built the Ford Motor Company. And by 1928, one out of every two cars in the world had his name on it!

Unfortunately, while failure has turned out to be a tremendous asset for the world's most successful people, the vast majority of adults view failure as a dead end sign on the highway to their dreams. Failure in one endeavor not only ends their hope of achieving success in that effort, it creates a fear of failing that can confine them to a lifetime of mediocrity. Fear of failure can create an insurmountable obstacle that stands between them and extraordinary success for the rest of their lives. So the question becomes, What do the world's most successful people know about failure that the vast majority of adults have never discovered? How have superachievers transformed failure from a feared and paralyzing enemy into a powerful ally in their pursuit of extraordinary success?

Conscious and Subconscious Fears of Failure

Our fear of failure can be both conscious and subconscious. Although our subconscious fears are less obvious, they are no less destructive. In fact, conscious fears are often more easily dealt with and resolved. Subconscious fears are more difficult to resolve because they are not easily detected. Consequently, they can remain unresolved for a lifetime. A friend of mine is a brilliant and very accomplished doctor and psychotherapist. Despite all of his training and experience, he has only recently learned that his greatest fear in life has been his fear of failure. His fear of failure has subconsciously guided his behavior in both his personal and professional life. And that is precisely why the fear of failure is such a limiting factor to anyone's success; it sets hidden boundaries all around us and can guide every aspect of our behavior and decision making. Henry Ford said it succinctly when he wrote, "One who fears failure limits his activities." In other words, we limit what we say, what we think, and what we do so we won't incur any risk of failing. If we set any goals at all, we set them so low that we have virtually no chance of failing to achieve those goals. Fear of failure forces an individual to accept mediocrity as a normal substitute for excellence. While this may have been your modus operandi in the past, it certainly won't work with the strategies you have been learning in our sessions. Fear of failure and shooting for the moon cannot coexist. One must give way to the other. That means you must learn an effective strategy for detecting and eliminating your fear of failure or it will sabotage the other strategies you have determined to begin using. To effectively deal with the problem of fear of failure, we must start by breaking it down into its component parts, namely fear and failure. Let's start with fear.

All Fear Is Not Created Equal

There are two types of fear—good fear and bad fear. Good fear motivates us to avoid wrong and destructive behavior and pursue good and beneficial behavior. It teaches us that there are natural limits and boundaries that we need to respect for our sake and the sake of others. For example, we should fear riding with a drunk driver. We should fear driving 120 miles per hour on a snow-covered highway. My father was a bomber pilot in World War II and flew 50 combat missions in the South Pacific. On nearly every mission the plane he was flying was hit by either antiaircraft fire or fire from enemy fighters. He and his crew were kept alive and his missions were successfully completed because of his good fear. Because he feared being shot down and never seeing his newborn daughter, he listened intently to each mission briefing. He performed thorough preflight checks of his aircraft. And once in the air, he was constantly vigilant, never relaxing his focus until his plane returned safely to his base. Had my father not possessed this good fear, he might have become arrogant, negligent, and careless in his attitude and performance on each mission. With the kind of missions he was flying, any one of these characteristics would have been deadly. Good fear is very healthy at any age. Unfortunately, younger people often possess very little of this positive kind of fear, and the result is thousands of deaths each year from car accidents, drug overdoses, and other careless and irresponsible behavior.

On the other hand, bad fear, which is our focus in relation to the fear of failure, has no redeeming value whatsoever. Simply stated, bad fear is fear that prevents us from doing that which is in our best interest and the best interest of others. Bad fear keeps a mother from visiting distant relatives because she's afraid of flying. Bad fear keeps students from raising their hands in class for fear of sounding stupid. Bad fear keeps an employee from taking unexpected initiative on a project for fear of failing in front of his or her peers. Bad fear whispers in our ear, "Don't swing for the fences, just try not to strike out." It causes us to remain in our comfort zone and just accept whatever comes our way. It causes us to accept what is okay in place of pursuing what is better or best. It was about this kind of fear that James F. Bell wrote, "Fear is an insidious virus. Given a breeding place in our mind, it will permeate the whole body of our work. It will eat away our spirit and block the forward path of our endeavors. Fear is the greatest enemy of progress."

The good news is that fear in general and the fear of failure specifically are very easily dealt with when you use the right techniques. You won't have to develop the courage of a gladiator or become a black belt in karate to overcome bad fear and the fear of failure. There are simple techniques that will enable you to detect your subconscious fears of failing and then to overcome both your subconscious and conscious fears of failure. Once fear's power is removed from your life, you will be able to clearly see opportunities that have been invisible to you in the past. And with no snow impairing your vision, you will be able to pursue those opportunities at full speed.

Dealing With the Fear Factor

If you say that you have no fear of failure, then either you are not being honest with yourself or your fears of failing are totally subconscious and more constraining than you can imagine. It doesn't mean you lack courage, because some of the most courageous people I have ever known, including highly decorated war heroes, have been under the influence and control of their fears of failure. For almost three decades I have used a four-step technique for dealing with my conscious and subconscious fears of failure that has worked wonders for me. It has radically reduced or completely eliminated my fear of failing with each project, venture, or dream in which I have applied it.

Four Steps for Overcoming Fears of Failure in Any Endeavor

1. **Define what you really want in each endeavor, project, or dream you are pursuing.** You simply ask the question, "If I could have absolutely anything in this situation, what would it be?" Forget how impossible it is; forget all of the potential obstacles that might be in the way. If you could have any outcome in this situation, what would it be? What would you really want? Determining what you really want and writing it down is the first step to detecting a subconscious fear and overcoming it. For example, let's say that you decide that what you really want at work is to be transferred to a different department that has better management and more potential for promotion.

2. **List the potential obstacles that could stand in the way of getting what you really want.** Returning to our example, you might list obstacles such as: "I'm not as qualified as others who are in that department," "My boss would prevent me from transferring to that department," or "There's too much competition for jobs in that department."

3. **List your reasons for not confronting each obstacle.** This is the step where the rubber meets the road. As you state your reason(s) for not confronting each obstacle, you are revealing your subtle or subconscious fears. In 1972, I was working for a large corporation and desperately wanted to transfer out of one subsidiary into a different one. My biggest obstacle was my boss, who was one of the most powerful individuals in the entire corporation and also the most defensive when it came to protecting his power base. As I worked through this exercise, I listed two reasons for not confronting him with my desire for a transfer. First, he would likely be deeply offended and would somehow punish me for requesting a transfer, and second, he would most likely deny my request and I would be stuck in his department for the rest of my time with the company. My subconscious fears that had kept me from asking for a transfer were now revealed.

4. **Create a risk-reward analysis chart for each of your fears.** This is the easiest and most important step in this technique. Most of the time, what we fear has been magnified in our mind to appear much greater than what it really is. This step puts that which we fear into a proper perspective. More often than not, when we see it in its true perspective, it's not deserving of the fear we have given it. The next table shows a little chart that I've used through the years that usually puts fear into its proper perspective, and how I used it in this situation.

As I studied this chart, I realized that the worst-case scenario was practically no different from what I would experience if I never asked for the

Risk-Reward Analysis Chart "If I Ask for a Transfer . . ."

Fear	Worst Case	Best Case	Likely Case
1. I'll be punished.	He'll give me more grunt work and pass me over at promotion time.	He'll be fine and give me better work assignments.	He'll be angry and things will remain the same.
2. I'll be turned down for the transfer.	I'll be turned down for the transfer and keep doing what I'd be doing even if I didn't ask for a transfer.	I'll get the transfer and start enjoying my work.	I'll get the transfer and be shunned by my ex-boss.
3. I'll be stuck in this department.	I'll have to put up with days or weeks of my boss's disdain.	I'll get the transfer and never worry about my boss again.	I'll get the transfer and feel awkward when I see my ex-boss in the cafeteria.

transfer. On the other hand, in both the best-case scenario and the likely case scenario, I would get the transfer and be a lot better off in the new subsidiary. This not only removed my subconscious fears, it provided all of the motivation I needed to go ahead and ask for the transfer. As it turned out, I got the transfer, and then my boss fired me from his department to save face with his peers and subordinates. I suffered a little more humiliation than I had anticipated in any of my scenarios, but I got the transfer and worked for a new boss who treated me more like a partner than an employee. Had I not charted out my fears, I would have never asked for the transfer, and life would have been much different. I would have never met and worked for the man who ultimately became my mentor and partner in my current business, which changed the entire course of my life.

This little chart has not only helped me work my way through countless fears over the years, it radically changed my life back in April of 1976. I had been working for a catalog company called Ambassador Leather for about three months. During those three months I had initiated an expanded television marketing campaign that was projected to double the company's annual sales from $30 million to $60 million. Bob Marsh owned the media company that was buying the commercial time for this campaign. One night Bob and I were at dinner and he made an offer that set my mind in motion. He said, "If you could find a product that you and I could sell on TV, we could go into business together and start our own marketing company." Within four weeks I had found a product that we both liked, and I handed my letter of resignation to Mike Siegal, Ambassador's CEO, saying,

"Mike, I have a chance to start a new business with someone I really admire so I've decided to give it a shot." In shock, Mike looked at me and said, "Are you crazy? These things never work out! I was planning to offer you the position of vice president of marketing. I'll double your salary and give you a company car. You name the terms. What do you want to stay with us?"

I was shocked. I was 27 years old and had just been offered all of my career goals in a single package. Now I had a major problem. Should I take the offer of my dreams, or should I take the mystery gift behind the curtain, a start-up television marketing business that might or might not work?

Even though I was only 27 at the time, I had already experienced a lifetime of failures. I had only been out of college for six years and I was already on my ninth job. I had started two other businesses from scratch a few years earlier and both had failed, leaving me broke and in debt. So on one hand I had the president of an established company offering me my dream job, a great salary, and a company car. On the other hand I had the offer of creating a start-up business 3,000 miles away from home with no promise of success. Making the equation even more unbalanced and appealing to my fear of failure were Mike's words, "Steve, don't be crazy! These things never work out!" I went home that night and created a risk-reward chart.

Well, I looked at my chart and all of the sudden there wasn't even a question. I wanted to get up to the plate and take the chance of hitting a home run. Even if I didn't hit a home run, I would be working with the man I respected and loved more than any businessman I had ever known. I would be building opportunities with him, and that would be fulfilling.

I went to work the next day and met with Mike. I told him that after a great deal of thought, I had decided to resign and start the new business.

If I Quit Ambassador and Start a Company with Bob Marsh

Worst Case	Best Case	Likely Case
Lose the opportunity of a lifetime (salary doubled to $36,000, vice president of marketing, company car, and stay home in Arizona) Move to Philadelphia, start new company, and be out of business in 6, 9, or 12 months and have to start all over	Start business with the man I really want to be in business with; hit another grand slam (like the one I hit with Ambassador) selling millions of dollars worth of products and making more money than I've ever dreamed of, maybe hundreds of thousands of dollars a year or even millions	Start business with the man I really want to be in business with, and hit a double to start the business that could grow year by year and maybe someday hit a home run on at least one TV product

Then Mike shocked me with his words one more time. "Steve, would you at least give us 10 hours a week of consulting—just 10 hours to oversee our television campaign—and I'll pay you a consulting fee equal to your full salary?" I said, "Of course!"

This simple little chart had empowered me to make the right decision. With Mike's new offer, I was going to have my cake and eat it too. I wasn't going to risk losing everything. I was going to have a full salary coming from Ambassador, and at the same time I was going to have a chance to start a business with Bob Marsh, and just maybe we would hit a home run.

As it turned out, our first project was a grand slam home run. Our $4,200 commercial produced $1 million of sales per week for 20 consecutive weeks. More important, it launched a business that has lasted 27 years, created the deepest friendships of my life, and produced billions of dollars in sales and millions of dollars in personal income for my partners and me. Ambassador was acquired by another catalog company that went out of business in 1988. Mike Siegal became one of my most ardent supporters and remained my esteemed friend until he died in 1995.

Turning Your Failures from Dreaded Enemies into Valued Allies

It's now time to look at the second component of fear of failure, namely failure. Failure is always painful at the time you experience it, and because it is human nature to avoid pain, we nearly always turn away from our failures and run away from them, never looking back. From that moment on, we enter similar situations with an increased fear of failure. Normally, rather than risk failure in those similar situations, we will simply run away and avoid failure as long as possible. As we have seen, this risk avoidance, whether conscious or subconscious, then becomes one of the greatest constraining factors in our life.

Earlier I mentioned that Zig Ziglar stated that "failure is an event, not a person." That is all it is, no more and no less. It is simply an event in which we did not achieve our desired outcome. However, failure is always an event that has a cause or group of causes. Earlier in this session I asked the question, "What do the world's most successful people know about failure that most people don't know?" Here is the answer: They have discovered that every failure contains real-life lessons that are more valuable than any theory you could ever learn from a textbook. These lessons are missed by nearly everyone, because they run away from their failures in order to avoid the pain that comes from revisiting them. On the other hand, the world's most successful people always revisit their failures long

The Sixteenth Law of Extraordinary Success

Failure when revisited will rarely be relived. Failure when analyzed will provide the building blocks for future successes that will be far greater than the failure itself.

enough to analyze all the causes of those failures to make sure that those causes are not repeated in future endeavors. Every failure has primary causes, secondary causes, and contributing factors. Each of those elements provides lessons on which future successes can be built and fortified. Failure can become one of your greatest teachers and mentors, or it can remain a tyrannical dictator that drastically limits or even destroys your hopes of future success. Do you want failure to push you that much closer to success? Then you have to revisit it and you have to analyze it. Or, you can do what comes naturally (which is what most people do) and run away from it. When you do that, you will repeat the same causes of that failure in future endeavors. The choice is yours.

How can you turn failure from a tyrannical dictator into one of your greatest mentors and teachers? Once again, all it takes is a simple technique and a little time. The first step is to reassign the role of failure, and that involves an exercise that will be the focus of the "Actions for Traction" section at the end of this session. You should go through this exercise in any area in which you've experienced failure, whether it's a marriage, a relationship, a business, or a project at work.

First, make a list of any personal or business failures that you can recall that were hurtful to you. Second, for each major failure, write down all of the possible reasons that caused or contributed to that failure. If you have trouble coming up with a thorough list of causes, you will need to go to others who witnessed or were involved with that failure and recruit their help in making a list of the causes they may have seen. Third, write down the lessons that you can learn from those causes. Finally, write down any similar situations you may likely face in the future in which you might repeat those same causes.

When I first began applying this technique to my business projects back in the late 1970s, the results were phenomenal. In only three years it took my hit rate from 25 percent to 75 percent in an industry where the average hit rate is less than 5 percent.

As you begin these exercises, I know you are going to think, "Do I really have to write these things down?" The answer is, only if you want to begin to fail less, succeed more, and free yourself from your conscious and subconscious fears of failure. So I urge you to complete these exercises. That's the only way they're going to become a part of your daily life and your routine and make a real difference in your life. It worked for Henry Ford. It was also the secret weapon of the man who turned more failures into successes than any man in history, Thomas Edison.

Actions for Traction

WHERE THE RUBBER MEETS THE ROAD

1. Take any area of your life (your career, your marriage or any other relationship, a hobby, finances, etc.) and write down the answer to this question: If you could have anything you want to happen in that area, what would it be?
2. List the obstacles that prevent you from seeing that wish fulfilled.
3. List any fears that keep you from confronting that obstacle and trying to overcome it.
4. Using one of the fears you've listed, answer the following three questions:
   a. What's the worst-case scenario?
   b. What's the likely scenario?
   c. What's the best possible outcome for you and others if the fear isn't realized and you overcome the obstacle?
5. List any personal or business failures that you can recall that were hurtful to you.
6. Using the list, write down all of the possible reasons that caused or contributed to each failure.
7. Write down the general lessons or principles these failures demonstrated.
8. Are you currently ignoring those lessons and repeating those factors in any relationships or projects you are currently involved in? If so, write them down.
9. List any similar relationships or projects you are currently involved in in which these failures could be repeated.
10. List the actions you can take to prevent repeating the lessons of past failures in current similar situations.

SESSION 12

Bring On the Critics . . . and Beat Them!

Using Criticism to Create an Unlimited Advantage

Your Porsche's New Megadecibel Horn Can Be Heard Two Miles Away! Your Porsche is equipped with a new type of electric air horn that is connected to your alarm system and can be easily heard for a distance of over two miles. Although it will irritate hundreds of people whenever your alarm goes off, its ultraloud scream will drive away any would-be thief and will also instantly stop anyone (even drivers of 18-wheelers) from ever cutting you off while changing lanes.

Several years ago I was eating dinner with some business associates at a quaint Beverly Hills restaurant. It was a nice summer evening, so we were eating on the curbside patio along with about 100 other people. All of a sudden, what sounded like a supersonic alarm started blasting from a car across the street. Everyone on the patio was annoyed to the point of disgust. To my horror, it was the car I had rented for the week. I was hoping it would stop in a few seconds so I wouldn't have to suffer the embarrassment of jumping up and running across the street to turn it off. Unfortunately, it just kept blasting. With 100 pairs of eyes glaring at me, I got up from the table, hopped over a wall, and ran across the street to turn it off. Needless to say, I wanted to break that horn to smithereens. A few hours later I was driving back to our company's beach house in Malibu. As I was winding my way up the Pacific Coast Highway, a pickup truck started to pull out from a side street directly into my path. I smashed my hand onto the horn as hard as I could. Fortunately, the driver heard the horn, slammed on his brakes, and stopped halfway into my lane, and I was able to swerve around him. If it weren't for that car's loud horn, that driver would have been killed, and I might have been killed as well. The irritating horn that I had wanted to bash into a thousand pieces earlier that evening had saved one life, and maybe two. Criticism is a lot like that loud horn. Even though it can irritate us to a degree that nothing else can, when we know how to receive it, it can produce benefits beyond measure. How do I know? Two people's criticisms have made me and my partners hundreds of millions of dollars, and the criticisms of a handful of people turned my marriage into the single most fulfilling aspect of my life. I'll share a few of those life-changing criticisms a little later in this session.

I once asked an audience of 3,500 men and women, "How many of you like being criticized?" Not one hand went up. I then asked, "How many of you hate being criticized?" Every hand in the auditorium shot up. I asked, "How many of you have been hurtfully criticized at least once in this past week?" Once again, hundreds of hands went up. Some shot up instantly, while others went up more slowly as people thought through their week. But within a matter of seconds it seemed like nearly three-fourths of the audience had raised their hands. I then asked the most telling question of all. "Thinking back to your childhood, how many of you can remember a specific criticism that you received from a parent, a brother or sister, a classmate or a teacher, that was especially hurtful?" Within a few seconds, every single person in the auditorium had raised a hand. They had all received a criticism that was so painful they could still remember it decades later. That shows the true pain that a criticism can inflict.

When I was 11 years old, my father gave me the only hurtful criticism that ever passed from his lips to my ears. Looking back, I know he didn't mean it. But it was so hurtful at the time that I can still remember where we were when he said it, what he was wearing at the time, and the look in his eyes when he said it. I can even remember the tone of his voice. That was 44 years ago, and I can picture it as clearly in my mind right now as if it had happened only a few minutes ago. That one criticism affected my self-esteem, my self-image, and much of my behavior for more than 30 years.

How about you? Do you like criticism or hate it? Have you been hurtfully criticized by anyone during this past week or month? Can you remember a particularly painful criticism that you received in your childhood? Criticism is unsettling at best and devastating at worst. Relationships are wrecked by it, and lives have been forever altered, even ended by it. Criti-

The Seventeenth Law of Extraordinary Success

Conscious or subconscious avoidance of criticism will short-circuit the ability to achieve extraordinary success and happiness.

cism can sting like a bee, or it can inflict deep wounds like a sharp knife. Like the deadly venom of a rattlesnake, it can fatally poison one's self-esteem and outlook on life. And yet, as painful and destructive as it is, most of us are faced with it in one form or another nearly every week or month of our lives.

Because criticism is so potentially painful and harmful, we often pattern our behavior to avoid it at all cost. Our natural avoidance of criticism can be as much of an obstacle to our personal and professional success as our fear of failure. It must be dealt with correctly or we have little hope of achieving extraordinary success and happiness. Although there are dozens of wrong ways to deal with criticism, I have found only one right way: a way that will transform criticism from one of your most dreaded enemies into one of your most valued allies. As this happens, you will no longer fear criticism, nor will you pattern your behavior to avoid it. In fact, critics and their criticism will lose their power to hurt you. For many, this strategy will be one of the most liberating and empowering skills you will ever learn.

Master Strategy 12—Overcoming Your Avoidance of Criticism

Why Criticism Is Such a Formidable Roadblock to Extraordinary Success

People are often surprised that I place such a high priority on the importance of learning how to deal effectively with criticism. That I include it as one of the 15 master strategies for achieving extraordinary success is baffling to many motivators and educators, especially business school professors. But the fact is, every superachiever I have ever known or studied knew how to deal with criticism effectively. I've also realized that when criticism is not dealt with in the correct manner, it reduces our ability to succeed by impacting seven areas critical to extraordinary achievement.

1. **It affects our self-image and our self-esteem.** When people that we value criticize us, their criticism can alter how we view our capabilities

and ourselves. It can also change what we think we are really worth. When my boss at my third job told me that I was the single greatest disappointment in his entire career and that I would never succeed in marketing, I believed him. His criticism became my personal self-image, and his classification of me as his greatest disappointment defined my self-worth for the next four years. In the vernacular of our first session, criticism throughout our life can continually reprogram our onboard computer with much lower capabilities of achieving success.

2. It stifles our initiative. No one ever achieves extraordinary success at home or at work unless he or she builds the habit of taking the initiative. No person in history has ever been prodded or coaxed into extraordinary achievement. And yet, criticism is poison to people's motivation, commitment, and ability to consistently take the initiative in an area in which they've received significant criticism.

3. It suppresses our creativity. Without creativity, no creative alternatives can be developed, and without the ability to develop creative alternatives, extraordinary success cannot be achieved in any endeavor. Criticism challenges our confidence in our creative abilities and causes us to suppress our creative thoughts and expressions for fear they will receive additional criticism.

4. It discourages risk-taking. No significant achievement can ever be accomplished without taking significant risks. When it comes to quashing the inclination and willingness to take risks, the conscious and subconscious avoidance of criticism is second only to fear of failure. One of the all-time most hated sentences is, "I told you so," and, to avoid hearing that sentence and its accompanying criticisms, people who are often criticized will choose not to take the risk in the first place.

5. It encourages and fosters dishonesty. It's often easier and safer to say what someone wants to hear than to say what is true and risk being criticized for it. In World War II, Adolph Hitler's greatest generals would often give him false reports of their battles rather than risk receiving his harsh criticism. The same thing happens with CEOs and their subordinates in nearly every company in America. During my brief tenure in the only major corporation I ever worked for, I can tell you that every single employee in my department (which included dozens of managers and assistant managers) was deathly afraid of receiving criticism from the two men at the top. This is also true at home. Husbands, wives, and children often choose not to say what they really think, feel, believe, or desire for fear of being criticized for those thoughts, feelings, beliefs, or desires. Half-truths and lies flourish in the fertile soil of avoidance of criticism.

6. **It wreaks havoc on our emotional health.** Criticism often generates destructive emotions that affect our mental, emotional, physical, and social well-being. These emotions can include hurt, anger, resentment, bitterness, depression, despair, and even hatred. As these emotions grow, they make achieving extraordinary success next to impossible, and the avoidance of criticism becomes necessary for emotional survival.

7. **It impairs relationships.** Considering that criticism fosters dishonesty and the negative emotions just listed, it's apparent that it can impair and even destroy relationships. It can even result in the inability to maintain any healthy relationship. Since achieving extraordinary success requires an individual to partner effectively with others, such success becomes out of reach to the person who has not learned how to deal effectively with criticism.

As you consider these seven areas that are so heavily impacted by criticism, it's easy to understand why the avoidance of criticism, either conscious or subconscious, is such a powerful constraint to the ability to achieve extraordinary success. It's also apparent why people hate criticism and treat it as an enemy to be avoided at all cost. I have known mature, intelligent adults who have avoided visiting their parents, brothers, or sisters for years because they just can't handle their criticisms. Without even knowing it, most people wage a subconscious war with criticism. And because you will never be free of critics at home or in the workplace, this war will continue to take its toll, and criticism will forever prevent you from achieving extraordinary success and happiness—unless you use a strategy that will completely disarm criticism and turn it from a dreaded foe into a valued ally. That is exactly what you are going to learn how to do in the remainder of this session.

Lessons from the Past

In World War II, getting an American spy behind enemy lines was very difficult, and our failure rate at doing this was high. We were much more effective at recruiting enemy spies and turning them into counterspies on our behalf. Foreign spies converted into counterspies could go back into their governments and enjoy easy access to strategic information that they could then pass on to American intelligence officers. The strategy that you are going to use with criticism is much the same. Instead of fighting criticism, you are going to turn it from one of your most destructive enemies into your secret ally for success. You are going to use criticism to gain beneficial intelligence that you

Side-by-Side Comparison

How People Deal With Criticism

Drifters	Pursuers	Achievers	Superachievers
Either ignore the criticism, deny it, excuse it, or criticize the critic. Quick to blame circumstances or others.	Listen to criticism and are bothered by it, but rarely take it seriously enough to make any significant or permanent changes.	Pay close attention to criticisms offered by people they respect. They try hard to effect change in respect to criticisms they consider valid.	Determine the validity of a criticism and then mine valid criticisms for gold. When they find the gold, they recruit any means necessary to implement the valid short-term and long-term changes the criticism warrants.

are not likely to get any other way. So your objective is neither to fight criticism nor to fight your critics. It's not to defend yourself against criticism. Most important, your objective is not to end criticism. That will never happen anyway. You can't end it, you can't avoid it, and you can't fight it. But you can turn it into one of your most valuable and productive allies.

Sir Winston Churchill wrote, "Criticism is often useful, and praise is often deceitful." He was saying he would rather be criticized than praised. Why? Praise doesn't make you do anything. It just makes you sit back and smile. Criticism, on the other hand, has the power to make you refocus and rethink something from a different perspective. The richest and wisest man who ever lived agreed with Churchill. In Proverbs 10:17, Solomon said that the person who ignores criticism makes costly long-term mistakes, and in Proverbs 15:32 he said that the person who listens to criticism and heeds its advice receives greater degrees of understanding. One of the most revered actresses of all time was a star of the silent screen era, Lillian Gish. She wrote, "I like people to come back and tell me what I did wrong. That's the kindest thing they can do." She had discovered the value of turning criticism into an ally.

A Bucket of Criticism–A Lot of Water, Some Sand, and a Little Bit of Gold

One of my family's favorite vacation spots is Coronado Island in San Diego. Anyone who has ever played on Coronado's beaches has noticed that when the waves recede they leave what appears to be millions of flakes of gold. Imagine for a minute that those flakes were really gold. Criticism is like somebody grabbing a bucket of that water and throwing it on you. A bucket of criticism is full of water, has a few inches of sand, and nearly always has a little bit of gold buried somewhere in the sand. A whole bucket of criticism might have a great big gold nugget, or it may only have one tiny little flake of gold—one that requires a lot of searching to find.

When a bucket of criticism is thrown at us, the first thing that hits our face is the water. It's cold, and it's shocking, but it's really quite harmless. All we have to do is grab a towel and dry it off. Some of the sand in the bottom of the bucket also hits us in the face, and a few grains get into our eyes. That's a little more painful and irritating and needs to be removed from our eyes, not only to end the pain and irritation but so we can see more clearly. And finally there's the gold. It's hidden in the couple inches of sand left in the bottom of the bucket.

Here are the points of the analogy. The water is the invalid part of the criticism, the emotional part. It's the use of an exaggeration or blanket statement. "You always do this! You never do that! I can't believe you did that again!" What does water do? It gets you wet. Does it kill you? Does it injure you? Does it maim you? No! It's just water! What do you do? You grab a towel and you wipe yourself off. Realize that the emotional part of the criticism—the exaggerations and superlatives—are only water, and nothing more.

And then there's the sand. The sand is the stinging part of criticism. It's the part of the criticism that irritates and hurts. It can be the spirit of the critic—a spirit of harshness, judgment, condemnation, condescension, anger, hatefulness, and so on. This spirit may be reflected in the words that are used, the critic's tone of voice, or nonverbal communication such as body language or the look the critic gives you. It can be a look of disappointment, disbelief, disgust, anger, or even hatred. It stings, and irritates, but it is also easily removed, and as soon as it is, the criticism loses its painful sting. The best way that I have found to remove it is to get away by yourself and to write down the criticism and then read it. When it's written down, it is usually devoid of the emotional sting of tone of voice and body language.

Finally, there is the gold. The gold is the truth of the criticism that can make us wiser and help us adjust our behavior, our attitudes, or our words for the better. There may only be a flake of truth that really needs to be searched for, or there may be a giant gold nugget of truth that will be of immeasurable value. This is what Churchill, Solomon, and Lillian Gish were talking about. They realized that with criticism, there's often a measure of truth that can be of great benefit to us and to those we relate to.

That's the analogy, but how do you turn that analogy into a practical skill? This can be accomplished with any criticism by taking only three steps.

Turning Criticism into Your Powerful Ally–A Three-Step Skill

The good news is that you don't have to be a Churchill or a Solomon to disarm criticism and gain the success-building benefits of converting it from a dreaded foe to a valued friend and teacher. All it takes is a single skill that anyone can learn and utilize. The purpose of implementing this skill is first to remove the sting of a criticism, and then to determine the valid elements of that criticism and draw as much benefit as possible from those valid elements. This simple skill involves three steps and can be applied to any criticism you receive, no matter who gives it or how painful it might feel.

1. Consider the Source of the Criticism. All critics are not created equal. The first step in effectively dealing with criticism is to consider the source of the criticism. The three questions that must be answered about the source of the criticism are: (1) How qualified is the critic to make the criticism? (2) What is the basis of the criticism? and (3) What is the critic's motive for making the criticism?

How Qualified Is the Critic? Some critics are highly qualified to give a particular criticism, others are somewhat qualified, and some are not qualified at all. Yet many people strongly react to criticism regardless of how qualified or unqualified the critic may be. So the first step in dealing with any criticism is to determine how qualified the critic is to give that particular criticism. Is he or she very qualified (VQ), somewhat qualified (SQ), or not qualified at all (NQ)? To help me visually evaluate and quantify a criticism, after I write the criticism down on paper and as I analyze the criticism, I place the appropriate abbreviation next to it.

My wife's father once delivered a stinging criticism to her regarding a visitation issue with her ex-husband concerning our son Devin. Shannon's father angrily pointed his finger at her and said, "If you really loved Devin, you would get the custody jurisdiction moved from California to Utah." My wife's father is a wonderful, loving father and grandfather. He had no intention of hurting my wife's feelings. But his criticism was delivered with such intensity that it devastated Shannon for days afterward. To help her through this criticism, I started with this first step of considering the source. I asked her, "How qualified is your dad to give this criticism? Is he a lawyer? Is he well versed in California's divorce and custodial laws? Has he researched all of the possible legal complications that could result from making such a move?" And then there's the issue of what was best for Devin's self-esteem. Was her dad a child psychologist? Was he even thinking about Devin's need to have a great relationship with his father? The answer to each of these questions was no. He was therefore not qualified (NQ) to give such a criticism, making his criticism 100 percent invalid.

In an earlier session I told the story of writing my first television commercial. When I read it to my partner, instead of patting me on the back he gave me a nicely presented criticism. He said, "I like it, but it doesn't have a hook. What it really needs is a good hook." In this situation, considering the source generated an entirely different score than in my father-in-law's criticism of my wife. My partner was a marketing and entrepreneurial genius. In the past he had successfully launched start-up businesses with creative and powerful advertisements he had written. Was he qualified to give a valid criticism of my commercial? Absolutely! He was very qualified and got a VQ.

And then there was my ex-boss who gave me the strongest criticism I have ever received. He's the one who said, "You are the single greatest disappointment in my entire career. You will never succeed in marketing." How qualified was he to make these two cutting criticisms? He was the senior vice president of marketing for a major conglomerate. His first criticism was related to his own personal career and the disappointments he had previously experienced. His second criticism was related to his field of expertise (marketing). So at first glance, it seemed that he was very qualified to give both criticisms. However, a closer look at his second criticism reveals he was predicting my future. No matter how qualified he may have been as a marketer, he certainly was not qualified as a fortune-teller. In fact, the only one who really knows the future is God, and my boss certainly wasn't divine. Therefore he got a VQ in relation to his first criticism and an NQ in relation to his second criticism. As it turned out, his second criticism with its prediction couldn't have been further from the truth. All of my successes in business have been built on my marketing skills—skills that helped create levels of success for my partners and me that turned out to be more than 100 times greater than any success achieved by my ex-boss.

What Is the Basis of the Criticism? Criticisms are usually based on one of several factors. These factors can reveal the degree to which a criticism may be valid. Some of these factors are:

1. The critic's emotions or feelings. (E)
2. The critic's past experience. (P)

3. Your past experience and track record. (YP)
4. The critic's failures. (CF)
5. Your past failures. (PF)
6. The critic's lack of understanding of your intentions, motives, goal, or vision. (LU)
7. The critic's inability to think creatively outside the box. The critic may be a conventional thinker trying to judge your creative thinking. (CT)
8. The criticism may be based on logic or wisdom that is greater than yours. (LW)

My wife's father's criticism was based on his emotions (E), which is usually the least valid basis for a criticism. My partner's criticism was based on his logic and wisdom (LW), which is usually the most valid basis for criticism. My ex-boss's criticisms were based on his emotions (E).

Once I made a suggestion to a boss that was both creative and outside the box. Being a conventional thinker, my boss believed that only the company's ad agency was qualified to come up with valid creative thoughts. When I presented my idea for a television campaign, he gave me a condescending smile and a pat on the shoulder and said, "That's not your job; our creative approaches are the responsibility of our ad agency." His rejection of my idea and his accompanying criticisms were based on his own conventional thinking (CT). Five years later my current company took that same idea back to his company and presented it to his boss, the company's founder. This time they bought it. It turned out to be the single most profitable marketing campaign in that company's history. The difference was that the company's founder was creative and recognized the value of the idea. They paid us millions of dollars for a campaign they could have owned five years earlier for the salary they were paying me—$12,000.

Perhaps the greatest example of executives missing the boat due to their confinement to conventional thinking is that of the executives at Xerox who rejected and criticized the ideas and inventions of their engineers at their Palo Alto Research Center (PARC). Their conventional thinking caused them to lose what could have been the sole patented ownership of the personal computer, the graphical user interface, and the Internet. Oops!

What Is the Motive of the Critic? Knowing the motive of the critic does not make a criticism valid or invalid. But if the motive is a positive one, it at least makes the criticism more tolerable. On the other hand, if the motive is a negative one, it may bring the validity of the criticism into question. However, just because the motive is negative does not necessarily invalidate the criticism, although it may make it suspect. In our industry one particular company has voiced strong criticisms of the deceptive practices of other companies in the industry. Even though that company's motives may have been totally self-centered, their criticisms were right on target and 100 percent valid. As you look at the motives of your critics, ask yourself, Are they motivated by positive factors such as their love and concern for you or their concern for a project or other people? Are they motivated by their commitment to excellence or ethics? Or are they motivated by negative factors such as selfishness, jealousy, fear, animosity, hurt, anger, immaturity, or ignorance?

Returning to our earlier examples, Shannon's father was motivated by his love and concern for Devin. So although he wasn't qualified to give that criticism, focusing on his motive made it easier for Shannon to handle it. In the case of the missing hook, my partner was motivated by his desire to see our first project—and me—succeed. My ex-boss's criticism, on the other hand, was motivated by his hurt feelings, his anger, and his pride.

In summary, considering the source involves three factors: the critic's qualifications, the basis of the criticism, and the motive for giving the criticism. Now that you have effectively considered the source of the criticism, let's move on to the next step.

2. Consider the Accuracy of the Criticism. Shannon's dad's criticism started with the statement, "If you really loved Devin, you would . . ." This criticism missed the target by a thousand miles. Shannon is the most loving mother I have ever known. In fact, it was her unselfish love for Devin that motivated her to want him to have a lot of quality time with his father. On the other hand, when my partner said, "It doesn't have a hook . . . what it really needs is a good hook," he hit the target right in the center of the bulls-eye. That was exactly what my script lacked and what it desperately needed.

And then there is the criticism of my ex-boss. He said that I was the single greatest disappointment in his entire career. Was that an accurate statement? He was the number three executive in the entire corporation, and prior to coming to that company he had experienced a distinguished career at another Fortune 500 company. I, on the other hand was only a junior manager making $12,000 a year. I had only worked for him for nine months. How on earth could I be the single greatest disappointment in his entire career? When I realized that his criticism was a gross exaggeration and couldn't possibly be accurate, the sting immediately vanished. You will find a few criticisms are extremely accurate, some are partially accurate, and many are totally inaccurate. The less accurate they are, the more easily their sting is removed.

Now that you've considered the source and the accuracy of the criticism, you are ready for the third and most important step in this skill. This is the step that will ultimately convert the criticism from an enemy to an ally.

3. Take Responsibility for Your Response to the Criticism and Mine It for Gold. Whenever someone criticizes us, our natural inclination is to react to them and their criticism. We usually want to defend our action or words that are being criticized. Deep down inside, we also want to counterattack. We want to belittle the criticism. We want to tell critics that they are all wet, or that they don't know what they're talking about. We often retaliate by criticizing them to someone else. We want to gossip about them, discredit them, and, if our feelings are really hurt, we want to hurt them back. Or we may choose to withdraw from the critic and run away from the criticism. These are a few of our natural human reactions to critics, their criticism, and the pain criticism inflicts. Unfortunately, all of these reactions are counterproductive and are actually in our worst interests. These reactions are not going to advance you to your dreams. To the contrary, they are going to prevent you from achieving your dreams. You have a choice: You can either yield to your natural inclinations and react to the criticism or you can choose to restrain your inclinations and respond to the criticism.

What's the difference between reacting and responding? My friend Zig Ziglar gives the perfect analogy. He says, "Suppose your doctor prescribes a medication and asks you to come back in 48 hours for a checkup. When you return for the checkup, if he examines you and says, 'Uh-oh, your body is reacting to the medication,' you know that you are in trouble. On the other hand, if he says, 'Ahhhh . . . your body is responding to the medication,' then you know you are on your way to feeling better." The same is true in relation to how you act when you are criticized. When you react, your negative natural inclinations are in control and they will rob you of your opportunity to benefit from the criticism and ultimately to achieve extraordinary success. When you respond to the criticism, you are taking control away from your nature and choosing to utilize the criticism correctly. You will analyze the criticism and then mine it for its gold. By choosing to respond, you will not only gain benefit from the criticism, you will increase your chances of achieving extraordinary success.

Don't feel bad if you blow it and react initially. Because you're human, that's going to happen some of the time. But blowing it in your initial reaction does not prevent you from going back to the criticism and responding to it. You do that by wiping off the water, taking the sand out of your eyes, and then mining it for gold. Sometimes those gold nuggets are right in front of us and easily lifted out of the sand. That was the case with my partner's criticism about my lack of a hook. I picked up that gold nugget, created my first hook, and generated $20 million in sales in only 20 weeks. More important, I added hooks to my creative model and have used them in every television commercial and infomercial I have since created.

Other times we have to dig long and deep before we find even a single gold flake, much less a nugget. That was the case with the criticisms from my ex-boss. Where is the gold nugget in his criticism about me being the greatest disappointment in his entire career, or in the statement, "You'll never succeed in marketing"? The nuggets I found in these criticisms were buried deep in the sand. As I searched his words, I realized that it was really my behavior and my work that had been disappointing to him. What had I done that was so disappointing? Then I found the nugget. I had not been a loyal member of his team. I had been moonlighting for other executives of other subsidiaries. I was also looking for another job with a different subsidiary. When he discovered that I had been moonlighting and that I was searching for a job in a different subsidiary, he felt betrayed and hurt by my disloyalty.

How did this become gold? When I started my next job, instead of always looking for a better opportunity, I made sure that I really focused on that job. I also let my new boss know that I was committed with my whole heart. Because of the gold nugget in my ex-boss's criticism, I would work hard to never again be perceived by future bosses as a disloyal employee. As I demonstrated loyalty in my jobs that followed, my bosses began handing me the bat and letting me swing for the fences, and after awhile I started hitting home runs. That's an awful lot of benefit from one little gold nugget that I mined from the criticism of my ex-boss.

In the "Actions for Traction" section, you are going to go back and look at some of the criticisms that hurt you at different points in your life and start mining them for gold. If you have recently been criticized by your spouse, your boss, your friends, or your coworkers, you will write down some of those stinging criticisms. You will then take the steps we have discussed and mine their criticisms for gold. As you do this, your fear of criticism will vanish and your conscious and subconscious avoidance of criticism will begin to abate. You will no longer guide your behavior based on your fear of criticism. You will find it much easier to take intelligent, calculated risks and pursue the opportunities and dreams that mean the most to you. Also, when you lose your fear of criticism, your valued relationships will grow stronger. You will be able to respond more effectively. Instead of people being afraid to criticize you, they will feel a greater freedom to offer constructive criticism. As you mine it for gold, you will acquire more wisdom and understanding to more effectively pursue and achieve your most cherished dreams.

Actions for Traction

WHERE THE RUBBER MEETS THE ROAD

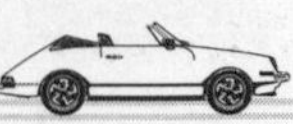

1. Make a list of some the more memorable criticisms that you have received either at home or at work.
2. Determine how qualified the person was to give such a criticism. Beside each of the criticisms, write VQ for very qualified, SQ for somewhat qualified, or NQ for not qualified.
3. Beside each criticism, write down as many of the following reasons as may have been the basis of the person's criticism.
   - (E) Emotionally based
   - (PE) Based on your or their past experiences or past failures
   - (LU) Based on their lack of understanding or fully comprehending your goal, intention, or vision
   - (CT) Based on their conventional thinking rather than creative thinking
   - (L) Based on logic
   - (RS) Based on the realities of the situation
4. What was the motive of the critic? Was it love, concern for you or the project, or his or her genuine concern for others, or was it selfishness, jealousy, fear, animosity, hurt, anger, or his or her own immaturity?
5. Looking back, how accurate was the criticism?
   a. Define the "water" in the criticism—that which was exaggerated, absurd, or meaningless.
   b. Define the "sand" in the criticism—that which was most irritating or hurtful (specific words, tone of voice, spirit of criticism, etc.).
   c. Determine the "gold" in the criticism—the truths that can be drawn from the criticism that can help you better perform in the future.
6. How did you respond to the criticism? Was it with anger, defensiveness, denial, blame, attack, or withdrawal? Or did you listen to, acknowledge, thank, or give the critic an explanation that helped him or her to better understand you or your action?
7. How could you have responded in a way that would have been better for you, your growth, and your relationship with the critic?
8. Write down the best ways you believe you could respond to criticism in the future.

SESSION 13

Taking Control and Keeping It

Prioritizing Your Days to Reflect Your Values and Goals

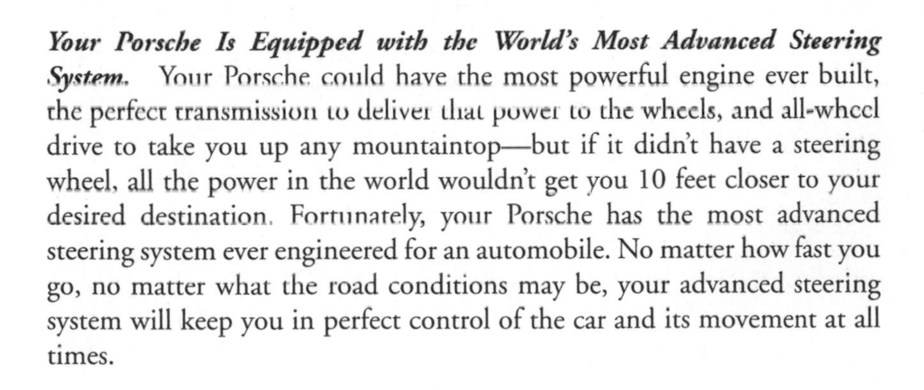

Your Porsche Is Equipped with the World's Most Advanced Steering System. Your Porsche could have the most powerful engine ever built, the perfect transmission to deliver that power to the wheels, and all-wheel drive to take you up any mountaintop—but if it didn't have a steering wheel, all the power in the world wouldn't get you 10 feet closer to your desired destination. Fortunately, your Porsche has the most advanced steering system ever engineered for an automobile. No matter how fast you go, no matter what the road conditions may be, your advanced steering system will keep you in perfect control of the car and its movement at all times.

The lifetime odds of dying in an airplane crash are 1 out of 4.6 million, while the odds of being killed in a car accident are 1 out of 125. In other words, you are nearly 39,000 times more likely to die from a car accident than from a plane crash. And yet, despite the odds, millions of adults who have no fear of driving have a fear of flying. Why? The answer is simple. In a car they feel like they are in control, while on an airliner they feel like they are totally out of control. Have you ever been riding in someone else's car when they are driving a little too fast or a little too close to the cars in front of them? My partner Jim will drive 80 miles per hour on a freeway, riding other people's bumpers and changing lanes the moment the car in front of him impedes his speed. When I'm riding with Jim, his speeding, tailgating, and lane changing stress me out. On the other hand, if I am driving, I can do all of the things that Jim does and not be nervous at all. Once again, the difference is being out of control versus being in control.

Being out of control in any form or situation is rarely an enjoyable experience, and the consequences of being out of control can be devastating. If you have ever stepped on a patch of ice and had your legs fly out from beneath you, you've known the heart-stopping panic of being out of control, even though it was only for a split second. A few years ago, I was driving my boys to school and hit a patch of ice. Even though I was only driving about 15 miles per hour, we started spinning out of control and hit a curb and a fence post. If you have ever experienced any situation where you have lost all control of a car, you can probably recall the panic you felt.

When we are out of control in any situation, even for the shortest amount of time, we can become frightened or even panicked. And yet, when it comes to pursuing their hopes and dreams, most adults move through their days, weeks, months, and years out of control and feel comfortable about it. Their time and what they accomplish with that time is more controlled by outside circumstances and the demands of others than by their own priorities, goals, desires, or needs. In a very real sense, they are moving through life in a car where others are always holding the steering wheel.

Whenever you ask yourself, "Where did this day go?" or "Where has this year gone?" you are really saying that you did not accomplish nearly what you wanted to achieve in that period of time. Your New Year's resolutions, whether silent or spoken, remain the same year in and year out: "This year I'm going to lose that weight," "This year I'm going to start exercising 30 minutes a day," "I really am going to do this or quit doing that." Sound familiar?

While most people are not in control of their time, such is not the case with superachievers. They start each new year far beyond the point where they started the previous year. They have either fulfilled some of their significant goals and dreams or they are much closer to fulfilling them than they were 12 months earlier. The world's most successful people typically accomplish more in a week than most people accomplish in a month; some accomplish more in a month than others accomplish in a year. Why? Is it because they are rich or because they have garnered the power to marshal hordes of subordinates to do things for them? Absolutely not! If you were to look back at their lives before they made any money or achieved their extraordinary success, you would discover that even then they were accomplishing much more in a week than their peers would in a month.

Another Secret of Superachievers

So what is their secret? First, they have employed many of the strategies that we focused on in our earlier sessions. They converted their dreams into goals, their goals into steps, and their steps into tasks. They dared to dream the impossible and effectively recruited and utilized partners to pursue those dreams. They became effective and persuasive communicators and learned how to creatively persist through extraordinary problems and setbacks. They overcame their fear of failure and converted criticisms from foes to friends. They did all of this from the time they first started moving on their paths toward extraordinary success. But this is not all they did. Just as important, they learned how to take control of their lives and their futures, one minute, one hour, and one day at a time. Each day they took the steering wheel in their hands and pointed their Porsche in the direction they wanted to go. Each day they accomplished goals they had predetermined to be in line with their priorities for that day—priorities that reflected their personal values and goals rather than the values and goals of someone else.

Side-by-Side Comparison

How People Take Control of Their Lives

Drifters	Pursuers	Achievers	Superachievers
Do not control their time, their direction, or the speed at which they move in any direction. They think they are in control, but they are not. They just go with the flow.	Try hard to get a lot done each day, and make slow progress toward achieving some of their modest goals. But too much of their time is controlled by outside circumstances and other people.	Have set their achievable goals and make steady progress toward those goals daily. They use time management skills to make the most of their working hours. They try hard to take control and keep it, and they succeed much of the time.	Have set extraordinary to impossible goals in their areas of greatest interest. They control nearly every aspect of their time, the direction of their paths, and the speed at which they move down those paths. They use nearly all 15 of the master strategies to stay on track to achieve their impossible dreams as quickly and efficiently as they can.

How about you? Who or what controls the use of your time? Even though you may think you are in control of how you use your time, chances are you only control a small portion of it. Before you start to argue with me, let me ask you a few questions. You might tell me that your children are more important to you than anyone or anything on earth, and I would believe that this truly reflects your core values. But say it's Saturday morning and you are playing with your children. Your wife is at the store, and your telephone rings. What do you do? Do you jump up and run over to see who's on caller ID, or do you keep playing with your kids and ignore the phone? If you jumped up to run to the phone, the phone's ring controlled that minute of your life. If it was your boss on the phone and you talked to him for 20 minutes, your boss controlled that 20 minutes of your life. I'm sure you would agree that neither the phone's ring nor your boss's conversation is as important to you as your children, and yet you replaced your time with that which you value most; with time spent on that which you value less.

Chances are pretty good that you are part of the 97 percent of America's adults who don't control their time or the steering wheel of their lives. After this session you will know how to take control of the wheel and become part of the 3 percent who do control their lives, minute by minute, hour by hour, day by day.

Master Strategy 13—Taking Control of Your Life, One Day at a Time

There are many aspects of our lives that are impossible to control. We can't control outside circumstances that influence and intrude into our lives, such as the weather, the ring of a telephone, whether an airline flight we have booked will take off and arrive on schedule, or whether we will be injured in an accident or contract an illness or disease. The list of things we can't control could fill a telephone book. However, there are also many important aspects of our lives that we can control very effectively—but most people fail to take or maintain control of these aspects as well. For example, we have the opportunity and the means of controlling our weight, and yet two out of every three Americans are overweight. We have the opportunity and the means of controlling how we spend our time and what we accomplish with it, and yet, 97 percent of America's adults fail miserably in this area as well. The fact is that in most of the important areas in our lives we have the means of exercising significant control, and yet most people fail to do so. Superachievers are great at gaining and maintaining effective control of the aspects

> ***The Eighteenth Law of Extraordinary Success***
>
> If you can't control your time, you won't achieve extraordinary success.

of their lives that they consider to be most important. But even superachievers fail to take control of the aspects of their lives that they consider to be less important. That's why even superachievers can be overweight or even addicted to various substances or vices.

Three Keys for Taking and Maintaining Control of Your Life

Contrary to popular belief, taking control of your life is not simply a matter of increasing your self-discipline or willpower. When I talk to a group about this subject, it's not uncommon for people to tell me that they control most of their time or most of their life. The error of this notion is quickly exposed by a single question. If you are driving your car at 65 miles per hour to your favorite destination, how long can you take your hands off the steering wheel before your trip will be ruined by a terrible crash? To reach your dreams, you have to keep your hands on the wheel at all times. That means you not only need to take control, you need to maintain that control until you reach your destination. To take and maintain control of the most important areas of your life requires three key elements: priority planning, sustained focus, and personal accountability. I don't know of anyone who has ever achieved extraordinary success without utilizing these three elements.

Replacing an Illusion with Reality

We live in a world full of illusions, and the most catastrophic illusion of all is that we have a lot of time to spare. You might think that *catastrophic* is too strong a word to use when applied to wasting time. If that was your thought, it's because you haven't yet realized how truly limited and valuable your time really is. Most people act as if there is no limit to the amount of time they have. There's always tomorrow. There's always next week, next month, or next year. We usually place no more value on our time than we place on the water we wash our hands with.

A while back, I was visiting my mother in a convalescent center about 600 miles from my home. We didn't spend a lot of time together on that trip because my niece was getting married in that same town and there were several festivities to attend. My last night in town I chose to take everyone out to dinner rather than spend the evening at my mother's bedside. The next morning before I left, I visited Mom and told her that I would see her the next month. She seemed discouraged that we had spent so little time together. Several days later I received a call from my sister telling me that my mother had taken a turn for the worse during the night. I rushed to the airport, jumped on a plane, and arrived 90 minutes later. I turned on my cell phone as soon as the plane landed, and it rang as I was walking toward the aircraft's door. It was my sister calling to tell me that Mom had passed away while I was in flight. There would be no next month. There wouldn't even be a minute to hold my mother's hand and tell her one more time how much I loved her. Time with my mother had been so free earlier that I had wasted it, and now not a single minute with my mother could be acquired for any price.

Time is truly the most precious and limited commodity we possess. Every single day we make dozens of choices about how to spend our time. If we don't plan how we are going to spend our time before the day begins, we will spend it on whatever comes up, regardless of whether or not it reflects our would-be priorities for that day. At the end of the day, we think, "Where the heck did this day go?" Most of the priority items on our to-do list are left undone. We then appease our frustration with, "Oh well, I'll take care of those tomorrow."

Your Dwindling Bank Account

Imagine for a minute that you could never go to work again and earn a single penny. Imagine that you have no source of income available to you at all. Imagine that the only money you have is in a bank account, and no money will ever be added to that account. This money is all that you will ever have to pay for your food, clothing, shelter, medicine, and other living expenses for the rest of your life. Finally, imagine that every single day you are using up a portion of the money in that account and your account balance just keeps getting smaller and smaller. How would you treat the remaining money? Would you spend it on anything and everything that you felt like spending it on? Or would you try to come up with a plan to make that account last as long as possible? Although this is not the case with your income and money, it is precisely the case with your time. As we discussed in our session on limited resources, you have a bank account of time, and its balance is declining every second of every day, even while you are fast asleep.

The good news is that you can take more control over how you use this precious resource so that at the end of your day, week, month, and life you will have little regret about how you spent your time. The first step in taking control of your life and destiny is taking control of your time. It all starts with what I call *priority planning.*

Priority Planning–The Key to Taking Control

Thomas Edison wrote, "The thing I lose patience with the most is the clock. Its hands move too fast. Time is really the only capital that any human being has and the one thing he can least afford to waste or lose." To make sure he didn't waste his time, Edison planned out every day before he started that day. That didn't mean that he always did every single thing he had planned, but it did mean that he had a plan to follow that would at least move him in the direction he wanted to go. There are two steps to priority planning: (1) Create a plan for the day that orders your activities to reflect your priorities for that day and (2) execute the plan according to your priorities. The first step is easy, while the second is more challenging.

To create an effective priority plan for each day, you only need three things: a pen, a day planner, and 10 to 15 minutes to create the plan prior to starting your daily activities. It's usually best to plan your day the night before, but if you're an early riser and can have an undisturbed 15 minutes in the morning, that's fine too. I highly recommend that you use a paper day planning system over an electronic one. If you like the electronic systems such as the Palm Pilot, use that for everything else, but still create your priority day plan on paper. The advantage of paper is simple: You can keep it in front of you throughout the day as a visual reminder and benchmark for working through your prioritized list. I use the Franklin Covey planner because of its simplicity. On its day pages there is a column for a prioritized task list to the left of the appointment schedule. If you don't have a day planner, you can follow this same procedure on any piece of loose-leaf paper.

1. Make a list of all the tasks that you would like to accomplish that day without regard to their priority.
2. After you have created the task list, place an A beside the most important tasks on that list. Then place B beside the tasks that are of secondary importance. Finally, place a C by the tasks that are the least important.
3. Now, starting with your A tasks, place a 1 next to your highest-priority A task, a 2 beside the next highest priority A task, and so on. After you have numbered all the A's, number all the B's starting with a 1 for your highest-priority B task. After you have prioritized your B tasks, prioritize your C tasks in the same manner.

In a matter of minutes you will have created a priority plan for your next day. Keeping this plan in front of you throughout the day will remind you to set your focus on achieving the most important tasks first and only moving to the lesser tasks after the more important ones have been completed. You've heard the adage, The squeaky wheel gets the grease. Often, low-priority tasks squeak louder than high-priority tasks. Without a plan, we may get distracted or irritated by their squeak and focus on handling them first. Also, higher-priority tasks are often more difficult to complete, so we tend to procrastinate and do what's easiest first, even though it's less important. Having a written prioritized list in front of you throughout the day enables you to ignore the squeaks and complete the higher-priority items even when they are more difficult. If you accomplish all of your A's and one of your B's, you've had a far more productive day than if you accomplished all of your C's and two of your B's.

The Best Plans in the World Are Worthless If They Aren't Effectively Executed!

Creating your priority plan is the easier step of priority planning. Executing the plan is a little more difficult. Creating a plan and keeping it in front of you points you in the right direction, but in order to execute the plan effectively you need to overcome three elements that will be competing for your time and attention: unexpected urgencies, time robbers, and procrastination.

Unexpected urgencies that draw your time and attention away from your priorities. Urgencies are interruptions that bring with them a sense that they need your immediate attention. Consequently, unless you have predetermined how you are going to handle them, they will pull you away from your priorities, even though you know your priorities are more important. For example, say you are working on your A-1 priority. Your boss walks up to your desk and tells you he wants you to stop what you're doing and come to a meeting. The meeting may be quite irrelevant to your priorities and your boss's, but he's going and wants you to tag along. Rather than putting your priority aside, you should say something like this: "Right now I'm working on this project that you and I both know should be finished this week. If I don't stay on it until I'm finished, there's a good chance I'll miss the deadline." Now it's up to your boss to weigh that priority against the meeting. There's a great chance he will respect your commitment to a matter that he also considers more important, and will excuse you from attending the meeting.

An even more common urgency is a ringing telephone. You should start each day making a commitment to yourself that you are not going to answer any unimportant phone calls until you've completed your highest-priority tasks. With caller ID and voice mail, putting calls off until later is a lot easier than it was a few years ago. Because urgencies always seem like they need to be dealt with instantly, you need to determine how you are going to deal with them before you start your day.

Time robbers—activities, events, and circumstances that interrupt and easily distract you from attending to your priorities. Franklin Covey, America's leading authority in personal time management, gives the following list of time robbers that steal our attention and time away from our prioritized tasks. The best way to overcome these distractions is to start your day with a predetermined strategy for dealing with any of these that are likely to come your way. Which of these are most likely to steal your time on any given day?

Time Robbers

Check the Robbers that Steal Your Time

____ Unexpected interruptions	____ Unrealistic time estimates
____ Unplanned phone calls	____ Lengthy phone conversations
____ Requests or demands of others	____ Shifting priorities
____ Mistakes of others	____ Mistakes
____ Equipment failures	____ Bureaucratic red tape
____ Poor communication	____ Indecision
____ Improper planning	____ Socializing
____ Inadequate listening	____ Personality conflicts
____ Conflicting priorities	____ Unwillingness to say no
____ Lack of self-discipline	____ Involvement with details
____ Meetings	____ Failure to delegate

The urge to procrastinate and put off the more important priorities until later. Hyrum Smith, cofounder of the Franklin-Covey organization, has been a close friend of mine for many years. As one of the world's experts on time management, he gives wonderful insight into the reasons people procrastinate. Here's a list of his six reasons.

1. **We sense no urgency in the activity, even if it's one of our highest priorities.** How much urgency do you sense in the activity of playing

with your child? If you're honest, you'll say close to none. And yet, it's absolutely critical to your child's self-esteem. How much urgency is in the activities of giving your children a hug or a pat on the back or listening to them tell you how they spent their day? No, it's not urgent, but it's important. But because we do not sense an urgency, it is easy to put off such activities until later.

2. The activity may not be fun or pleasant. There are a lot of things that I put off because I know they're the hardest things I'm going to have to do that day. I put them off until the end of the day. When the end of the day arrives, I put them off until tomorrow. I'm that way with expense reports. I hate expense reports. However, as much as I hate filling them out, they are absolutely critical to our accounting department and the filing of our corporate tax returns. So, like it or not, I have to complete them by an appointed deadline. I'm sure you can think of important tasks you put off because they are neither fun nor pleasant.

3. The activity is outside of our comfort zone. If your personality type is that of a golden retriever, you hate confrontation. If there is a need at home or on the job for you to have a confrontation, you will procrastinate about doing it for as long as you possibly can, no matter how important that event may be. If you are a lion, you hate committee meetings, and even if one is desperately needed, you will procrastinate about attending because it is outside your comfort zone. No matter how important an activity or task may be, if we are not comfortable performing it, we will put it off as long as possible.

4. We fear failure in the performance of the activity. If you are a salesman and you have been assigned to target a major account that the company is hoping for and counting on for next year, your fear of failure may cause you to procrastinate about soliciting that account and cause you to focus on chasing lesser accounts that you are more likely to succeed in acquiring. Now that you have learned how to effectively deal with your fears of failure, this should not be that much of a problem in your future.

5. We don't perceive the activity's real value. I used to watch the news as soon as I got home from work, rather than focusing on my kids. One day one of my sons tearfully said to me, "Daddy, you watch too much news." He had finally had enough of me putting off his need for love and attention in favor of watching the news. I had underestimated the importance of playing with my sons as soon as I got home. A new rule was invoked in the Scott household: Dad can't watch TV until the kids are in bed.

6. We lack the knowledge that is needed to do that activity now. While this may be a good reason for other people to procrastinate, it's certainly not a good reason for you and me. If we don't know how to do it, we recruit and utilize a partner who either can show us how to do it or will do it with us or for us.

The priority planning process is the single most important step in taking control of our lives, minute by minute and hour by hour. By setting our focus on the plan each day, we can minimize our tendency to procrastinate or be distracted by time robbers. But there are two other elements that are also critical to taking and maintaining the control of our lives and achieving extraordinary success: sustaining our focus and becoming personally accountable.

Sustained Focus—The First Key to Maintaining Control

Thomas Edison wrote, "The first requisite for success is to develop the ability to focus and apply your mental and physical energies to the problem at hand—without growing weary." If Edison were a student in our school system today, he would have certainly been diagnosed as a victim of severe attention deficit disorder (ADD). Even in his day he was considered retarded by the headmaster of his school because he couldn't stay focused on the lessons. Consequently his mother removed him from school after three months of first grade and home-schooled him from that point on. And yet, despite his obvious affliction with ADD, he was able to maintain higher levels of focus than any businessman, entrepreneur, or superachiever I have ever studied. During his lifetime he was deeply concerned that colleges were not teaching young people how to think or how to maintain their focus. As bad as it was in his day, it's even worse today. The lack of this skill is a tremendous detriment to personal achievement at all ages and occupational levels. From preschool all the way to the executive suite of Fortune 500 companies, people are losing the battle of staying focused on the tasks needed to accomplish a goal quickly and effectively. Why is this so much more prevalent today than it was with our parents and grandparents? I believe we lack the skill of sustained focus for three reasons. First, since the 1950s we have been raised in the "entertain me" society. Our focus is dependent on the entertainment value of whatever we are doing. As soon as a project (whether coloring in kindergarten or working on a presentation to a board of directors) loses its entertainment value, our mind begins to wander.

Second, our inability to stay focused is due to the fact that we have short attention spans. Hollywood's producers are pros at playing to this aspect and consequently have increased our inability to stay focused on anything longer than a few minutes. Television, movies, and music are delivered to us in very short bursts. For example, even a three-hour movie like *Titanic* will usually have changes in camera angles every seven seconds or less. Why? Because it's the only way the film can hold our attention for a lengthy scene or piece of dialogue.

The third reason we do not have the skill of sustained focus is that we live and work in a world full of distractions and interruptions: telephones, cell phones, televisions, noise pollution, and lots of personal interruptions. The good news is that it is possible to maintain a sustained focus even in today's world, even if you have been diagnosed as having ADD. All it takes are the right techniques. (By the way, ADD is not necessarily bad. I have ADD off the charts, and most of the superachievers I have known or studied exhibit the characteristics of ADD. So don't panic if you or any of your children have ADD.)

Edison used four techniques to maintain his focus—the same techniques you have already learned in our previous sessions. He defined every dream or idea in writing; drew a picture so he could gain a visual image; wrote down the broad ramifications of achieving a dream; broke each dream down into digestible parts (goals, steps, and tasks); and infused his dream into the hearts and minds of others. These techniques have served me well for the past 27 years. However, because some of my children have also been diagnosed with ADD, I have found three additional techniques that are quite helpful to each of them.

1. When possible, bring entertainment value or a competitive aspect into each project or effort. Make everything you or your children do as fun as you can. Look for ways to add excitement, challenge, or competition to your projects and theirs.

2. Take short mental breaks every 10 to 15 minutes. These breaks should be one to two minutes long, and you should completely disengage your mind from whatever you are doing. Get up and walk around if possible, or get one of your short phone calls out of the way.

3. If you or a child truly have ADD, performing multiple tasks can enhance the ability to remain focused. For some kids doodling really helps. For me, even though I'm usually working on one primary television production at a time, I am always working on multiple secondary projects as well. For example, while I'm producing one show, I'll start writing another.

Most of my day will be focused on my primary project, but any time I begin to lose my focus or become bored, I'll quickly shift to one of the other projects and work on that for awhile. Then I am able to return to my main project with 100 percent focus and a renewed energy level. This was another technique that Edison used throughout his life. I don't think there was ever a time after his twelfth birthday when he was only working on one project. Also, always keep a pen or pencil close at hand. When a distracting thought begins to draw your focus away from what you are doing, quickly jot your thought on a note. Once you've done that, your mind will be instantly freed to return its focus to what you were doing.

We've now looked at the key to taking control (priority planning) and the first key to maintaining control (sustained focus). The second key to maintaining control of our time and any important project or area of our life is acquiring personal accountability.

Personal Accountability—The Second Key to Maintaining Control

Some of the companies I have created with my partners have been in the fitness and weight loss industries. We created Deal-A-Meal and *Sweatin' to the Oldies* with Richard Simmons, a treadmill business with Jane Fonda, a fitness business with Suzanne Somers, and of course our Total Gym with Chuck Norris and Christie Brinkley. I mention this to show that I am fairly well versed in the weight loss and fitness industry. Every year millions of Americans lose weight on various diets. Unfortunately, the vast majority regain all of their lost weight within two years. This happens because they do not stay on the diet and exercise plans that brought about their weight loss. However, year in and year out, Weight Watchers has been wonderfully successful in helping dieters to maintain their weight loss for years. Their secret? They have built their entire program around personal accountability. Because you have already learned that the most powerful strategy for achieving extraordinary success is effective partnering, if you begin to incorporate that strategy into each of the important areas of your life, you too will experience the incredible power of personal accountability. If there is any area of your life in which you feel you are hopelessly out of control, your only hope is to become honest and accountable to someone else.

When you use the vision mapping process, you are becoming accountable to a plan and a process with which you can measure your progress against your stated goals. When you create a priority plan, you are becoming accountable for the high-priority tasks you have listed. These provide a measure of accountability that will serve you well. But nothing is more effective than being accountable to someone you can be honest with and who will hold your feet to the fire, even if it means an occasional confrontation. I have had wonderful partners who have held me accountable for the past 27 years. Even Edison made himself accountable in different ways to his staff, his advisors, and his investors.

Our goal at the beginning of this session was to provide you with the strategies and skills to take and maintain control of your time and the aspects of your life in which you have the ability to exercise control. Using the strategies of priority planning, sustained focus, and personal accountability in combination with the other 12 master strategies we have previously discussed, you will be able to grasp the steering wheel of your life and take charge of where you go and what you achieve. In the "Actions for Traction" section that follows, I'm going to introduce you to a one-week exercise that is fun and eye-opening, and at the same time will provide you with an extra 10 to 15 hours in your week that you will be able to allocate to activities that reflect your personal values and your highest priorities. It will take a little bit of work, but what a difference it will make in the weeks, months, and years ahead!

Time Inventory Form

	SUN	MON	TUES	WEDS	THURS	FRI	SAT
6:00							
7:00							
8:00							
9:00							
10:00							
11:00							
Noon							
1:00							
2:00							
3:00							
4:00							
5:00							
6:00							
7:00							
8:00							
9:00							
10:00							
11:00							
Midnight							
1:00							
2:00							
3:00							
4:00							
5:00							

Actions for Traction

WHERE THE RUBBER MEETS THE ROAD

TAKING A PERSONAL INVENTORY OF YOUR TIME

1. On the preceeding page is a template for a time inventory form. If you have our preprinted notebook, you'll find two full-size copies of this form in the section titled "Taking Control of Your Life." If you don't have our preprinted notebook, use the template to make two copies of this form on lined paper from a standard loose-leaf notebook.
2. On your first form, fill in how you think you spend each hour in your typical week. Then, after you have filled in every block of time, circle every hour block that is an elective block of time where you have no weekly obligations. For example, my elective times are each weekday evening from 6:00 P.M. until 11:30 P.M. and most of Saturday and Sunday.
3. Using the second form, every few hours that you are awake, record what you did in the preceding hours. Take this form with you everywhere you go for a week. Once again, after you have finished filling in all of the blocks of time, circle every hour block that is an elective block of time. At the end of the week, compare this actual log of your time with your guesstimate log.
4. Begin to consider how you can replace the poor and good uses of your elective hours with better and best uses that reflect your greatest values, highest priorities, and most important dreams.

SESSION 14

It's Easy to Become Positively Amazing

Unleashing the Power of Redirected Focus

Your Porsche Comes with a Plush Leather Interior that Makes Every Trip a Delight. Going back to our analogy of your Porsche, imagine owning this beautiful, powerful Porsche with its turbocharged 415-horsepower engine and all-wheel drive that can take you anywhere. It's not only the most powerful Porsche ever built, it's also the most beautiful. Imagine, however, that instead of its plush leather seats, there was no upholstery at all, and the springs were protruding from the seats. Imagine that the stereo didn't work and all you heard was noise coming in from the outside. All of that, coupled with the fact that it has no heating or air conditioning, could make driving that beautiful and powerful machine miserable.

Two months before we started our business in 1976, I flew to Omaha to meet with the owner of a telephone answering service that was taking calls for my Ambassador television campaign. When I arrived, the owner met me outside the baggage claim area. As we walked through the parking lot, I noticed a car that stood out from all of the other cars in the lot. It was rusty, beat up, and looked like it had been dumped there as a practical joke. To my shock, my host walked over to the door on the driver's side, looked at me, and said, "Hop in." As I opened the door, I noticed that all the upholstery was gone. When I saw the springs protruding out of the passenger seat, I became a bit apprehensive. But my host grabbed a pillow in the backseat and handed it to me to lay it over the springs. The heater wasn't working, and neither was the radio. As we began to move forward, a loud screech blasted from beneath the hood, and each time he stepped on the brakes, an even louder screech came from his wheels. We drove for 10 or 15 minutes until we arrived at a nice restaurant. By the time I got out of the car I had a backache. My whole body had been cocked at an awkward angle from sitting on the springs protruding from the seat. Once we were in the restaurant, my host explained that he was driving the junker because he owed back taxes to the IRS and he hoped that their examination of his car would convince them that he didn't have enough money to pay all of his back taxes in a single payment. It worked. They let him arrange payments over a three-year period.

The master strategy that we're going to look at in this session is analogous to the interior of your Porsche. You can either have an interior like that of my friend's beat-up car, which will make any drive you take miserable, or you can have the most luxurious, the most comfortable, and the best-smelling leather interior ever put into an automobile. The choice is yours. Our fourteenth master strategy deals primarily with your inner attitudes and how you can acquire a positive personality.

Positive Thinking Can Be Positively Stupid!

A few years ago, I was invited by a close friend to attend an all-day success seminar at which he was going to speak along with a dozen other speakers. The 15,000 people who attended responded enthusiastically to each speaker and mobbed their booths during the breaks to buy their books and tapes. While nearly everyone in the arena was psyched up about all that they were hearing, I was grieved. Speaker after speaker was challenging the audience to bring the power of positive thinking into their lives. It reminded me of the pep rallies I used to attend in high school: lots of cheerleading and very little substance. Unfortunately, when it comes to winning a game or winning in life, positive thinking rarely wins anything. On the other hand, becoming a positive person not only results in more wins and bigger wins, it can produce winning benefits even in the midst of losses!

The Critical Difference between a Positive Thinker and a Positive Person

While this may seem like a simple difference in semantics, in reality it's a difference as great as that between flying a glider and flying a supersonic jet fighter. I received my private pilot's license for flying gliders or sailplanes

Side-by-Side Comparison

How People React or Respond to Negative Situations

Drifters	Pursuers	Achievers	Superachievers
React to each negative situation with an equal or greater negative reaction. They tend to be cynical because they see little reason to be positive or optimistic.	Overreact to negative situations. Try hard to be positive thinkers, but tend to "run out of gas" when good things don't happen quickly or easily.	Tend to react to problems by coming up with quick solutions. Are positive more often than they are negative.	Respond to negative situations rather than react, because they know that responding will serve their purposes more quickly and effectively than reacting will. Control their attitudes because they like to have a lifestyle of taking control and keeping it.

when I was 16. I thought nothing could beat flying an airplane without an engine. In a glider, the only noise you hear sounds like wind through pine trees. It's so quiet and graceful that you feel like *you* are flying instead of the plane. However, gliders do have their limitations. Even though they are lots of fun to fly, they really aren't practical for flying from one place to another. Typically you can stay aloft for 15 minutes to an hour, flying at speeds of 50 to 80 miles per hour. A few years later, I took the controls of an Air Force supersonic jet fighter. Wow! We could get anywhere we wanted to go, faster than you could imagine. Unlike the glider, we had an engine that gave us all of the power we needed, and if we wanted to fly farther than our fuel tanks allowed, we could refuel in the air. No destination was too distant.

To continue our analogy, like a glider, positive thinking can make life more enjoyable for a little while, but it really can't get you from one location to the next: It has no engine, no fuel, no power. On the other hand, becoming a positive person gives you a supersonic engine that can jet you to any dream you want, no matter how far away or how impossible it might seem.

Master Strategy 14—Acquiring a Positive Personality

As you learned in our second session, we all have a personality type with its own natural inclinations, strengths, and weaknesses. Of the four personality types, otters have the strongest natural inclination to be optimistic and positive, followed closely by lions. Beavers, on the other hand, tend to be more cautious and pessimistic. Golden retrievers can go either way. But the fact is, we cannot rely on our natural personality type to determine whether or not we will become a positive person. Becoming a positive person is first and foremost a matter of choice, and like all of the other master strategies it is acquired by developing and utilizing a specific set of skills.

You may or may not be familiar with Helen Keller. When she was about two years old, an illness left her totally deaf and blind. All she could see was darkness. All she could hear were her own thoughts. She could never see her mother's smile or hear her father's comforting voice. She couldn't see the beautiful country in which she lived, and she couldn't hear the sounds of nature or an orchestra playing a symphony. All of the things that you and I take for granted in our world were locked out of hers. If anyone ever had a reason to complain or to be a bitter, negative person, it was Helen Keller. By the time she was six, she had become nearly impossible to deal with. Then a 20-year-old woman entered her life. Anne Sullivan became a teacher, a partner, and a mentor to Helen, and to the world she became known as the Miracle Worker. She achieved a breakthrough with Helen, teaching her to spell and communicate before Helen turned seven. Anne opened up the world to Helen, and spent the rest of her life with her.

Although life never became easy for Helen Keller, she became one of the world's most inspirational writers and speakers. She wrote, "No pessimist ever discovered the secrets of the stars, or sailed to an uncharted land, or opened a new heaven to the human spirit." She also wrote, "Character cannot be developed in ease and quiet. Only through experience of trial and suffering can the soul be strengthened, ambition inspired and success achieved." Do these sound like the words of someone who lived in darkness and silence? She also wrote, "Be of good cheer. Do not think of today's failures, but of the success that will come tomorrow. You have set yourselves a difficult task, but you will succeed if you persevere; and you will find a joy in overcoming obstacles." What on earth happened to Helen Keller that enabled her to become such a positive person in her negative world? Neither sight nor sound ever entered her world. Her life was never smooth sailing. She endured the heartbreak of a broken engagement; the devastation of losing all of her possessions in a fire; even the death of her lifetime partner and mentor. And yet, with her positive nature and her words of love, kindness, and hope, she continued to inspire people of every rank and station, from servants to kings. She had become a truly positive person to her very core. The skills you are going to learn in this session can enable you to experience that same positive nature.

The Nineteenth Law of Extraordinary Success

No matter how much success a person achieves, if he or she becomes a positive person, he or she will achieve more and enjoy the journey a lot more.

Why is this so important? Why is becoming a positive person so critical to your future success and happiness? First of all, nobody likes riding in a Porsche with a gutted interior and sitting on springs. It's no fun to go through life being negative. Remember, I am not talking about the power of positive thinking. I'm not talking about ignoring reality and psyching yourself up to be happy when you feel like being sad. Instead I am talking about a particular skill that is as real and tangible as any of the other skills we have focused on.

I've heard lots of motivational speakers talk about psyching yourself up and looking in the mirror and engaging in self-talk. If that has helped you in the past, that's great, but it has nothing to do with the strategy and skills that are the focus of this session.

Chuck Norris is one of my best friends in life. He is truly one of the nicest guys in the world. If you met Chuck's mother you would understand why he and his brother Aaron are the way they are. Their mother weighs about 98 pounds, and every ounce is packed with love and kindness. Besides being an actor, Chuck is a six-time world champion in tae kwon do (karate) and the only non-Korean ever awarded the rank of Grand Master. If Chuck asked me to get in the ring with him and spar for a few rounds, no amount of self-talk in front of a mirror would change the outcome of the first 10 seconds of our match. Chuck would throw a punch or a kick and all of my positive thinking would vaporize with the impact of that first blow. Then, when the paramedics would revive me back to a semiconscious state, no amount of positive thinking or self-talk would make the pain go away.

Four Steps to Becoming a Positive Person in a Negative World

It's easy to be positive when everything is going great. It's quite another thing to be positive when things are going badly. My goal is not to give you a set of skills that will simply help you to have a more positive outlook on life or an ability to be occasionally positive. Rather, my goal is to provide you with the skills that will empower you to become a positive person right to your very core. As I have looked at a number of positive people, I have found that they have all taken four steps—some consciously, and others without much thought. I have taken these same steps that have enabled me to move through life as a much more positive person than I used to be. Perhaps you have already taken these steps either consciously or just in the natural course of your own development. If you have not, I can tell you that taking these steps will make a radical change in you that will also have an impact on everyone you relate to.

Step One—Taking Responsibility for Your Responses. The first step to becoming a positive person is to begin to consistently take responsibility for how you respond to negative situations. As easy as this may sound, it's not. We live in a very negative world that easily stirs up negative attitudes and reactions. Did you know that by the time children reach their teens, for every pat on the back they've received, they've received at least 17 criticisms? That's our national average. For many kids it's much worse. For many kids there is no safe harbor from criticism. They get it at home, they get it at school, and if they are in sports, they get it on the athletic field. One of my sons is extremely athletic and is involved in football, baseball, basketball, wrestling, and track. At some of his various events, I have been appalled by the way that some coaches and parents ride their kids. I have watched dads scream at their sons for missing a tackle on the football field or for striking out in baseball. Unfortunately, the world is even more negative for adults.

So how can you become a positive person in a very negative world? The answer is that it won't flow naturally from your human nature. When we are confronted with a negative action, our human nature wants to counter that action with an equally negative reaction. If a driver cuts you off on the freeway, nearly running you off the road, what is your natural reaction? If you get to the airport, check your bags, and an hour later find out that your flight has been canceled, what are your impulses? How about if the person behind the counter tells you there are no other flights he or she can get you on for at least two days? How do you react when you find out that someone is bad-mouthing you behind your back? Our natural inclination is to always react negatively to negative situations. This might not be so bad if we were only confronted with one or two negative situations a month. Unfortunately that is not the world we live in. Our weeks are usually filled with lots of negative circumstances, situations, and events, and until we make a certain choice, all of those negative circumstances will produce lots of negative reactions.

That certain choice is to choose to respond to negative events rather than react to them. Do you remember the difference between the two from our session on criticism? Reacting is what your body does to medications it doesn't like, and responding is what your body does to medications it does like. As is the case with criticism, each time we encounter a negative situation, we have a conscious choice to make. If we react, we will only make matters worse for us and for those we are reacting to. If we choose to respond, we will improve any negative situation, both for us and for the people we are responding to. Since our natural inclination is to react, we are likely to do so instantaneously, until we build a habit of responding. But, just as with reacting to a criticism, as soon as you catch yourself reacting to a negative situation, you can put the brakes on, shift gears, back up, and change your reacting to responding.

The Incredible Power of Resetting Your Focus. Now that you know you need to take charge of your attitudes and respond rather than react, the question is, How do you do that? The good news is that you don't have to wait for your feelings to change before you change your reaction to a response. Once again it comes down to an easily learned skill that you will be able to master in no time. Before I introduce you to the skill, let me explain the mechanics.

Picture yourself on a beautiful summer day somewhere in the Rocky Mountains of Utah or Colorado. You're walking along and you see a beautiful stream next to a 100-acre meadow covered with purple and yellow wildflowers. It's a gorgeous day and you're thinking, "Wow, I'm just grateful to be alive. It doesn't get any better than this!" Then, all of a sudden a gunshot rings out to your left and you instantly jerk your head to the left and see a beautiful elk stagger a few feet and then fall to the ground. Your heart starts to race and you think, "That just ruined my day." Not that you are necessarily against hunting, but you just weren't into thoughts of death prior to the gunshot. You were into life and all the beauty around you, but that gunshot has changed everything.

Look what really happened. The gunshot drew your focus away from something very positive and turned your focus from that positive sight and feeling to a negative sight and feeling. That's what every negative situation does. No matter where our focus is set, a negative situation instantly jerks that focus away from the positive and directs it to the negative. Whether it's a situation that doesn't involve another human—such as your computer crashing or a weather-delayed flight—or a negative situation induced by a person, the mechanics are exactly the same. The negative situation takes charge of your focus and directs it toward the negative.

Last year I was shooting a show in New York. A half hour before I left for the set, I decided to make some script changes on my laptop. As I was typing a change that I was really excited about, I reached across the table for my cup of coffee. To my horror, I spilled the coffee right onto my keyboard. All of a sudden, the cursor started moving right to left, deleting my script one line at a time. I tried to stop it, but to no avail. I finally held my finger down on the power button and turned the computer off. When I tried to restart the computer, nothing happened. It was toast! I instantly reacted and started to panic. A moment later I remembered—don't react, respond; reset your focus. You see, just as a negative situation grabs our focus and resets it on the negative, *we can choose to grab it right back and redirect it to the positive.* I thought, "I'll borrow my producer's hard copy of the script, make the changes on it, and hand it to the TelePrompTer operator to change it on his computer." No sweat. My laptop was fried, but Apple had just come out with a brand-new, vastly superior laptop that I wanted to buy anyway. But since my old laptop was only eight months old I couldn't justify a new purchase. Now that my old laptop was history, I could justify a new one and would have one within a day of arriving home. With my focus reset in less than a minute, I left the hotel for the set in a great mood. Had I not reset my focus, my attitude would have been bad all day. In 27 years I've never arrived on a set angry, because as the director, I know it would affect my work with the celebrities in front of the camera. With millions of dollars at risk, the last thing I would ever want to do is show up angry and risk the outcome of the shoot.

Martin Luther said it this way: "You can't stop a bird from landing on your head. But you can stop it from building a nest." In other words, we can't stop a negative situation from coming our way, but we don't have to let it retain our focus and wreck our day—not for an hour or even a minute. We can instantly reset it to the positive.

In our session on communication I quoted a statement of Solomon's that is also appropriate here. In Proverbs 15:1 he said, "A soft answer turns away wrath, but grievous words stir up anger." This means that a soft or gentle response causes wrath (hateful anger) to recede and disappear. It also says that the converse is true. A harsh response increases anger and stirs it up into something even more destructive than the precipitating situation. Our natural inclination is to react to negative situations, which will only stir them up into something more destructive, whereas choosing to respond with softness will reduce tensions and turn the negative situation in a positive direction. A soft response not only reduces the tension in the situation, it will reduce your tension and stress as well. By the way, if you think the word *destructive* is a little overdramatic, think again. Doctors have discovered that stress causes our body to release a hormone called cortisol, which breaks down cellular integrity, making us more susceptible to cancer, and also contributes to heart disease, increased fatigue, reduced sex drive, wrinkled skin, and weight gain. Was Solomon wise or what!

Also, when we react rather than respond, we are letting negative situations or negative people take control of our happiness for the entire time we are reacting. We spent an entire session focused on taking and maintaining control of our time and happiness. What a waste to let a negative situation rob us of that which we work so hard to gain and maintain!

Helen Keller was a consummate pro at keeping her focus set on the positive. She warned that not resetting our focus can cause us to miss the opportunity to remain happy or regain it if it is lost. She said, "When one door of happiness closes, another opens; but often we look so long at the closed door that we do not see the one that has opened before us." But perhaps her most inspiring words on the power of resetting our focus from the negative to the positive are in this quote: "They took away what should have been my eyes. But I remembered Milton's *Paradise Lost.* They took away what should have been my ears; Beethoven came and wiped away my tears. They took away what should have been my tongue, but I had talked to God when I was young. He would not let them take away my soul, and possessing that I still possess the whole." No matter what negatives came into her life, she never lingered before she reset her focus on the positive.

Step Two—Building an Attitude of Gratefulness. The second step to becoming a positive person is building an attitude of gratefulness. Have you ever noticed that people who are genuinely grateful are also extremely positive? That's because it's impossible to be grateful and negative at the same time. When you are grateful, you are not angry, resentful, or bitter. When you are grateful, you are not critical, judgmental, or vengeful. That doesn't mean that grateful people can't become angry; they can. But they can't be both at the exact same time. Also, even though grateful people can become angry, sad, or depressed, if their gratefulness is firmly rooted in their core, they can't stay angry, sad, or depressed for very long. Ultimately, their gratefulness will regain control of their heart and mind.

"I'd Like to Be a Grateful Person, But . . ." Whenever I talk about the subject of gratefulness, people invariably come up to me and say, "I'd like to be grateful, but . . ." What follows are a myriad of reasons that people think prevent them from being grateful. Their spouse doesn't appreciate them; their boss treats them like a piece of dirt; their ex-wife took them to the cleaners, or their ex-husband ran off with his secretary; they've lost their job; their kids are on drugs; and on and on. While all of these are very legitimate

problems, they have nothing to do with whether or not the person should be grateful. The other cop-out is stated this way: "I'll be grateful when . . ." And then you can fill in the blank with another long list of words. "When I get a new job; when my husband starts helping around the house; when my wife starts meeting my sexual needs; when my kids get straightened out;" and on and on. Once again, these are all legitimate things to look forward to, but they have nothing to do with being grateful.

If gratefulness were truly dependent on all of the circumstances in one's life being good, then no one would be grateful. We would all be waiting for a day in the future—one that will not come in this life. Despite her dire circumstances, Helen Keller's life exuded gratefulness from the time she was seven years old until the time she died. However, in this she is not alone. I have known countless men and women who have experienced heartbreaks, disappointments, injustice, emotional and physical injuries, and even the deaths of children and spouses, who through it all maintained a heart of gratefulness. So the question now becomes, What does it take to build an abiding attitude of genuine gratefulness? Here again, we need to start with a correct definition.

Gratefulness Is Not a Feeling. Many people make the same mistake with gratefulness that they make with love. They think it is a feeling. Nothing could be further from the truth. Both love and gratefulness can produce feelings, but over time feelings are inconsistent and often change. Gratefulness starts with an awareness and is confirmed every day with a decision. For people to be grateful, they must be aware of two things. First, they must be aware that no matter what they don't have, they have more to be thankful for than they may have ever imagined. That means gratefulness may require a resetting of your focus from what you don't have to what you do have. Next, it requires awareness that everything you have that is good, you have gained through the contributions of others. If you believe in God, you would acknowledge that everything you have has been given to you by God and others. If you don't believe in God and want to give credit somewhere else, that's up to you. Some of you might say, "Wait a minute, I have everything that I have because I've worked hard to get it, not because anybody gave me anything!" To those people I would ask, Who prepared your food for the first three years of your life? Who changed your diapers? Where would you be right now if no one had done either of these two seemingly mundane chores? Did you educate yourself, or did you have teachers? Did you do all of your laundry, your dishes, your cooking? Did you choose where you would be born or that you would even be born at all? Did you give yourself your first job, and every job after that? In reality,

I have never had one person name one good thing in his or her life that he or she could take all of the credit for.

So gratefulness starts with an awareness of all of the good things you have in life, and an awareness that those good things have been provided not by your efforts alone, but through the efforts and contributions of others. Because both my father and mother had a period of their lives where each breath they took was either a struggle or painful, I am grateful for every breath that I take so easily without experiencing any pain. My mother just passed away and I miss her terribly. I have a long way to go in the grieving process. But even though my heart is breaking, I am so grateful for everything I have had in the past and everything I have right now. Even in my grief, I am so very grateful that I was raised and nurtured by the most loving, kind, and selfless woman I have ever known.

Awareness is the first step to building a grateful attitude. The second step is a daily decision to be thankful for all that you have and to express that thankfulness to God and those around you who have made and continue to

To Those Who Are Wondering Why I'm Including This in a Book about Personal Achievement

At this moment you might be thinking, "I thought this book was about business and making money. This session is sounding more and more like a course on behavior." You're right on both counts. This is a book about business, making money, and becoming a superachiever. But even though it may not be taught in business school, how you behave either accelerates or stifles your potential to achieve. If you were looking for a partner in your business and you had to choose between people who were equally qualified in every area, but one was truly happy, optimistic, and positive and had the ability to make everyone around him or her feel good and the other was pessimistic, unhappy, cynical, and neutral to miserable to be around, who would you choose? Obviously you'd choose the first person. If you were applying for a job, and you were competing against someone who was equally qualified, would you rather appear to be the more genuinely positive person or the more subdued or negative person?

The other consideration is your happiness. I have known people who were worth hundreds of millions of dollars, and yet they were unhappy individuals. Why wait until you're rich to be happy and fulfilled? Being fulfilled along the way makes the journey a whole lot nicer.

make such wonderful contributions to your life. In the "Actions for Traction" section at the end of this session, there is an exercise that will be extremely helpful in helping you to build an attitude of gratefulness.

Overcoming a Huge Roadblock to Gratefulness. Everything I have learned about building an attitude of gratefulness was taught to me by my personal mentor, Gary Smalley, a world-class expert on relationships. Gary has told me of times when he has taught on this subject and people would come up after the meeting and tell him horrific stories of personal tragedies that have made it impossible for them to experience the kind of gratefulness he talks about. In those situations Gary leads these people on a treasure hunt for pearls. You probably know that every beautiful pearl starts with a painful irritation caused by a grain of sand. Given the choice, an oyster would much rather have a life free of pain, but sandy oceans make a pain-free life nonoptional. However, without the painful grain of sand, there would be no pearl; and without a doubt, it is the pearl that is the oyster's crowning glory. So when people bring their painful stories to Gary, he takes them hunting for the treasure that pain has created. Often, the greater the pain, the more beautiful and radiant the resulting pearl will be. More often than not, the treasure hunt is over before these people leave, and usually, their hearts are filled with gratefulness.

For example, the wife of a famous professional football player had been a victim of incest as a child from the time she was 8 years old until she was 16. Over and over again she was raped, not just by her father but by her uncles as well. She had been so hurt by all this that it was beginning to erode her relationship with her husband. They came to Gary for help, and she told him her painful story. Gary spent one hour treasure hunting with her and the pearls she found changed her life. Her burden was not only lifted, it was replaced with a heart full of gratefulness. Several months later she went to work for a shelter that helps abused young children, including victims of incest. After her first week on the job, one little girl came up to her and said, "Will I ever be as happy as you are?" This little girl whose heart had been so utterly broken was attracted to this woman, because she was the happiest person at that shelter. Her marriage completely changed as well. She became the kind of wife and mother she had always wanted to be, all because she had learned to treasure-hunt her tragedy.

If you have had a personal tragedy in your life that has kept you from building a grateful attitude, Gary leads readers through this treasure-hunting process in his book, *Making Love Last Forever* (Thomas Nelson, 1997). In my opinion, this is one of the most beneficial books ever written on the subject of relationships. If you are married or involved in any serious relationship, this book should be required reading.

Step Three—Striving for and Achieving Excellence. The third step to becoming a positive person is striving for and achieving excellence. If you are working on implementing the master strategies we have focused on, such as the vision mapping process, shooting for the moon, effective partnering, and so on, then you have already begun your lifetime quest of adding excellence to all of your most important endeavors. As you utilize these master strategies, your levels of excellence and achievement will skyrocket. The more excellence you bring to your personal and professional efforts, the more positive you will become.

Step Four—Maximizing Your Relationships at Home and at Work. The fourth step to becoming a positive person is maximizing your relationships at home and at work. Although it's possible to have unhappy relationships and still be a positive person, it's much more difficult. This is when many people tell me, "There's no way I can have a good relationship with my spouse, my boss, or my coworkers." I tell these people that my wife and I were separated for 14 months and then divorced because we believed there was no way on earth we could get back together and be happy. And yet, after a 14-month separation and a six-week divorce, we were happy beyond imagination to remarry each other in November of 1999. Since we've been back together, our marriage has been more joyful and fulfilling than any other aspect of our lives. The exclamation point to our reuniting was the birth of our fourth child 16 months after we got back together.

So what's the key to maximizing any relationship? According to Gary Smalley, there are seven keys. These keys have worked like magic for Shannon and me, and I really believe they can work in any relationship when they are given a legitimate try.

Seven Keys to Maximizing Your Relationships

Key 1–Honor

In many relationships honor is an unknown commodity, and yet it is the foundation on which any fulfilling relationship must be built. The good news is that honor is something we can choose to give whether we feel like it or not. You might say, "There's really not much to honor about my spouse." Well, honoring or valuing someone is not dependent on them but on you. Honoring is a choice. It's something we choose to do, even if there's no reason to honor another person. We choose to bring honor into any relationship not because someone deserves it, but because that is the right thing to do in any relationship. How do you honor others? You honor them with words of encouragement and by listening to them. You honor people by looking into their eyes when they're speaking or by giving them a smile or a pat on the back. As you begin to honor them, you'll not only see a change in them, you'll see a change in yourself. We honor with our expressions, our words, and our tone of voice. We also can *dis*honor someone with a look, harsh words, or a condescending tone of voice.

Key 2–Encouragement

Have you ever received encouragement and not appreciated it? We all need encouragement. We encourage people with our spirit and our attitude as well as with our words and tone of voice. We can encourage people just by responding to them instead of reacting to them. A few words of encouragement or a willingness to just listen can make all the difference in the world in how people will face the rest of their day. Other forms of encouragement include nonsexual touch, a hug, even a pat on the back. When you are listening to someone as a means of encouraging him or her, don't try to solve any problems he or she voices. Just listen.

Key 3–Security

One of the greatest needs of a woman is security. She wants to feel safe in a relationship. She wants to know that her mate is 100 percent committed to her for the long term. She wants to feel secure enough that she can express whatever she thinks or feels and not be judged or criticized for her thoughts or feelings. But women aren't the only ones who want security in a relationship. Men need it as well. We can increase people's sense of security by reducing the amount of criticism we give them. Criticism makes people feel insecure. As we remove criticism from a relationship, everyone will begin to feel more safe and secure. You might say, "But they need criticism." No, they need correction. I will shortly show you the only right way to criticize. There are a thousand wrong ways to criticize but only one right way. It's the only way in which you gain all of the positive benefits of correction with none of the negative results. We also infuse security in the relationship by showing appreciation.

Key 4–Respect and Admiration

Just as a woman needs to feel safe and secure, the single greatest need of a man is to feel respected and admired. How do you communicate respect and admiration? By giving genuine praise, not just flattery. Flattery is when you comment on something someone has rather than on what he or she has done. Praise and respect are communicated by focusing attention on something he or she has accomplished. While flattery is appreciated, praise, admiration, and respect meet a much deeper need. The more specific the praise is, the more believed and appreciated it will be.

Key 5–Effective Communication

The single greatest problem in most relationships is the lack of effective communication. The skills and techniques we discussed in our earlier sessions will work wonders for any relationship in which they are used. Ladies, because most men are left-brain dominant, the only way you will ever get a man to understand what you're feeling is by using an effective emotional word picture. It's the only communication technique that stimulates the right side of a man's brain.

Key 6–Fighting by the Rules

We need to quickly resolve conflicts the right way. The following list was provided by Gary Smalley and shows you the do's and don'ts of conflicts. Research has shown that when couples honor the rules of conflict, their relationships are strengthened by the conflict rather than weakened by it. Conflicts either drive us apart or take us to deeper levels of intimacy, depending on how we respond or react to them. When a couple becomes familiar with these rules and uses them, their chances of resolving each conflict in a positive way are significantly increased.

Rules for Constructive Conflict

Conflict Do's

1. Take a timeout to gain control, become more calm, and reduce your anger before you engage in the confrontation.
2. Prepare for the confrontation before you engage in it.
   - Determine your specific goal for the confrontation. Do you simply want to resolve a current problem? Do you want to stop a behavior pattern? Do you want to replace a destructive behavior pattern with a constructive one? Do you want to correct, encourage, or punish?
   - Determine what specifically you want to say and how you want to say it. Write it down if time permits so you can make sure you avoid all of the don'ts in your message.

- Determine how to begin the confrontation in the least inflammatory way. Include your positive goal for the confrontation. (For example, "I really want to be the best friend I can be to you" or "Because our relationship is so important to me, I wanted to share something that could make it better for both of us.")

3. Approach the confrontation in the spirit of a learner who also makes mistakes and has weaknesses.
4. If criticism is to be given, use the sandwich method discussed later in this session.
5. Use as many encouraging and positive statements as you can in the context surrounding the central issue you are trying to address or resolve.
6. Be willing to offer and accept a progressive resolution of the problem or issue. In other words, be willing to come up with a solution that involves a period of time. Don't demand that the solution be agreed on, enacted, or achieved by the end of the confrontation.
7. Ask for advice on what you can do to help resolve the problem on your end, or to reduce your contribution to the problem.
8. If the person attacks you, don't defend yourself or retaliate. Assure him or her that you too have weaknesses that you need to work on.
9. Keep the confrontation on track. Don't be diverted to side issues or opportunities to deal with problems other than those you have planned to address. If the other person won't proceed unless you do address side issues, you can always agree that he or she has a legitimate concern and ask if you can set aside time later to deal with that issue.
10. Control your words, tone of voice, and nonverbal communication. Respect and honor the person, even in the midst of conflict. Remember the wisdom of the proverb of Solomon, "A soft answer turns away wrath, but grievous words stir up anger." In other words, giving a soft answer defuses and prevents anger, while destructive, divisive, or inflammatory words or answers turn up the heat and cause the other person's anger to boil over.
11. Reassure the person of your ongoing care and commitment to him or her and to your relationship.

Conflict Don'ts

1. Don't bury the problem or the hurt it's causing you.
2. Don't deny or run away from the problem or the confrontation required to address it.

3. Don't let your addressing the problem degenerate into an attack on the person or his or her character. (If character is the issue, address, don't attack the specific character failing, not the character in general.)
4. Don't use inflammatory remarks, sarcasm, or name calling.
5. Don't enter a conflict in the spirit of a self-righteous know-it-all.
6. Don't let the conflict broaden to issues other than the one(s) you are trying to address.
7. Don't use generalizations, exaggerations, or blanket statements such as "you always" or "you never."
8. Don't use ultimatums or threats.
9. Don't use body language or nonverbal communication that shows disbelief or lack of respect (such as rolling your eyes or shaking your head).
10. Don't interrupt.
11. Don't raise your voice.
12. Don't withdraw or walk away or hang up the telephone in the middle of a confrontation.

Key 7—Correct Criticism

It's better to give than receive. That's true for just about everything, except criticism. Now that you've learned the right way to receive criticism, you are safe from being harmed when you receive it. However, until you begin to give criticism the right way, you can inflict a lot of pain and damage with critical words. To my knowledge, there is only one right way to give criticism. Gary Smalley taught me this method 30 years ago, and after 30 years of using this method, I can tell you it really does work. It provides correction without the normal collateral damage inflicted by ordinary criticism. It's called the sandwich method. Remember, the goal of criticism is to provide correction and encourage a change of behavior. Even though our natural inclination is sometimes to want to inflict pain, to do so is often counterproductive in accomplishing a goal.

The Sandwich Method of Criticism: The Only Wise Way to Criticize. In a nutshell, the sandwich method of criticism places one slice of criticism between two slices of praise. You begin by pointing out a positive quality about the individual or his or her performance and offering specific (not general) praise for that quality or performance. "*Hallie, that was so nice of you to get a bottle of chocolate milk for Daddy. You are so thoughtful.*" Next comes the slice of specific criticism, addressing a wrong activity or choice, but not attacking the person's character: "*Hallie, even though I* *love chocolate milk, the bottles are too heavy for you to carry. Because you dropped it on the carpet, we're going to have to take a lot of time to clean it up. So next time ask one of your big brothers to carry the bottle of milk for you, Okay?" Do you understand?"* After the criticism has been delivered and has been acknowledged and understood, it's time to put the last slice of bread on the sandwich. *"Hallie, you are the sweetest little girl. Thank you for trying to be so nice to me."*

This is how I recently dealt with my two-year-old. If you're dealing with an older child, a teenager, or an adult, make sure that your praise is not just a transparent veil for getting to the criticism. That will be sensed as condescension. The slices of bread are just as important as the meat in the middle. The praise should be specific, sincere, and well thought out.

In closing, remember that becoming a positive person has nothing to do with just positive thinking or psyching yourself up. First and foremost, it's taking responsibility for your attitudes, taking charge of those attitudes, and deciding where your focus is going to be set once a negative situation has distracted it.

Actions for Traction

WHERE THE RUBBER MEETS THE ROAD

1. Write down recent situations or circumstances in which you reacted rather than responded. Describe your reactions and any negative consequences they produced with you or someone else.
2. Looking at the situations you've described, write down how you could have responded to those situations or circumstances that would have produced more positive outcomes for you or others.
3. For the next week, take a few minutes each night to write out any situations that occurred during the day that you reacted to and the negative consequences of those reactions. Then, for each situation, write how you could have better responded to that situation.
4. Take a few minutes each night during the next week to write out any situations that occurred during the day that you responded to and the positive outcomes you experienced because you responded rather than reacted.

SESSION 15

Discovering the High-Octane Fuel of the World's Most Successful People

Igniting the Passion You Never Knew You Had

Without Igniting Your Fuel, Your Porsche Will Only Stand Still! Imagine your sparkling cobalt-blue Porsche is inside your garage just waiting for you. Its 415-horsepower turbocharged engine is just waiting to be revved up. You jump into the driver's seat ready to pursue your first dream, slide your master key into the ignition switch, and turn it—and nothing happens. Your $100,000 Porsche is just sitting there, silent. There's one thing missing from your car, and without it you can't even get out of your garage, much less to your destination: There's no gas. Imagine, a $100,000 car at your disposal, waiting to speed you toward your dreams, and it's rendered totally worthless for the lack of a $25 tank of gas! As wonderful as that car may be, it can't take you anywhere without a tank of fuel. And for this automobile there's only one grade of fuel that will even turn the engine. It's the highest-octane fuel ever produced. With it, there's no limit to where you can go. Without it, you will remain stuck in your garage. The fuel for your Porsche—the only fuel that can ignite its engine and power it to any destination in the world—is the fuel of passion.

As we begin our last mentoring session, I want to tell you how honored I am that you've opened up your mind and heart to the strategies and skills that have radically changed my life and the lives of so many others who have had the joy of achieving their impossible dreams. Hopefully, as we start this session you have already defined your dreams in writing using the vision mapping process and have adjusted many of your dreams and goals upward using the shooting for the moon approach. You are now ready to begin your journey to your most important dreams.

If you have ever watched an episode of *America's Most Wanted,* you've witnessed the passion of John Walsh as he attempts to motivate his viewers to help law enforcement locate hardened criminals. If you have ever watched *Oprah,* you've probably been impressed with her passion for virtually any subject featured on her show on any given day. As I've mentioned before, I've worked with some of the biggest names in the entertainment industry, but two of the most passionate workers I've ever known aren't from Hollywood. One I knew simply as Brother Hicks. While I was in college I worked with Brother Hicks on a janitorial crew on the graveyard shift. He spent 12 hours, five nights a week, cleaning the toilets on 12 floors of an office building. He was in his sixties and was one of the most positive and passionate workers I have ever known. His passion and positive nature didn't come from the quality of his job or his circumstances at home, as he spent most of his time there caring for his invalid wife. He had no car and took the bus to work each night. His shift didn't start until midnight, but since the last bus left his area at six, he showed up for work six hours early every night, and he did that for 25 years. Everybody loved being around Brother Hicks because he was always happy. He said he loved working in the bathrooms because he could sing loud, hear the echo, and not be heard by anyone else.

I recently met the second most passionate worker I have ever known at a Harlan's Barbeque stand at the George Bush International Airport in Houston. This guy was truly amazing. His name is Rick Maddox, and if you ever eat at that Harlan's you won't have to ask, "Which one is Rick?" You'll see him entertaining everyone around him, and if no one's around him you'll hear him singing. Watching him work, I realized that his passion isn't for the wonderfully delicious barbeque that he prepares on that hot stove; it's for the people he serves. If I owned any retail business, I would hire him in a second. He makes every customer smile, and gets them excited about the barbeque that he prepares for them.

How about you? How much passion do you bring to your job each day, to each project you tackle, or to your personal relationships at home? Most people have lots of reasons why they've lost their passion for their work, their spouses, their children, or even life in general.

Unfortunately, your level of success at work and at home is inextricably bound to your level of passion in each area. "But I'm not a passionate person," you say. Or, "If you had my job, there's no way you could be

Side-by-Side Comparison

How People Develop Passion

Drifters	Pursuers	Achievers	Superachievers
Don't use the fuel of passion because they don't need fuel to drift and simply go with the flow, which is what they do.	Catch their passions and are controlled by them, rather than develop passions for the pursuit of their dreams.	Often gain a degree of passion for the pursuit of their goals, but do not follow a routine to develop positive passions in areas where they do not occur naturally.	Develop the fuel of passion for the pursuit of each of their important dreams and projects. Outsiders think that they were born passionate, but the reality is that they develop passion for each of their important pursuits.

passionate about it!" And then there's the most depressing comment of all, "If you were married to my spouse, you wouldn't be passionate either!" Wrong, Wrong, Wrong! Even though these statements may accurately reflect your feelings and the feelings of millions of adults, all three also reflect a crippling and terribly erroneous belief about passion. You see, all three of these statements reflect the belief that your level of passion is dependent on someone or something else besides you. Nothing could be further from the truth. The good news is, there are a few specific steps that you can take that will quickly raise your level of passion in any important area of your life, regardless of your circumstances. As your passion rises, fulfillment and success will follow.

Master Strategy 15—Gaining Passion for Your Visions

Just as there are particular personality types that have a natural inclination to be positive and optimistic, there are also personality types that have a natural inclination to be passionate. Once again, lions and otters have more of an inclination to be passionate than beavers and golden retrievers. Otters are usually passionate by nature, as long as the focus of their passion remains fun or there's a group of people to cheer them on. Lions are passionate by nature, as long as the focus of their passion is challenging. But when Lions get bored because there is no challenge, they quickly lose their passion, and when Otters' passion ceases to be fun or the crowd disappears, their passion subsides as well. In either case, inherent passions are rarely sustained. To sustain a passion, it must have a higher octane rating than that which is produced inherently by one's personality type. It must come from a different refinery.

I've had people tell me, "I know people who have been highly passionate from the day they were born." I usually answer, "So do I." But the passion they are born with is simply related to their personality type. They may be a strong otter or a strong lion. But the fact remains that that kind of passion isn't adequate to sustain the pursuit of distant, extraordinary dreams. That requires a whole different kind of passion. And that's the kind of passion we're going to talk about. This kind of passion is one that you or anyone else can acquire. You just have to know which gas station to go to and have the right credit card. Now I am going to give you the location of the right service station and I'm going to give you a credit card that you can use for the rest of your life.

There are two ways you can get a passion. First, you can catch a passion in the same way a person catches a cold. Second, you can purposely acquire it. You catch a passion by getting around something that has some appeal to you. First you dabble in it, then you begin to chase it, and finally you have caught a full-blown passion. The problem with this kind of passion is that it can take control of you instead of you controlling it. Before you know it, it can cause you to lose sight of your most important values and your highest priorities and goals.

For example, a man can catch a passion for women. If he is single, it can distract him from his educational or business priorities. If he's married, it can destroy his family and ruin his reputation. Even presidents of the United States, the most powerful leaders in the world, have let their passions take control of their behavior and destinies. For all of the things Bill Clinton might have accomplished, he will forever be remembered as a man who was out of control when it came to his passion for women. As we saw in an earlier session, to achieve your dreams it is critical that you take and maintain control of your life and your time—and the last thing you want to do is to lose control to anyone or anything that can sabotage your dreams.

Speaking of this kind of passion, Ben Franklin said, "A man in passion rides a wild horse." In other words, if you let your passion control you, it takes you wherever *it* wants to go, and ultimately throws you to the ground.

A close friend of mine caught a passion for golf. On weekends his children are without their dad and his wife is a golf widow. How sad for his

> ***The Twentieth Law of Extraordinary Success***
>
> Without developing a controllable passion for a vision, extraordinary success is impossible.

family. They are a million times more important than chasing a white ball on the grass for hours on end. Imagine the return on the investment of his time if he would make that same kind of commitment to spending quality time with his wife and kids. Franklin was right, passions like his are like riding a wild horse.

Thomas Hobbes wrote, "Passions unguided, for the most part are mere madness." When a passion takes control of us, it's like madness. Nobody wants to live with a madman or a madwoman. This is not the kind of passion we are interested in. Instead of a passion catching me and pulling me away from that which I value most, I want to acquire and maintain passions that will reflect my values and power me to my dreams. I want to have a passion for my wife. Not just sexually, but as a person. She is the most priceless treasure that has ever been given to me, and I want to have a passion for meeting her deepest emotional, physical, and spiritual needs. I also want to have a passion for my children. I have seven of the most wonderful children on this planet. They deserve my focus, love, energy, encouragement, direction, thought, and more. I want to have a passion that will drive me to do those things that are best because I know that controlled passion is the fuel to excellence. Without passion, you cannot achieve excellence in a marriage, you can't achieve excellence as a parent, and you certainly can't achieve excellence in your career.

So how do you acquire the right kind of passion? How do you fill up your tank every single day as you begin to pursue your dreams? Henry Ford acquired a passion for making the automobile affordable for the masses. Ray Kroc gained a passion for bringing low-cost, inexpensive fast food to America.

Thomas Edison gained a passion for every project he worked on. He never approached any project without fuel in his tank. He didn't approach his projects slowly, and he didn't approach them methodically, gradually, or drudgingly. He had a passion that burned as brightly as a raging fire in the night! Even in his later life, when he had very little natural physical energy, his workers said he always came to work with a passion for the project of the day. He was so passionate it was hard for him to leave work. He often slept in his laboratory so that if a thought came in the middle of the night he could begin to work on it instantly. Edison had learned how to acquire a passion for virtually anything he took on as a project.

All of this is to say that if you don't acquire a passion for pursuing and achieving your dreams, your projects, your goals, and even your appointed tasks, you will never leave the garage. Your creator has given you this incredible Porsche, the car of a lifetime that can take you anywhere. It's got the best of everything, but you're not even going to get out of your garage without the fuel.

So how do you acquire passion for things that you're not naturally passionate about? How do you acquire a passion that lasts—that doesn't just peter out with the first obstacle that appears in your path or the first resistance you encounter along the way? As is the case with the other master strategies we have looked at, here again it's simply a matter of learning and applying the right skills and techniques. This kind of passion is made up of only three ingredients. When those three ingredients are present, then you will have this kind of passion. If you are missing even one, you will not have it. You must have all three ingredients to have this passion.

The Three Essential Ingredients of Passion

Passion is made up of vision, hope, and fulfillment. As has been the case with so many of the terms we have looked at, here again there are a lot of misconceptions about each of these terms. People tend to associate a vision with something mystical; hope is usually equated with wishful thinking; and fulfillment is often thought to be synonymous with contentment. All three of these notions are wrong. None of these terms describe an abstract quality, but instead are as tangible as gold or silver. They are specific elements.

Critical Definitions for the Three Ingredients of Passion

Vision: **A clearly defined dream with a precise and detailed map or plan to achieve that dream within a defined amount of time.**

Hope: **A well-founded and confident expectation that a specific dream, goal, step, or task will be accomplished within a defined amount of time.**

Fulfillment: **The inner joy and excitement that comes from achieving meaningful goals, steps, and tasks that reflect your core values.**

Vision—the Ingredient that Passion Must Always Start With. Gaining a vision is the first ingredient of passion, and you can't have the other two ingredients without it. It must come first. To gain true passion, you not only need all three ingredients, you need to introduce them to the mix in the right order. The first ingredient in creating or acquiring passion is gaining a clear and precise vision for your dream. How do you do that? While millions of other adults don't have a clue, you already know the answer: You use the vision mapping process that you learned in our eighth session.

Charles A. Lindbergh gained a vision for becoming the first man to successfully cross the Atlantic Ocean in an airplane. Others had tried, and all had failed. Using the same vision mapping process you have learned, Lindbergh converted his vision into goals, his goals into steps, and his steps into tasks. When he successfully achieved his vision, the world gave him the nickname "Lucky Lindy." In reality, luck had little to do with it; acquiring a passion did! Gaining the vision became the first ingredient in his passion.

Years later, Lindbergh acquired another passion. Having visited a private medical research facility, he became intrigued with two of the major medical problems that no researcher had been able to develop a solution for. He gained a vision for two different mechanical devices that might solve these two "unsolvable" problems. Driven by a newly acquired passion, Lindbergh developed the first successful blood centrifuge and the first mechanical heart-lung machine. Both devices were considered milestones in medicine, and both were developed because the pilot who first crossed the Atlantic gained a passion for two problems that medical researchers could not solve. Lindbergh received no money for this incredible contribution to medical science and chose to have his role remain anonymous.

If you have started your vision mapping journal, defining and mapping out your dreams for the areas of your life that are most important to you, then you have provided the first ingredient in the development of a passion for your dreams.

Hope—the Second Ingredient Essential to Producing Passion. Hope is the second ingredient critical to producing passion. Most people think of hope as simply wishing, as reflected in these common uses of the word: "I hope she'll go out on a date with me." "I hope he'll fall in love with me." "I hope my boss notices that I'm doing a good job." That's not the kind of hope I am talking about. True hope is the well-founded and confident expectation that a specific vision, dream, goal, step, or task will be accomplished within a defined amount of time. The vision mapping process generates true hope because it first converts a dream into a tangible set of goals, steps, and tasks that a person can mentally and visually grasp. That grasp begins to create a well-founded and confident expectation. Then, as each task, step, and goal is completed, the expectation that the dream will be fulfilled becomes more and more well-founded and confident as each completed task, step, or goal brings us closer to the full accomplishment of that dream.

When Lindbergh first gained his vision of becoming the first person to cross the Atlantic in an airplane, he had no funding and no airplane, and didn't know of any airplane already built that could do the job. He converted his vision into a list of specific goals, steps, and tasks, and began tackling that vision one task at a time. He found a group in San Diego that he believed could build a plane to his specifications, which would significantly raise his probability of success. He then started raising the money to pay for the building of that plane. As he and the partners he recruited started accomplishing his list of goals, his expectation of success became more and more well founded and confident, and his hope grew accordingly. How confident did his expectations become? Instead of building a plane with two engines for his 3,600-mile trek, he only wanted one engine. That meant a lot less horsepower and no backup plan if the engine failed during the journey, but it also meant each gallon of fuel would be used up at half the rate it would be by two engines.

How confident were Lindbergh's expectations? So confident that, instead of taking another pilot with him to serve as a backup and give him time to occasionally sleep during the 30-plus-hour journey, he chose to fly solo. His expectations were high and so was his confidence. They were well founded because of the continued progress he and his team made in completing their tasks, steps, and goals within the time limits he had set. His passion for this effort was growing. The same will be true with you. Each time you complete a task, step, or goal, you get that much closer to achieving your dream and your expectation becomes more well founded and confident, producing even more hope.

Fulfillment—the Third Ingredient Essential to Producing Passion. Fulfillment is the third ingredient necessary to produce a passion. The good news is that you don't have to do anything extra to develop this ingredient. It happens automatically as you complete each step toward your dream. Each time you complete a task, step, or goal, you think to yourself, "Wow! I did it! I'm that much closer to fulfilling my dream." That's fulfillment!

Back to our example of Lucky Lindy. With each new task, step, or goal that Lindbergh or his team completed, fulfillment (the final ingredient) was added to the mix of vision and hope, producing a passion for his dream that captivated his heart and mind. As his passion grew, it motivated him to go forward with even more enthusiasm and commitment. As Lindbergh saw his team complete each new task, step, or goal, the level of his hope and fulfillment also increased. When the day came, his passion was so powerful that he took off on his 33-hour, 30-minute solo flight having had no sleep for over 24 hours. Would you get behind the controls of a small experimental single-engine plane and begin a solo flight across the Atlantic if you hadn't slept for 24 hours? No one else on earth would have tried such a feat, but no one else on earth had Lindbergh's passion for such a dream. His dream was realized, and 33 hours and 30 minutes after taking off, he landed at 10:22 P.M. in Paris before a frenzied crowd of over 100,000 people. That is the power of passion.

This same passion that provided all of the fuel Lindbergh needed to convert his impossible dream into reality is available to you and your pursuit of each of your most important visions. Using the vision mapping process, you can create true, well-defined visions. As you begin to complete the tasks necessary to make each step toward the completion of each goal, your hope will gain a firm and confident foundation. With each completed task, with each completed step, and with each goal you achieve, your hope and fulfillment will increase, producing a heartfelt passion that will fuel your pursuit of that vision all the way to its completion.

So passion isn't something mystical. It's not something you have to wait to catch. You may catch a good passion, or you may catch a bad one. You may catch one that fuels your dream, or you may catch one that destroys it. But you don't have to wait to catch either. You can bring passion into any one of your dreams and significantly raise your probability of success.

You may say, "Wait a minute! I'm working at a dead-end job that's so miserable I could never have a passion for it!" Yes, you can! First you have to bring a new vision to that job. Maybe it's to perform it better and faster than anyone else has ever performed it. Maybe your vision will be to perform that job so well that you will be noticed for a promotion out of that job. As you gain that passion, it will fuel your achievement on that job and become the key to moving upward in that organization or outward to an opportunity with another company.

Passions are like a nuclear chain reaction. When passions catch us and control us, they produce a chain reaction gone wild that can be incredibly destructive. How many marriages have been ruined by adultery? What's the beginning of adultery? It's a passion that catches a husband or wife. How many people have lost their jobs because they became passionate over something negative, such as gambling, drinking, or drugs? Those passions catch us and destroy our lives.

But what happens when we develop a passion that we control to enhance the pursuit of our most cherished dreams? It too produces a nuclear reaction. But that reaction is controlled rather than out of control. Instead of producing destructive consequences, it produces beneficial results. That kind of passion becomes like a nuclear fuel that provides electric power to entire cities. That's the power of a controlled chain reaction. That's the power of an acquired or developed passion.

One of my favorite figures in American history is a man that you probably never heard of. He's quite obscure. Yet he made one of the most remarkable contributions to you and me, our families, and our nation, ever made by a single individual. He ended his career as a paymaster on a railroad. Right now you might be wondering, What kind of contribution could this guy have made? His name was Nathan Trist.

In 1847, President Polk dispatched Trist to Mexico to negotiate a peace treaty to end the Mexican-American War. Shortly after Trist began his journey from Washington to Mexico, he had a vision for the kind of settlement he wanted to pursue. The more he thought about it, the more passionate he became. He sent a message to Polk telling him what he was going to attempt to achieve in these negotiations. When Polk read the dispatch, he became extremely concerned that such a demand of Mexico would infuriate that country's leaders and motivate them to continue the war rather than settle it. Polk sent a message to Trist telling him to abandon any such notion. But Trist not only had a vision, he had gone through the vision mapping process, converting his vision into precise goals, steps, and tasks. As he began to complete the tasks and take the steps, his vision became infused with hope and fulfillment, producing a passion that not even the president of the United States could quench! Trist sent a message back to the president assuring him that he could get the concessions he had envisioned. President Polk was so infuriated by Trist's persistence in pushing for such a dangerous proposition that he sent a message back firing him and demanding that he return to Washington at once. Polk would send someone else to negotiate a much less demanding treaty that would be more likely to be accepted by Mexico.

But President Polk did not comprehend the power of Trist's passion for his vision. Trist ignored the president's demand and negotiated the treaty. His vision wasn't fueled by his desire to please the president, but rather by his passion to achieve what he considered the best possible outcome. The result? It was not what Polk had predicted—namely a greater determination to keep fighting. Rather, Trist talked Mexico into signing the exact treaty he had envisioned, with all of its unbelievable concessions. When he brought it back to Washington, Polk signed it and the Senate ratified it.

However, Polk was so upset that he banned Trist from ever serving in a government role for the rest of his life.

What did that treaty give you and me, and our nation? We got the states of California, Utah, Nevada, New Mexico, and Arizona, part of Colorado, and part of Wyoming. We received more land and wealth in that single treaty than has ever been acquired by any nation in history. Without this acquisition, we would not have had the strategic metals, oil, and wealth that were critical to fighting and winning World War I and World War II. Thanks to Nathan Trist, we not only live in the richest country in the world, we live in a nation and a world that was able to preserve freedom from totalitarian domination.

How much did all of this cost the United States? Trist negotiated it for the exact price he said he could: $15 million. We got California, the Southwest, and the Rocky Mountain West for only 4 cents an acre, the single most remarkable land purchase in U.S. and world history. And it all came about because an unknown, unsung, and unjustly treated Nathan Trist added the fuel of passion to his incredible vision.

Now, as we come to the close of our mentoring sessions, it's your turn to begin your pursuit of your impossible dreams. You've been provided with the perfect vehicle to take you to each of those dreams. Your Porsche is made up of 14 master strategies. You've now been given the fuel and a credit card to utilize the fifteenth master strategy. Only one thing is left for you to do, and you are the only one who can do it. You must place the key in the ignition switch and turn it. Do you know what an ignition switch does? It provides the electrical current that produces a spark that ignites the fuel. And just like everything else in this very lengthy analogy, the ignition switch is critical. Without that one spark, the car will not take you anywhere. That ignition switch can be described in a single word. But that word is so misunderstood that I want to give you a word picture first.

In 1859, an unknown tightrope walker named Charles Blondin ran an ad in the *New York Times* claiming that he was going to cross Niagara Falls on a tightrope. About 5,000 people turned out to see if this man could do the unfathomable or take a plunge into the millions of gallons of water that pour over those falls every single minute. The falls are about 1,100 feet across, a distance equal to the length of nearly four football fields. Can you imagine walking across a tightrope that long? And then there's the height. The falls are 16 stories high. Every minute, 40 million gallons of water pass over the falls. That's 1,000 swimming pools a minute.

Before Blondin began his first attempt to cross the falls, he asked the crowd a question. "How many of you believe I can cross the falls on that tightrope?" The crowd applauded their belief and he crossed the falls and returned back across the rope to their amazement. He then asked the crowd, "How many of you believe I can cross the falls pushing a wheelbarrow?" Once again they applauded their belief, and once again he crossed the falls back and forth pushing a wheelbarrow. To the further amazement of the crowd, he crossed the falls two more times, once on stilts and once blindfolded. The crowd was now worked up into a frenzy. He then asked what seemed like a very simple question. "How many of you believe I can cross Niagara Falls with somebody on my back?" Well, that seemed like a piece of cake compared to what they had already witnessed. The crowd applauded and cheered this man they now believed could do anything he wanted to do on a tightrope. Then, with a single question, he silenced the crowd. "Which one of you would like to volunteer?" That crowd of 5,000 people who had professed to believe in his ability, who had cheered and rallied with praise and belief to each of his previous questions, now stood silent. Even though all 5,000 had professed their faith in Blondin and in his ability to carry a person across the falls on his back, not one truly believed.

You see, true belief always has a corresponding action. If the action isn't there, then neither is belief. If you don't believe that a plane is going to safely fly you to your destination, you will not get on board. If you think and believe that it will, you will get on the plane.

This kind of belief is appropriately called faith. Faith always has corresponding action that gives evidence of its presence. Out of that crowd of 5,000 people who professed their faith in Charles Blondin's ability, not one truly believed. The only person who really did possess faith in Blondin and his skill was his best friend. He climbed up onto Blondin's back and became the only man in history ever to cross Niagara Falls on the back of a tightrope walker. That's true belief. That is true faith.

Faith can be applied to anything. Even if you say, "I'm not religious," you still exercise faith a thousand times a day. When you flip on your light switch, that's expressing faith. You're saying you believe there's power going through those wires, and the wiring is good enough not to short out and burn your house down. When you get into a car with somebody else driving, you are expressing faith that that person is going to get you safely where you are going.

What am I telling you here? I am saying that the ignition switch needed to ignite your passion to use the 15 master strategies to pursue your dreams is the ignition switch of faith. In this case, the expression of that faith will be to spend the time necessary to do the exercises at the end of each session with the goal of learning, mastering, and utilizing the strategies and skills we have discussed. If you truly believe that these strategies and skills can perform for you like they have for me and for countless others who have achieved their impossible dreams, then you will do the exercises, master the skills, and begin to use them in your daily pursuit of excellence and your dreams. In addition to doing the exercises, you will begin to use the vision mapping process. You will learn the communication techniques we've talked about. You will learn how to reset your focus from the negative to the positive in any given situation. You will learn and commit yourself to honoring the people around you, whether they're your children, your spouse, your coworkers, your clients, or anyone else whose path you cross. You will choose to value them.

It all takes faith. You have to believe that the outcome is going to be what I've told you it will be. I promise you, it will. These are techniques that have been proven through the centuries. They have been used by every person who has ever achieved his or her impossible dreams. They work! They have worked for me over and over. They have worked in my relationships. They have worked on my projects. They have worked in my television shows. They work!

But you are the one who has to turn the switch. Nobody else is going to put that key into your ignition and turn it for you. If you do not do the exercises; if you do not manage your time and prioritize your day; if you do not put your dreams into writing and convert them into goals, steps, and tasks, you will not achieve extraordinary success in any area of your life.

You have a Porsche. It's you! You have the world's most advanced computer inside of your skull. It's been there from your birth. You can use it to achieve mediocrity or you can use it to achieve the extraordinary. But you have to turn the switch.

In closing, I want to tell you how honored I have been for the time you have given to our sessions together. I would love to hear from you as you begin to put these strategies to work in your life. You can visit my Web site at either stevenkscott.com or mentoredbyamillionaire.com, where you'll be able to take a closer look at our preprinted vision mapping journal, our *Mentored by a Millionaire Workbook* with all of the exercises in this book, and the forms to complete these exercises. You'll also be able to look at our audio series on this subject and my newest audio series, *Solomon's Treasures: Secrets to Wealth, Success and Happiness from the Richest Man Who Ever Lived.* This site also has a link to my e-mail address. If you wish to order any of these or our other mentoring supplements you can call (800) 246-1771. My assistant, Karen, is wonderful, and she'll be happy to help you any way she can. May God bless you with all that is needed to pursue and achieve all of your most cherished dreams.

Actions for Traction

WHERE THE RUBBER MEETS THE ROAD

1. If you are like most readers of most self-help books, there's a good chance you haven't yet started your vision mapping journal. Without taking this first step of faith, it will be nearly impossible for you to convert your dreams into reality. So if you haven't yet started completing the exercises at the end of each chapter, now is the time to create your notebook and Vision Mapping Journal. If you prefer to order a preprinted notebook with all of these exercises and a vision mapping journal, you may do so by visiting my Web site or calling Karen at my office.
2. If you have started the exercises in this book, continue to do so at a marathoner's pace. One chapter's set of exercises per month is the slowest pace you should consider, and two chapters' sets of exercises per week is the fastest pace you should follow.
3. When working with your vision mapping journal, remember that this is a lifetime project. Unlike your notebook, your journal will not be completed in a matter of weeks or months. Don't be in a hurry. Start with your most important dreams in the most important areas of life, and simply work from there. With each year that passes, you will discard some dreams and add new ones. The goal of your journal is to provide a clear road map and schedule for achieving each of your most important short-term, long-term, and lifetime dreams. It's your map; it's your life. Take it seriously, but have fun with it. If you do, it will become your genie in a notebook.

INDEX

Accountability. *See* Personal accountability
Achievers, 3. *See also* Comparison charts
Admiration, need for, 250–251
Allen, Paul, 57, 171–173
Altair 8800 computer, 171
Ambassador Leather, 202–204
American Telecast:
  partners in, 9
  productivity of, 80
Attention deficit disorder (ADD), 78, 231, 232
Attitude:
  adjusting for success, 24–26
  of gratefulness, 245–248
  know-it-all, 50, 253
  responsibility for, 254
Authority, in effective partnering, 77

Back to the Future (movie), 192
Ballmer, Steve, 173
Baxter, Meredith, 103
Blondin, Charles, 265–266
Book of Proverbs, 105–106, 136
Boone, Debby, 103
Boone, Pat, 103
Brinkley, Christie:
  annual guarantee for, 183
  marketing idea by, 145
  as Total Gym spokesperson, 69, 103, 104, 107, 166, 178, 233
Brother Hicks, 256
Budget, adhering to, 193

Carter, Jimmy, 108
Celebrities. *See also specific celebrities*
  in effective partnerships, 69
  guarantees received by, 183
  as personal references, 102–103
  recruiting, 165–166
Cher, 87, 103, 104, 145, 166, 197
Chik-fil-A, 80
Churchill, Winston, 212, 213
Clark, Maurice, 63–64
Clinton, Bill, 258
Commitment, in partnerships, 81
Communication, effective. *See also* Presentations
  barriers to, 88–90
  challenges to, 94–97
  critical elements of, 93–94
  with financial partners, 61
  foundation for, 90–93
  persuasion versus manipulation, 87–88, 116
  in relationships, 251
  role of, 83–87
  techniques for, 99–115
  of vision, 74–75, 81, 186
  written, 94
Comparison charts (by type of person):
  achievement levels, 4
  brain "reprogramming," 23
  communication, 84
  dealing with criticism, 212
  dealing with failure, 180, 198
  explanation of, 4
  goal setting, 164
  lack of know-how/resources, 52
  in negative situations, 239
  pursuit of dreams, 5, 136
  taking control, 223
  use of partners, 65
  use of passion, 257
  use of resources, 56
  use of strengths/weaknesses, 45
Competitive advantage, through partnering, 68–69
Computer operating systems, 172–173
Conflict, resolving, 251–253
Consideration, communication role of, 91–92

Control:
in conflict resolution, 251, 252
human need for, 221–222
of passion, 258, 259, 264
Coppola, Francis Ford, 10
Credentials, for mentors, 11–12
Credibility:
of celebrities, 102–103
in presentations, 120
Criticism:
anticipating, 187–188
benefits of, 211–220
effects of, 208–211, 250
methods for, 253–254
prevalence of, 242

Deal-A-Meal weight loss program, 146, 187, 233
Delegating work, 57, 67
Detroit Automobile Company, 66, 71, 76, 77, 138, 197
Disney, Roy, 64, 72
Disney, Walt, 64, 68, 72, 76
Dot-com companies, 134
Downs, Hugh, 166
Dream Index, 141, 142
Drifters, 3. *See also* Comparison charts
Drive-through talking, 92–93

Edcouch-Elsa High School (Texas), 175
Edison, Thomas:
ability to focus, 231, 232, 233
creative persistence of, 180, 183–187, 190, 191
failures of, 197
goals set by, 161, 162
IQ level of, 19, 50
limited resources of, 57
as mentor of Henry Ford, 10
partnering by, 68
passion of, 259–260
time management by, 227
vision of, 139, 144, 186
Edison Electric Company, 138
86-DOS, 173
Elsa, Texas, 174–175
Emotional word pictures:
creating, 113–115
defined, 100, 109, 118
effectiveness of, 110–111, 251
example of, 111–112
in persuasive communication, 94
role of, 108
Emotions:
communication role of, 94, 96
criticism and, 211, 213, 215–216
Encouragement, role of, 250
Environment, for effective partnering, 77–78
Excellence, achieving, 249

Failure:
accelerating, 71
analyzing, 188–189, 205
anticipating, 187–188
fear of, 198–204, 230
magnitude of, 70
other people's, 190–191
overcoming through creative persistence, 178–180, 190
recognizing, 192–193
reducing risk of, 69
role in success, 196–198, 204–206
as springboard, 191–192
Faith, role of, 266–267
Fax technology, 192–193
Fear:
of failure, 198–204, 230
as motivator, 78–79, 80, 199
types of, 199–200
Federal Express, 192–193
Financial rewards:
as incentive, 78
sharing, 76–77
Flagler, Henry, 63, 64
Focus:
redirected, 243–245, 254
sustained, 225, 231–233
Fonda, Jane, 87, 103, 145, 166, 197, 233
Ford, Henry:
failures of, 197–198, 199
goals set by, 161, 162
mentor of, 10
partnering by, 66, 68, 71, 77
passion of, 259
as visionary, 138–139

Ford Motor Company, 66, 139, 198
Founding fathers (of U.S.), 58, 59
Fox, Michael J., 192
Frame of reference:
  communication role of, 89, 92–93
  for emotional word pictures, 113
Franklin Covey organization, 162, 227, 229
Fulfillment:
  as life goal, 23
  as passion ingredient, 260, 262–263

Gates, Bill, 57, 79, 171–173
Gender, communication role of, 89, 111, 112, 251
General Dynamic, 161
Geniuses, as superachievers, 50
Get Clark Smart (Howard), 59
Gifford, Kathie Lee, 87, 177
Gish, Lillian, 212, 213
Goals:
  shooting for the moon, 163–175
  in vision mapping, 147–157
Graphical user interface (GUI), 79, 216
Gratefulness, 245–248
Grinding It Out (Kroc), 134
Guajardo, Frank, 174–175

Heaton, Patricia, 87, 106–107, 146
Heston, Charlton, 87, 166, 197
Hitler, Adolf, 117, 210
Honor:
  communication role of, 90–91, 119
  in relationships, 249–250
Hook (in communication):
  defined, 99, 118
  role of, 100–101
  types of, 101–105
Hope, as passion ingredient, 260, 261–262
Howard, Clark, 59
Human brain:
  processing power of, 21–22
  right versus left, 30, 89, 94, 108–111, 251

IBM, 171–172
Industrial Light and Magic, 48
Integrity:
  of mentor, 11
  in partnerships, 81
Internet:
  family-safe service for, 106–107, 146
  origins of, 80, 216
Iwerks, Ubbe, 63, 64, 72

Jefferson, Thomas, 59, 63
Jesus Christ, 108
Jobs, Steve, 79
Jurassic Park (movie), 48

Keller, Helen, 51, 240, 245, 246
King, Larry, 37
Knowledge:
  through effective partnering, 66–67
  expanding, 68
  overcoming lack of, 48–54, 231
Kroc, Ray:
  goals set by, 164–165
  partnering by, 64
  passion of, 259
  resources lacked by, 47, 57
  vision of, 134–135, 144

Landon, Michael, 18, 54, 87, 102–103, 166
Laws of extraordinary success:
  first: on master strategies, 2
  second: on mentors, 2
  third: on attitude reprogramming, 22
  fourth: on overcoming lack of know-how, 48
  fifth: on overcoming limited resources, 55
  sixth: on effective partnering, 64
  seventh: on effective partnering and success level, 66
  eighth: on effective communication, 85
  ninth: on communication techniques, 100
  tenth: on clear vision of achievement, 134
  eleventh: on impact of vision, 137
  twelfth: on goals/steps to achieving dreams, 157
  thirteenth: on shooting for the moon, 163

Laws of extraordinary success *(Continued)*:
fourteenth: on creative persistence, 181
fifteenth: on dealing with fears of failure, 196
sixteenth: on analyzing failure, 205
seventeenth: on avoiding criticism, 209
eighteenth: on controlling time, 225
nineteenth: on being a positive person, 241
twentieth: on developing passion, 259
Lear, Bill, 18–19, 161, 162, 193
Life expectancy, 54
Lindbergh, Charles, 49, 261, 262–263
Listener:
attention of, 95–96, 99–100
communication role of, 89
honoring, 90–91
Llano Grande Center for Research and Development, 175
Lucas, George, 10

Maddox, Rick, 256
Making Love Last Forever (Smalley), 248
Manipulation:
avoiding, 97
through fear of loss, 115
versus persuasion, 87–88, 116
Marketing, as career, 5
Marriage. *See also* Relationships
counseling for, 11–12
failure rate of, 189
goal setting in, 173–174
personality type and, 42
ramifications of success in, 186
Marsh, Bob, 10, 190, 202, 204
Marsh, Dave, 183–184
Marsh, Henry, 181
Mask (movie), 191
Master strategies:
#1: reprogram mind/attitude, 18–22
#2: play to strengths, 33–35
#3: overcome lack of know-how, 48–54
#4: overcome lack of resources, 54–61
#5: partner effectively, 64–72
#6: communicate effectively, 86–94
#7: gain vision of achievement, 133–140
#8: use vision mapping, 145–157
#9: dream big, 162–175
#10: use creative persistence, 182–193
#11: overcome fears of failure, 196–206
#12: stop avoiding criticism, 209–219
#13: take control of life, 224–235
#14: acquire positive personality, 239–249
#15: gain passion for visions, 257–267
MAX.com Internet service, 106–107, 146
McDonald brothers, 135, 164
McDonald's, 47, 64, 135
McGraw, Ali, 103
Memory technique, 27–30
Mentor:
defined, 9
recruiting, 10–13, 34, 75
roles of, 10, 12
Mentored by a Millionaire Workbook (Scott), 267
Mentoring, as success strategy, 2, 8–9
Mentoring Session Notebook, 15, 117
Microsoft, 171, 172
Mintz, Charles, 72, 76
MITS, 171
Money, maximizing as resource, 57–61, 67
Monoghan, Tom, 19
Morris, Robert, 59, 63
Motivation:
for criticism, 216–217
criticism effect on, 210
factors in, 115–116, 119
fear as, 78–79, 80, 199
through manipulation, 87, 88, 97
in partnerships, 80–81
MS-DOS, 173
Multitasking, 78, 232–233

Networking, to find partners, 74
Norris, Chuck:
annual guarantee for, 183
martial arts skill of, 241
as MAX.com spokesperson, 106, 107, 146
as Total Gym spokesperson, 69, 87, 103, 104, 166, 178, 233

Palo Alto Research Center (PARC), 79–80, 216
Partnering, effective:
- benefits of, 66–71
- creative persistence and, 186–187
- defined, 64–66, 71
- for financial resources, 60–61
- historical examples of, 63–64
- motivators in, 80–81
- to overcome know-how lack, 49, 51, 53
- process of, 73–77
- recruiting for, 81–82
- utilizing, 77–80

Partnering, ineffective, 71–72
Partnership categories, 73
Passion:
- acquiring, 258–260
- effect of, 263–264
- ingredients of, 260–263
- need for, 256–257
- personality type and, 257–258

Persistence, creative:
- example of, 182–184
- personality type and, 181
- role of, 178–180
- as success factor, 181–182
- techniques for, 184–193

Personal accountability, 225, 233–235. *See also* Personal responsibility
Personal computers (PC), 79, 171–173, 216
Personality types:
- characteristics of, 37–45, 240
- as communication barriers, 89, 92
- determining, 34–37
- for effective partnerships, 73
- passion and, 257–258
- persistence and, 181
- role of, 32–34, 46

Personal life. *See also* Marriage; Relationships
- goal setting in, 173–174
- gratefulness in, 245–248
- maximizing relationships in, 249–254
- ramifications of success in, 186

Personal responsibility. *See also* Personal accountability
- for attitudes, 254
- for failure, 188
- for response to negative situations, 242–243

Persuasion:
- challenges in, 95–97
- versus manipulation, 87–88, 116

Phillips, Frank, 47–48, 51
Phillips Petroleum, 48
Polk, James, 264–265
Positive personality, 81–82, 239–249, 254
Positive thinking, 238–239
Presentations:
- preparation for, 93, 116–117, 119–120
- in recruiting partners, 74, 75

Presentation Worksheet, 121–130
Priority planning, 225, 227–231, 233–235
Procrastination, 229–231
Proverbs (Bible), 105–106, 136
Pursuers, 3. *See also* Comparison charts

Reagan, Ronald, 108, 166
Reese, Della, 87
Relationships. *See also* Marriage
- love as manipulative in, 116
- maximizing, 249–254
- respect in, 250–251

Resources:
- for creative persistence, 191
- through effective partnering, 67
- lack of, 53–54
- money as, 57–61
- in shooting for the moon, 170
- time as, 54–57

Respect:
- communication role of, 90–91, 119
- in relationships, 250–251

Responsibility. *See* Personal responsibility
The Richest Man Who Ever Lived: His Breakthrough Strategies for Wealth and Happiness (Scott), 105
Risk:
- avoidance of, 204, 210
- partnerships and, 69, 71–72

Risk-reward analysis, 78, 201–204
Ritter, John, 87, 166
Rockefeller, John D., 64, 133, 134, 144
Ruth, George "Babe," 19, 169

Salt (in communication):
defined, 99–100, 118
role of, 105–108
SAS software company, 80
Schedule, in vision mapping process, 156–157, 193
Scott, Shannon, 6, 36, 42, 177, 195, 214, 217, 249
Scott, Steven:
attention deficit disorder of, 78, 232
business success rate of, 67, 188–189, 205
children of, 24, 195, 214–215, 217, 230
in choral group, 49, 75
commercials by, 94–95, 99, 101–107, 182–184
contact information for, 119, 140, 143, 267
early career of, 5–8, 86–87, 201–202, 217, 219
failures overcome by, 196–197, 202–204
marriage of, 85, 249
mentors of, 10, 20
parents of, 115–116, 119, 225–226, 247
partnering by, 50–51, 68, 76–77, 186–187
qualifications as mentor, 13–14
in ROTC, 160, 167–168
start-up companies by, 166–167, 177–178
wife of (*see* Scott, Shannon)
Seattle Computer Products, 173
Security, need for, 250
Self-image, criticism and, 210
Selleck, Tom, 87, 166
Semantics, communication role of, 89, 94
Shaughnessy, Jim, 10, 111–112, 181
Shaughnessy, Patty (Plant), 111–112
Shineberg, Sid, 10
Shooting for the moon:
applications for, 167–175
defined, 165
fear of failure and, 199
partnering in, 82
process of, 165–167
role of, 163–164
Siegal, Mike, 202–204
Simmons, Richard, 103, 145, 146, 187, 233
Smalley, Gary:
communication techniques of, 92, 94
criticism method used by, 253–254
on marriage, 189, 249
as mentor, 10, 248
personality types defined by, 36
relationship videos produced by, 11
Smith, Fred, 192–193
Smith, Hyrum, 229
Solomon, 105–106, 136, 138, 212, 213
Solomon's Treasures: Secrets to Wealth, Success and Happiness from the Richest Man Who Ever Lived (audio series), 267
Somers, Suzanne, 233
Sonneborn, Harry, 63, 64
Southwest Airlines, 80
Spielberg, Steven:
creative persistence of, 191
goal setting by, 163, 168
know-how of, 48, 51
mentor of, 10
success of, 1–2
Standard Oil, 64, 134
Stoltz, Eric, 191
Strengths/weaknesses:
assessing, 53, 62, 73
in complementary partnerships, 69
Stress:
destructive power of, 244–245
partnering to reduce, 70–71
Success. *See also* Laws of extraordinary success
definition of, 142–143
level of, 66, 67–68
pace of, 68
passion as factor in, 256–257
rate of, 67, 188–189
standards for, 23–24, 142–143
Sullivan, Anne, 240
Superachievers. *See also* Comparison charts
achievement level of, 3
attention deficit disorder and, 232

control of time by, 222, 223, 224–225
criticism handled by, 209
intelligence of, 50
as overcoming knowledge lack, 48
Sustained focus, 225, 231–233
Sweatin' to the Oldies videos, 146, 187, 233

Testimonials, 120
Time:
communication role of, 90, 91
control of, 222–235, 245
maximizing as resource, 54–57, 67
Time Inventory Form, 234, 236
Time robbers, 229
Total Gym, 69–70, 178, 182, 184, 193, 233
Trist, Nathan, 264–265

Urgencies, handling, 228–229

Vision:
communicating, 74–75, 81, 186
in creative persistence, 184–185
defined, 138
gaining, 138–139
passion for, 257–260
as passion ingredient, 260, 261, 263
role of, in achievement, 131–138
written, 139–140
Vision Mapping Journal, 15, 119, 140, 143, 147, 176, 267, 268
Vision mapping process:
accountability in, 233
to acquire passion, 261, 263
defined, 141
in financial partnerships, 60–61
in identifying partners, 73
preliminary steps in, 141–143
role of, 26, 145, 146
setting lofty goals in, 162–163
using, 145–157

Walsh, John, 256
Washington, George, 59, 60, 63, 64
Weight Watchers, 233
Wendy's restaurants, 80
Williams, Ted, 188
Winfrey, Oprah, 256
Winston, Stan, 48
Workload:
delegating, 57, 67
partnering to reduce, 70

Xerox Corporation, 79–80, 216

Zemeckis, Robert, 191–192
Ziglar, Zig, 10–11, 196, 204, 218

Take the next step on the path to extraordinary success ...with your own, personal, one-on-one Millionaire Mentor

You've just discovered the master strategies known and practiced by the world's most successful people. Now continue your journey ... and your learning! In this how-to packed program, Steve Scott expands the strategies and insights he shared in *Mentored by a Millionaire* and takes them to a whole new level, with an audio program that puts him right in the room with you!

Steve Scott

With the ***Mentored by a Millionaire Audio System*** you'll have Steve Scott as your personal, one-on-one millionaire mentor. He'll be available to you whenever you need him, so you'll never forget your focus or lose momentum. You can check in *anytime* you want a strategy review, a shot of willpower, or a fresh dose of inspiration. And you can experience a mentoring session *anywhere*: while you're commuting, traveling, even exercising! There's no more powerful or convenient learning system in the world.

The Mentored by a Millionaire Audio System is packed with even more tips, techniques, secrets, strategies and critical insights you won't find anywhere else. The complete system includes:

Steve Scott's Best-Selling Audio Series, *Mentored by a Millionaire*

- ✓ 15 one-on-one mentoring sessions on 10 Compact Discs or 8 audiocassettes
- ✓ Resource CD-ROM with simple exercises that will empower you to put Steve's secrets into action

Order *Mentored by a Millionaire* TODAY!

Call toll-free 1-800-373-6086

Order online at www.nightingale.com